Distributed Programming with Java

Distributed Programming with Java

QUSAY H. MAHMOUD

 MANNING

Greenwich
(74° w. long.)

For electronic browsing and ordering of this and other Manning books,
visit http://www.manning.com. The publisher offers discounts on this book
when ordered in quantity. For more information, please contact:

> Special Sales Department
> Manning Publications Co.
> 32 Lafayette Place   Fax: (203) 661-9018
> Greenwich, CT 06830   email: orders@manning.com

Library of Congress Cataloging-in-Publication Data
Qusay H. Mahmoud 1971-
    Distributed Programming with Java/Qusay H. Mahmoud
       p.   cm.
    Includes bibliographical references and index.
    ISBN 1-884777-65-1 (alk. paper)
    1. Java (Computer program language).   2. Electronic data processing—
Distributed processing.   I. Title.
    QA76.73.J38M32   1999
    005.2'762—dc21   99-27785
                                            CIP

Manning Publications Co.   Copyeditor: Kristen Black
32 Lafayette Place   Typesetter: Jimmie Young
Greenwich, CT 06830   Cover designer: Leslie Haimes

Printed in the United States of America
2 3 4 5 6 7 8 9 10 – CM – 02 01 00

To the loving memory of my father (1937 – 1998)

contents

Part III   CORBA

preface

"Java is the language of network computing."
Lawrence J. Ellison, Chairman and CEO, Oracle Corporation

The introduction of the Java programming language to the computer market marked a turning point in the computer industry. It is a clean, rich, and powerful programming language. More importantly, its elegance makes it a pleasure to program in, and the Java Virtual Machine (JVM) enhances the portability of software across a heterogeneous network.

As a truly platform-independent language, Java allows applications written in it to run on any system that has a Java interpreter. This is an important feature, since network-based applications should run on all of the different Internet platforms. Java is described as a distributed language since it provides high-level support for networking.

Java provides a number of mechanisms for networking and distributed computing, including high-level APIs for sockets programming and the Java remote method invocation (RMI) system. Once Java was introduced, a number of vendors began building systems and tools that make the task of developing distributed applications easier than ever. For example, Inprise Corporation provides an implementation of CORBA 2.0. It's known as VisiBroker, and it is completely written in Java. A number of other vendors also began exploiting the idea of mobile agents, since Java represents an ideal language for developing them. One in particular is ObjectSpace; they developed Voyager ORB, which provides a simple way for developing distributed and mobile agent applications easily and quickly.

This book grew out of my experience writing distributed applications in Java. I started using Java when it was first released to the public. However, unlike many other developers, I did not start with applets; rather, I started experimenting with building network-based applications using the java.net package. This book, therefore, covers everything for writing distributed applications in Java; its purpose is to provide practical advice about how to build those applications. You can think of this book as a complete tutorial on developing distributed applications in Java using different paradigms, including sockets, RMI, CORBA (using VisiBroker), and mobile agents (using Voyager). The sample programs shown throughout the book will give you an excellent starting point for writing your own distributed applications in Java.

I hope this book will provide you with a starting point for building distributed applications in Java. If it does help you get started building distributed applications quickly, then I have accomplished what I set out to do.

acknowledgments

First and foremost, I would like to thank Andrea Ondak, my initial contact at Manning, for getting me started with this project in the first place. Also, I owe many thanks to Marjan Bace, my publisher, for his patience and guidance throughout the writing process.

Of course, the book itself would not be what it is now without my review editor at Manning, Ted Kennedy, who helped guide the direction of the book. The technical reviewers, namely Robert Resendes, Michael Katchabaw, Bruce Arbuckle, Klaus Glahn, John Anderson, Juan Jimenez, Frank Gruetzmacher, Eva Coscia, Klaus Glahn, and Andy Czerwonka, provided invaluable comments. Rhett Guthrie and Graham Glass provided invaluable comments on the Voyager chapters.

Mary Piergies, production manager at Manning, provided me with guidance and answers to all my questions on formatting required for publishing. Thank you, Mary! And thanks to everyone on the production team for this book. Thanks also to Leslie Haimes for designing such a neat cover for the book.

I also would like to thank Dr. Weichang Du of the University of New Brunswick, Canada, for being my supervisor during my undergraduate and graduate studies.

Finally, I would like to thank my family, especially my brother, Dr. Mohammad H. Hamdan, and his wife, Carol, for their support and encouragement during my studies. Special thanks to my lovely fiancée, Reema, for her continuous encouragement during the last couple of months of my work on this project.

guide to this book

This book is divided into four parts.

PART I: SOCKETS PROGRAMMING   In the first six chapters you'll get an introduction to distributed programming and a tutorial on sockets programming with Java. I've also implemented many interesting network applications in this part of the book. You'll see examples of sockets in real-world applications, and we'll discuss threads, security issues, and object serialization.

PART II: RMI   In chapters 7 through 10, I'll introduce a new paradigm for easily developing distributed applications. You'll get an overview of RMI, then we'll discus the anatomy of an RMI-based application, along with advanced RMI programming techniques (such as dynamic servers and factories, signed messages, and callbacks). Full working examples will accompany each technique.

PART III: CORBA   Chapters 11 through 19 will give you an overview of CORBA along with the anatomy of a CORBA-based application. I'll explain IDL-to-Java mapping as well. Advanced CORBA topics (such as activation, inheritance, the tie mechanism, and the interface repository) are covered through examples. This part ends with a discussion of Caffeine.

PART IV: MOBILE AGENTS AND VOYAGER   In the final five chapters mobile agents are discussed, then Voyager is introduced, along with many examples on how to use it to build distributed and mobile agent applications. We'll also discuss advanced Voyager features such as publish/subscribe, activation, and timers. As you read, you'll see examples on how to integrate Voyager with CORBA.

This book is written in a way that lets you get the most out of the topics in a short time. Each part is independent of the others. If you are new to programming distributed applications in Java, I recommend that you start reading on page 1 and continue on to the last page of this book. This way, you will start with low-level (sockets) distributed programming and progress to the highest level (using Voyager). On the other hand, if you have some background in internet-working, and you are interested in mobile agents and Voyager, for example, then you can jump to part four of this book without getting lost in the discussions. In short, this book can be read in any order you want, depending on your experience and interest.

intended audience

This book targets a number of groups of people:

- Java developers who want to get started developing industrial-strength distributed applications. Using examples, this book explains several technologies for developing distributed applications in Java.
- Client/server architects who would like to know the various approaches for developing client/server systems and want to be able to choose a paradigm for a specific project. The book enables you to determine which approach to use for a particular application.
- Distributed applications developers who would like to familiarize themselves with the approaches of developing distributed applications. For example, you might be familiar with CORBA, but here you will learn about RMI and Voyager.
- Distributed- or network-computing instructors who want their students to have a practical book that can be easily read and understood. This book shows students how to solve one problem using different technologies, thereby allowing them to easily compare these technologies.
- Seniors and graduate students in computer science (or a closely related field) who want to understand distributed objects programming and experiment with the different technologies for developing distributed applications

author online

Purchase of *Distributed Programming with Java* includes free access to a private Internet forum where you can make comments about the book, ask technical questions, and receive help from the author and from other users. To access the forum, point your web browser to http://www.manning.com/Mahmoud. There you will be able to subscribe to the forum. This site also provides information on how to access the forum once you are registered, what kind of help is available, and the rules of conduct on the forum.

All source code for the examples presented in *Distributed Programming with Java* is available to purchasers from the Manning website. The URL http://www.manning.com/Mahmoud includes a link to the source code files.

about the cover illustration

The cover illustration of this book is from the 1805 edition of Sylvain Maréchal's four-volume compendium of regional dress customs. This book was first published in Paris in 1788, one year before the French Revolution. Its title alone required no fewer than 30 words.

Costumes Civils actuels de tous les peuples connus dessinés d'après nature gravés et coloriés, accompagnés d'une notice historique sur leurs coutumes, moeurs, religions, etc., etc., redigés par M. Sylvain Maréchal

The four volumes include an annotation on the illustrations: "gravé à la manière noire par Mixelle d'après Desrais et colorié." Clearly, the engraver and illustrator deserved no more than to be listed by their last names—after all they were mere technicians. The workers who colored each illustration by hand remain nameless.

The colorful variety of this collection reminds us vividly of how culturally apart the world's towns and regions were just 200 years ago. Dress codes have changed everywhere and the diversity by region, so rich at the time, has faded away. It is now hard to tell the inhabitant of one continent from another. Perhaps we have traded cultural diversity for a more varied personal life—certainly a more varied and interesting technological environment.

At a time when it is hard to tell one computer book from another, Manning celebrates the inventiveness and initiative of the computer business with book covers based on the rich diversity of regional life of two centuries ago, brought back to life by Maréchal's pictures. Just think, Maréchal's was a world so different from ours people would take the time to read a book title 30 words long.

PART I

Sockets programming

C H A P T E R   1

Introduction to distributed programming

1.1   INTRODUCTION

A distributed system consists of a collection of autonomous computers linked together by a network; the network is equipped with distributed system software that enables computers to coordinate activities and to share the resources of the system. The resources can be hardware, software, or data.

Distributed applications are based on the client/server architecture in which a set of server processes acts as a resource manager for a collection of resources of a given type, and a collection of client processes each performs a task that requires access to some shared resources.

Computer networks provide the necessary means for communication between the components of a distributed application. In this chapter, we will discuss the basic communication architecture on top of which distributed applications can be developed. I'll then summarize the principles of protocols and protocol layering and show how they can be used to provide a unified method for communication between components of a distributed application.

1.2 OVERVIEW OF INTERNETWORKING

To understand networking protocols, it is useful to know a little about networks. The term *network* usually means a set of computers and peripherals (printers, modems, plotters, scanners, and so on) that are connected together by some medium. The connection can be direct (through a cable) or indirect (through a modem). The different devices on the network communicate with each other through a predefined set of rules, which is commonly referred to as a *protocol*.

1.2.1 Network architecture

The devices on a network can be in the same room or scattered throughout a building. They can be separated by many miles through the use of dedicated telephone lines, microwaves, or similar systems. They can even be scattered around the world, connected by a long-distance communication medium.

If the devices on a network are in a single location such as a building or a group of rooms, they are commonly called a local area network, or LAN. In a typical LAN, all the devices on the network are connected by a single type of network cable. If the devices are widely scattered, such as in different buildings or different cities, they are usually arranged into several LANs that are joined together into a larger structure called a wide area network, or WAN.

1.2.2 Protocols

The term *protocol* is used to refer to the set of rules that two or more computers must follow to exchange messages. A protocol describes both the format of messages that are sent and the way a computer should respond to each message. The existence of well-known protocols enables the separate software components of a distributed application to be developed independently and implemented in different programming languages on computer systems that may have different data representation and order codes. The key communication protocol used in the Internet is called the *Internet Protocol*, which is usually abbreviated IP. Messages on the Internet travel in *packets*, which are usually called Internet packets or Datagrams. In chapter 2, you'll learn more about communication protocols such as Transmission Control Protocol (TCP) and User Datagram Protocol (UDP).

1.2.3 The OSI reference model

The Open Systems Interconnection (OSI) reference model is specified and implemented by the International Standard Organization (ISO). This model forms a protocol stack, which is a suite of protocols that are layered as shown in figure 1.1. There are seven layers in this stack; each is described below.

- *The application layer*   This layer is responsible for delivering data to the user. It mainly defines an interface to a service. Examples of this layer are File Transfer Protocol (FTP), remote login (Telnet), and Simple Mail Transfer Protocol (SMTP).
- *The presentation layer*   Protocols that implement this layer are responsible for transmitting data in a network representation that is independent of the underlying platform. If encryption is required, it will be provided at this layer. Examples of this layer include eXternal Data Representation (XDR) and Abstract Syntax Notation-1 (ASN.1).

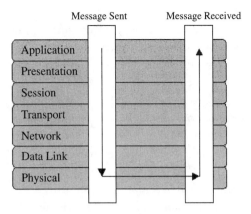

Message Sent   Message Received

Application
Presentation
Session
Transport
Network
Data Link
Physical

Figure 1.1 Protocol layers in OSI

- *The session layer*   This layer is responsible for establishing communication between processes, as well as performing error recovery. It is important to note that in the case of connectionless communication, this layer is not required.
- *The transport layer*   In this layer, messages are addressed to communication ports. The transport layer can either be connectionless (as in the case of UDP) or connection-oriented (as in the case of TCP), as we will see in chapter 2.
- *The network layer*   In this layer, data packets are transferred between computers. This layer is also responsible for generating routing paths. (This is true in the case of a WAN; however, no routing is required for a LAN.) Examples of this level include the IP and X.25.
- *The data link layer*   This layer is responsible for the error-free transmission of packets between computers.
- *The physical layer*   This layer contains the actual circuits and hardware that drive the network.

If you need detailed information on each layer, I suggest you refer to Andrew S. Tannenbaum's book *Computer Networks*, which provides comprehensive coverage of the OSI reference model.

1.2.4   Naming and routing

To make datagram delivery possible, each computer attached to the network must be assigned a unique address. One computer must know the address of another computer before it can communicate with the second system.

The Internet uses symbolic names for hostnames and networks, such as *prep.ai.mit.edu* or *utoronto.ca*. These symbolic names are called domain names, and they are convenient for us humans; however, they have to be translated to IP addresses before they can be used as communication identifiers. IP addresses are 32-bit numeric identifiers containing a network identifier and a host identifier that uniquely identify the network and a host on that particular network. The translation from symbolic names to IP identifiers is usually done by a naming service known as the Domain Name System (DNS).

IP identifiers are used when a host is sending packets to other hosts on the same network or another network, and in receiving packets from hosts on the same network or another network. If a host is sending packets to another host on the same network, only the host identifier is used to locate that host on the network. On the other hand, if a host is sending packets to a host on another network, then both the host and the network identifiers are used to locate that foreign host. The process of locating networks and hosts and delivering packets to them is called *routing*. A router on a network contains an IP layer that implements a routing algorithm that moves packets to their destinations.

It is the IP layer's responsibility to move packets from source to destination on the Internet. The IP layer forwards each packet based on a 32-bit destination address known as the IP address. Ranges of IP addresses, as discussed in section 1.2.5, are assigned to different organizations, which in turn each assigns numbers to departments. This is done by the Network Information Center (NIC), which is the only organization with the authority to do this.

While data is being routed, it can be lost in intermediate networks. The underlying transmission protocol has the responsibility to verify the correct delivery of the data from source to destination. For example, TCP has support to detect errors or lost data and to retransmit data until it is correctly received.

1.2.5   Internet addresses

There are five classes of Internet addresses: A, B, C, D, and E. The classes are all different; each meets the requirements of different organizations. For example, Class A addresses are used for large networks that have more than 65,536 hosts. Class B addresses are used for medium-size networks that have more than 256 but fewer than 65,536 hosts. Class C addresses are used for networks that have up to 256 hosts.

Class D is used for multicast, which is implemented on some Internet hosts. This class has the range 224.0.0.0 to 239.255.255.255. Class E is reserved for future use; it has the range 240.0.0.0 to 247.255.255.255.

The decimal representation of the various classes of Internet addresses is shown in the following tables.

Table 1.1 Class A addresses

Network ID	Host ID		
1 to 127	0 to 255	0 to 255	0 to 255

Table 1.2 Class B addresses

Network ID		Host ID	
128 to 191	0 to 255	0 to 255	0 to 255

Table 1.3 Class C addresses

Network			IDHost ID
192 to 223	0 to 255	0 to 255	0 to 255

Table 1.4 Multicast: Class D addresses

Multicast			
224 to 239	0 to 255	0 to 255	0 to 255

Table 1.5 Reserved: Class E addresses

Reserved			
240 to 247	0 to 255	0 to 255	0 to 255

The numbers shown above represent the permissible range of values for each class of addresses. The numbers 0 and 255 have special meanings. The number 0 is reserved for machines that do not know their own addresses. In certain cases, such as misconfiguration, it is possible for a machine not to know its own identifier or the identifier of the network it is running on. For example, a machine in class C with the number 0.0.0.42 would represent a machine that knew its number (42) but didn't know the number of the network it is running on. The number 255 is used for broadcasting. A broadcast is a message that you want to be seen by every machine on the network when it is sent out.

1.3   *INTRODUCTION TO DISTRIBUTED PROGRAMMING*

A distributed system consists of a collection of autonomous computers linked by a network and equipped with distributed system software that enables computers to coordinate their activities and share the resources (hardware, software, and data) of the system. Resources in a distributed system are physically encapsulated within one of the computers; other computers can only access them via communication. The resources are managed by a resource manager, which is an important component of a distributed system. Therefore, in a distributed system, resource users communicate with resource managers to access the shared resources of the system.

The world wide web, or web for short, represents a good example of a distributed system. Many web servers run on various computers, and each server holds a wide range of documents and information in other media on diverse topics. These web servers act as resource managers.

The two major types of applications of distributed systems are distributed computing and parallel computing. In distributed computing, a set of computers connected by a network are used collectively to accomplish a distributed job such as teleconferencing. On the other hand, in parallel computing, a solution to a large problem is divided into many small tasks. The tasks are distributed to, and executed on, multiple computers to achieve high performance.

Distributed systems can be implemented using two models: the client/server model and the object-based model.

1.3.1 The client/server model

The client/server model is an important model for distributed systems. It contains a set of server processes, each one acting as a resource manager for a collection of resources of a given type. It also contains a collection of client processes; each one performs a task that requires access to some shared hardware and software resources. Resource managers may themselves need to access resources managed by another process, so some processes are both client and server processes. However, in the client/server model, all shared resources are held and managed by server processes.

The client/server model is a form of distributed computing in which one program (the client) communicates with another program (the server) for the purpose of exchanging information. In client/server computing, both the client and server usually speak the same language—a protocol that the client and server both understand—so they are able to communicate.

In the client/server model, if a process acts as both a client and a server depending on its role, then it is an example of the *peer-to-peer* model of communication. Networked games are a perfect example of this model.

1.3.2 The object-based model

A distributed object-based system is a collection of objects that isolates the requestors of services (clients) from the providers of services (servers) by a well-defined encapsulating interface. In other words, clients are isolated from the implementation of services as data representations and executable code.

In the object-based model, a client sends a message to an object, which in turn interprets the message to decide what service to perform. This service, or method, selection could be performed by either the object or a broker.

In part II of this book, we will discuss Remote Method Invocation (RMI), in part III we'll discuss CORBA, and in part IV we'll discuss Voyager. All of these systems are object-based, as clients and servers are isolated by interfaces.

1.4 DISTRIBUTED PROGRAMMING TECHNIQUES

The client/server model can be implemented in various ways. It is typically done using low-level sockets or remote procedure calls (RPCs). Using low-level sockets for developing client/server systems means that we must design a protocol, which, as you've learned, is a set of commands agreed upon by the client and server through which they will be able to communicate. RPC is a high-level paradigm that abstracts the interface between the client and server to a local procedure call. Therefore, in RPC there is no need to design a protocol for the client and the server to use. In this section, you'll learn more about sockets and RPC.

1.4.1 Sockets

Facilities for interprocess Communication (IPC) represent a major addition to the Unix operating system. The basic idea was to make IPC similar to file input/output (I/O). The IPC primitives are provided as system calls, which are implemented as a layer over the TCP and UDP protocols. Message destinations are specified as socket addresses.

IPC operations are based on socket pairs; one socket belongs to each of a pair of communication processes. With IPC, information is exchanged by transmitting it in a message between a socket in one process and a socket in another process. Messages are queued at the sending socket until the networking protocol has transmitted them and an acknowledgment has arrived, if the protocol requires one. When messages arrive, they are queued at the receiving socket until the receiving process makes an appropriate system call to receive them. In client/server terms, the server is the process that listens for requests and the client is the process that sends the requests. Once the server process receives a request it tries to process that request, and it sends the output to the client.

1.4.2   Remote procedure calls

The RPC approach, which was conceived in the 1970s, views computer-to-computer communication as enabling one computer to call a procedure in another. In RPC, all messages go through the network; each either requests or acknowledges a procedure's action as shown in figure 1.2.

Figure 1.2 RPC-based client/server computing paradigm

An RPC is a high-level communication paradigm that allows network applications to be developed by way of specialized procedure calls which are designed to hide the details of the underlying network mechanism. With RPC, the client makes a procedure call which sends requests to the remote server, which in turn serves the procedures registered at the remote machine as necessary. When these requests arrive, the server calls a dispatch routine, executes the requested procedures, and sends back the reply, and the procedure call returns to the client.

Programs that use RPC mechanisms have the advantage of avoiding the details of interfacing with the network. They therefore provide network services to their callers without requiring that they be aware of the existence and function of the underlying network. This feature solves the tedious issues of distributed programming by making the calls transparent.

However, the RPC approach has its own limitations. Most notably, all interactions between the client and server must go through the network, as shown in figure 1.2. In chapter 20, we will discuss a new paradigm (mobile agents) for developing distributed applications.

1.4.3   Why distributed programming is good

A number of key characteristics are primarily responsible for the usefulness of distributed applications. In this section, I'll define and elaborate on some of them. Note that the following characteristics are not automatic consequences of distributing programming; software has to be designed carefully in order to achieve these characteristics.

- *Multiuser applications* A good example of a multiuser application is electronic mail (email). Distributed computing makes such applications possible by interconnecting stand-alone systems.
- *Resource sharing* Distributed computing allows an organization to make the best use of the available physical resources. For example, office workers can share the same expensive color printer.
- *Scalability* Since distributed systems are built out of multiple components, it is possible to add more components as needed. Distributed systems may be used to solve problems of any size since they scale with the problem.
- *Efficiency* Multiple platforms in a heterogeneous environment can be utilized so that each computer has to solve only part of the problem.
- *Fault tolerance and availability.* Components of a distributed application can be configured to survive most types of failures.
- *Transparency* The system is perceived as a whole rather than as a collection of independent components. Therefore, local and remote objects can be accessed using identical operations, without knowledge of their location.

1.4.4 Why distributed programming is hard

Along with all the advantages of distributed applications comes the fact that developing distributed applications is hard for a number of reasons:

- *Multiple failure modes* Distributed applications may fail in many different ways since they are built of many more components than a stand-alone application. For example, a distributed application with two components (A and B) running on different machines may fail in three modes: component A may fail, component B may fail, or the network connecting both components may fail.
- *Security issues* When developing distributed applications, you have to worry about protecting communication channels. Communication channels are accessible to eavesdroppers; therefore you have to devise and implement some security policies for distributed applications to protect information to stop illegal access to it.
- *Use of multiple technologies* A distributed application may require the use of multiple technologies. These technologies may be from different vendors, so consequently, they may not work with each other.
- *Testing and debugging* Testing and debugging distributed applications is much harder than testing and debugging stand-alone applications, because a distributed application can be running on more than one machine.

1.5 DISTRIBUTED PROGRAMMING SUPPORT IN JAVA

The Java Virtual Machine (JVM) enhances the portability of software across a heterogeneous network. Being platform-independent, Java allows its applications to run on any system that has a Java interpreter. This is a very important feature, since network-based applications would run on all of the different platforms on the Internet. The built-in security that Java provides, along with the security APIs, allows developers to incorporate low-level and high-level security functions in their applications.

In part, the Java environment is highly regarded because of its suitability for writing programs that use and interact with resources on the Internet and the web. Some of the features and mechanisms that Java supports for networking and distributed computing are listed here:

- *Sockets* Java supports connection-oriented (TCP) and connectionless (UDP) protocols over which sockets communicate. Throughout part I of this book, I will show you how to write distributed applications in Java using sockets.

- *RMI* Remote Method Invocation allows a programmer to write distributed applications in which the methods of remote Java objects can be invoked from other Java Virtual Machines on different hosts on the network. In this model, communicating distributed objects all have to be implemented in Java. Under RMI, Java objects cannot communicate with other objects on the network if they have been implemented in other languages. Part II of this book discusses RMI and shows you how to use it to develop distributed applications. For more information on RMI, go to http://java.sun.com/products/jdk/rmi.

- *JavaIDL* JavaIDL enables a programmer to define remote interfaces in the Interface Definition Language (IDL), which is an industry standard defined by the Object Management Group (OMG). Once the programmer has defined the remote interfaces in IDL, he then can compile that definition using a special compiler to generate Java interface definitions, client stubs, and server skeletons. JavaIDL allows a Java client to transparently invoke an IDL object that resides on a remote server, and it allows a Java server to define objects that can be transparently invoked from IDL clients. In part III of this book, we will discuss CORBA in greater detail and I'll show you how to develop distributed applications using VisiBroker for Java, which is a complete CORBA implementation. For more information on JavaIDL, go to http://java.sun.com/products/jdk/idl.

- *JavaSpaces* JavaSpaces is an attempt to provide distributed application developers with a simple, fast, and unified mechanism for sharing, coordination, and communication of distributed resources, services, and objects in a network. JavaSpaces has its own proprietary tuple-spaces, which are based on the tuple-spaces of the famous Linda prototype that was originally developed as a global communication buffer for parallel-processing systems. For more information on JavaSpaces, go to http://java.sun.com/products/javaspaces.

- *Jini* Jini is an R&D project at Sun Microsystems that expands the power of Java to enable spontaneous networking of a wide variety of hardware and software—anything that can be connected to the network. Sun envisions Jini as a system that will allow people to use networked devices and services as simply as they use a phone today. For more information on Jini, go to http://java.sun.com/products/jini.

- *JavaPC* JavaPC is a software system that provides an easy and flexible migration path to the Java platform and to network computing. JavaPC allows corporations to deploy Java applications on PCs running MS-OS and Windows 3.x. For more information on JavaPC, go to http://java.sun.com/products/javapc.

1.6   NETWORK MOBILITY

As programs begin to travel across networks, both the network and the programs begin to take on new characters. Network-mobile code makes it easier to ensure that an end-user has the necessary software to view or manipulate data sent across the network.

Mobile agents, which are discussed in part IV of this book, represent an evolutionary approach for developing distributed applications. They are attractive because the reliability of the network is not important. This topic is discussed in more details in chapter 20.

Java support for network mobility starts with its support for platform independence and security. These two features of Java help make network mobility practical. Platform independence makes it easier to develop a program across the network since you do not have to maintain a separate version of the program for each different platform. And Java security gives users confidence in downloading class files from untrusted resources.

1.7   OVERVIEW OF JAVA SECURITY

The Java security model is comprised of three layers:

- The Java language itself.
- The Java compiler and run-time system.
- The SecurityManager class.

At the language layer, Java achieves its safety in different ways. First, Java strictly defines that all primitive types are of a specific size, and independent of the machine architecture. Second, pointer arithmetic and forging access to objects cannot be done. Third, Java provides array-bound checking. Therefore, an attempt to index an out-of-bound element of an array will throw an exception. Finally, Java ensures that casting one object to another is a legal operation.

The Java compiler and run-time system security layer provide the necessary features to ensure that the Java system is not subverted by invalid code. It provides a simple, secure execution environment that consists of three sublayers:

- The Java bytecode interpreter and class format verifier.
- Amechanism for dynamically loading and checking libraries at runtime.
- An automated garbage collector.

The first two layers, namely the language and the compiler, mainly ensure that the Java system is not subverted by invalid code; however, they do not provide any mechanisms to protect against malicious instructions in a client/server program. The JDK1.0 introduced the SecurityManager class, which defines and implements a security policy by centralizing all access-control decisions. Web browsers, such as Netscape's Navigator and Microsoft's Internet Explorer, use the SecurityManager class to implement a customized security manager that will be installed when executing untrusted code or applets, to reflect their own security policies.

The three layers are used together to provide a very restricted environment known as a sandbox, in which untrusted code or applets can be run. The essence of the sandbox is that local code is trusted and can have full access to the underlying file system. Likewise, downloaded remote code is untrusted and can access only limited resources provided inside the sandbox. The sandbox model is illustrated in figure 1.3.

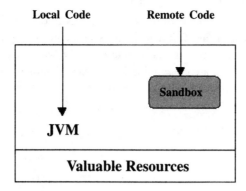

Figure 1.3 The JDK1.0 security model

JDK1.1 has introduced the concept of signed applets. A correctly signed applet is treated as trusted local code, and so it can access the file system. Signed applets, together with their signatures, are delivered in the JAR (Java Archive) format. This new evolving sandbox model is illustrated in figure 1.4.

While this evolving sandbox opens up interesting possibilities, it is still crude in the sense that all local Java applications enjoy full access to the underlying system resources while remote code is running in the sandbox, unless the code is signed by a trusted entity.

This, however, has changed in Java 2, where signed code, in addition to remote, has been extended to local code. With the new security model in Java 2, all code (remote and local), signed or unsigned, will get access to system resources based on what is mentioned in a *policy file*. A policy file allows you to specify what permissions you wish to grant to code residing in a specified code source, and what permissions you wish to grant to code signed by specific persons.

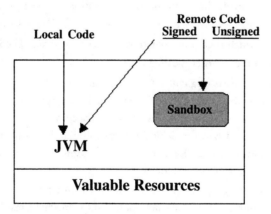

Figure 1.4 The JDK1.1 security model

Protection domains are new features in Java 2. Prior to Java 2, the `SecurityManager` was used to enforce the security policy. However, this has changed with the new Java version, and the `SecurityManager` is kept in Java 2 just to be backward-compatible with JDK1.0 and JDK1.1. Protection domains implement the site's security policy, which is defined by stating explicitly what permissions you want code running in a particular domain to have. As an example, consider the following policy file with two policies:

```
codebase    "http:///www.company.com"
signedBy    "12345678901122334455"
permission File "/local/emerge/*"
action "read, write"

codebase    "http://www.company.com"
signedBy "12345678901122334455"
permission Net "http://www.company.com"
action "connect"
```

The two policy entries state that any class downloaded from the site www.company.com and signed by the principal with the certificate 12345678901122334455 is allowed to only read and write, but not delete, for example, any file in the directory /local/emerge. It can also open a socket connection to port 80.

As a final note, the protection domain policy-based system allows you to control access to the file system, the network, and other functions in the Java run-time. As editing the policy file manually is an error-prone process, the Policy Wizard provided by JavaSoft helps you properly customize the site.

1.8   SUMMARY

- Computer networks provide the means of communication between the components of a distributed application. These components communicate with each other through a predefined set of rules, which is commonly referred to as a protocol. The key communication protocol used in the Internet is called the IP.

- A distributed system consists of a collection of autonomous computers linked by a network and equipped with system software that enables computers to coordinate their activities and to share the hardware, software, and data resources of the system. Such a system offers a number of benefits, including scalability and transparency. Developing such a system, however, is hard for a number of reasons, including multiple failure modes and the use of multiple technologies.

- Java is a programming language particularly well-suited for writing applications that use and interact with resources on the Internet. Some of the mechanisms that Java supports for networking are sockets, RMI, JavaIDL, JavaSpaces, and Jini. Java's built-in security features and security API allow developers to incorporate low-level and high-level security functions in their applications.

C H A P T E R   2

Introduction to sockets programming

The Unix operating system is highly regarded as a development platform that has many programming tools and provides great support for networking. In Unix, two related processes can communicate via a pipe. But how can two processes running on two different machines communicate? Berkeley Unix provides a mechanism for just this sort of communication across machines: sockets.

In this chapter, I'll start off by discussing the building blocks for interprocess communications. I'll also discuss communication protocols such as TCP and UDP, and how to choose the right protocol for your application. Then I'll discuss sockets and I'll show you how to do basic sockets programming in Java. Finally, I'll show you how to use the `InetAddress` class to resolve Internet addresses.

2.1   INTERPROCESS COMMUNICATION

The Unix I/O system follows a paradigm usually referred to as *Open-Read-Write-Close*. Before a user process performs I/O operations, it calls *Open* to specify and obtain permissions for the file or device to be used. Once an object has been opened, the user process makes one or more calls to *Read* or *Write*. Read reads data from the object and transfers it to the user process, while Write transfers data from the user process to the object. After all transfer operations are complete, the user process calls *Close* to inform the operating system that it has finished using that object.

In Unix, two related processes can communicate via a *pipe* if they inherit file descriptors for that pipe from a common ancestor. A pipe is a pseudo-file that can be used to connect two processes together, as shown in figure 2-1. When process A wants to send a message to process B, it writes to the pipe as if it were an output file. Process B can then read the data by reading from the pipe as if it were reading from an input file.

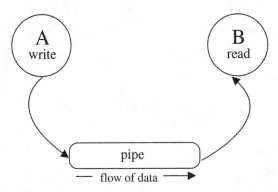

Figure 2.1 Two processes connected by a pipe

As an example, when a user enters a command such as

```
cat myClass.java | lpr
```

to a Unix shell, the shell creates two processes with a pipe between them. `cat` is the program that reads a file in sequence and writes it to the standard output (however, in this case it will be sent to the printer instead), and `lpr` is the program that sends the result to the line printer. Note that the two processes in this example are somehow related. Remember, two unrelated processes *cannot* communicate via a pipe.

Two unrelated processes may, however, communicate through files. For example, process X may append a message to a file, and process Y may check the file at regular intervals and read from it whenever it contains any new messages. This approach, however, is rather inefficient, and we're still left with the question of how two processes on two different machines communicate. The Berkeley Unix system provides a solution to this problem in the form of *sockets*.

2.2   WHAT ARE SOCKETS?

When facilities for IPC and networking were added to Unix, the idea was to make the interface to IPC similar to that of file I/O. In Unix, a process has a set of I/O descriptors that one reads from and writes to. These descriptors may refer to files, devices, or communication channels (sockets).

Sockets are analogous to telephones in the sense that they provide the user with an interface to the network just as telephones provide the user with an interface to the telephone system. Figure 2.2 shows how sockets provide an interface between the user and the network.

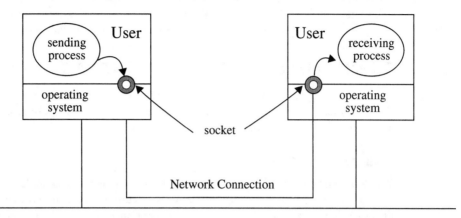

Figure 2.2 Sockets: the interface between the user and the network

Think of a socket as the end point of a Unix pipe. Actually, a pipe in Unix is implemented as a pair of sockets. A socket is used in exactly the same way as a file descriptor. Thus, the lifetime of a descriptor is made up of three phases: *creation* (opening the socket), *reading and writing* (receiving and sending to the socket), and *destruction* (closing the socket).

The IPC operations are based on socket pairs; each pair belongs to a communication process. IPC is done by exchanging data as it is transmitted in a message between a socket in one process and another socket in another process. When messages are sent, the messages are queued at the sending socket until the underlying network protocol has transmitted them. When they arrive, the messages are queued at the receiving socket until the receiving process makes the necessary calls to receive them. Message destinations are specified as socket addresses; each socket address is a communication identifier that consists of an Internet address and a port number. The port number is an integer that is needed to distinguish between services running on the same machine. Note that port numbers between 0 and 1023 on Unix systems are reserved for use by *root* or *superuser*.

Two or more sockets must be connected, as in TCP, before they can be used to transfer data. There are a number of connections to choose from, but most system software which performs socket communication between computers uses either TCP or UDP as described in section 2.3. To further complicate matters, there are three types of sockets. They will be explained in the next section.

2.2.1 Types of sockets

Three kinds of sockets may be used: SOCK_STREAM, SOCK_DGRAM, and SOCK_RAW. SOCK_STREAM provides byte-to-byte stream communication, and it can be used for transmission in either direction. SOCK_DGRAM is used for datagram transmission, and it also can be used in either direction.

The third kind, SOCK_RAW, is provided for users who want a high level of control over message transmission. This interface, for example, may permit the user to specify the exact path to use when sending packets over a complicated network. It is important to note that for security reasons, Java does not support the SOCK_RAW type of sockets. See chapter 3 for more information on how this may affect the development of some system services such as *ping*, which is a Unix program used to check the aliveness of a remote machine.

2.3 TCP/IP AND UDP/IP COMMUNICATIONS

You can use two communication protocols for sockets programming: *datagram communication* and *stream communication*. Both are supported in Java. I will discuss each protocol in detail, then I will compare them and tell you when to use what.

2.3.1 Datagram communication

The datagram communication protocol, known as UDP, is a connectionless protocol, meaning that each time you send datagrams, you also need to send the local socket descriptor and the receiving socket's address. As you can tell, additional data must be sent each time a communication is made.

2.3.2 Stream communication

The stream communication protocol is known as TCP. Unlike UDP, TCP is a connection-oriented protocol. In order to communicate over the TCP protocol, a connection must first be established between the sockets. While one of the sockets listens for a connection request (server), the other asks for a connection (client). Once two sockets have been connected, they can be used to transmit data in both (or either one of the) directions.

Now, you might ask, "What protocol should I use—UDP or TCP?" The answer depends on the client/server application you are writing. The following section briefly describes the differences between the UDP and TCP protocols; this may help you decide which protocol you should use.

2.3.3 UDP vs. TCP

In UDP, every time you send a datagram, you have to send the local descriptor and the socket address of the receiving socket along with it. That is not necessary with TCP, but since TCP is a connection-oriented protocol, a connection must first be established between the sockets before communication begins. Therefore, there is a connection setup time in TCP, but more information is needed for UDP.

In UDP, there is a size limit of 64 kilobytes on datagrams you can send to a specified location, while in TCP there is no limit. Once a TCP connection is established, the pair of sockets behaves like streams—all available data are read immediately in the order in which they are received.

UDP is an *unreliable* protocol—there is no guarantee that the datagrams you send will be received in the same order by the receiving socket. In comparison, TCP is a reliable protocol; it is guaranteed that the packets you send will be received in the order in which they were sent.

In short, TCP is useful for implementing network services (such as remote login (rlogin, Telnet) and FTP) which require data of indefinite length to be transferred. UDP is less complex and incurs fewer overheads. It is often used in implementing client/server applications in distributed systems built over local area networks. You are better off using TCP since it provides reliable, connection-oriented communications. Programs only use UDP if the application protocol handles reliability, the application requires multicast, or the application cannot tolerate the overhead involved in TCP. In this part of the book, most of the examples use TCP.

2.4 CLIENT/SERVER COMMUNICATION

As you learned in chapter 1, the client/server model is a form of distributed computing where one program (the client) communicates with another program (the server) for the purpose of exchanging information. Figure 2.3 shows the sequence of steps normally taken to set up socket communication and data exchange between a client and a server. Note that the server in the figure is a single-threaded server in the sense that it is only capable of serving one client. In the next chapter, we will discuss multithreaded servers.

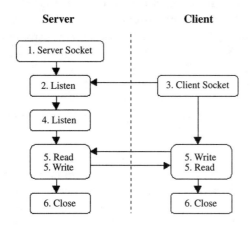

Figure 2.3 Client/server socket communication

In order for both the client and server to communicate, they will need to speak the same language, or protocol, which is a set of commands that allows the client and server to exchange information.

2.5 SOCKETS PROGRAMMING IN JAVA

Programming sockets in Java is seamless. At the core of Java's networking support are the Socket and DatagramSocket classes, which are part of the java.net package. As I mentioned earlier, there are two flavors of sockets: those that use TCP and those that use UDP. In this section, I will describe the basics of sockets programming for TCP and UDP. I will also give you an introduction to multicast sockets. However, before we delve into sockets, we first need to discuss data streams, which are used heavily in sockets programming for sending and receiving data.

2.5.1 Data streams

The core of all input/output in Java is the data stream. Think of a data stream as a pipeline of data. You can put information in the pipeline (in other words, write it to the stream), or you can get information from the pipeline (read it from the stream).

With sockets, information is read and written by wrapping it up in various kinds of streams. You can write information by constructing an `OutputStream` (which provides the `write()` method), and you can write information by constructing an `InputStream` (which provides the `read()` method). When a socket connection is successfully established, each end-point creates an `InputStream` and an `OutputStream`. The `InputStream` is created using `getInputStream()`, and the `OutputStream` is created using `getOutputStream()`. These streams allow you to read and write either single or multiple bytes. Here are some of the other streams included in the `java.io` package:

- `BufferedReader` and `BufferedWriter` buffer data while reading or writing, thus reducing the number of accesses required on the original data. Note that buffered streams are more efficient than nonbuffered streams.
- `FilterInputStream` and `FilterOutputStream` are constructed using an instance of nonbuffered `InputStream` and `OutputStream`. They improve performance by caching and flushing.
- `DataInputStream` and `DataOutputStream` provide higher-level services for reading and writing primitive data types.
- `FileReader`, `FileWriter`, `FileInputStream`, and `FileOutputStream` are used collectively to read from or write to a file.

It is important to note that data streams are not object-friendly. In chapter 5, we will discuss specialized streams that allow you to read and write objects. For more information on data streams, please refer to the `java.io` package. For an excellent reference on streams, please refer to *Java Network Programming* by Merlin Hughes, Michael Shoffner, and Derek Hamner (Manning Publications Co., 1999).

2.5.2 TCP sockets

TCP socket connections are created through the `Socket` class. There are four steps to programming a client or a server using sockets:

1 Opening a socket.
2 Creating a data input stream.
3 Creating a data output stream.
4 Closing the socket(s).

And, of course, you have to develop the protocol (language) that the client and server should understand or be able to speak in order to carry on a useful conversation with each other. Now, let's take a detailed look at each of the steps involved in programming sockets.

Opening a socket   If you are programming a client, open a socket like this:

```
Socket MyClient = null;
try {
   MyClient = new Socket("host", PortNumber);
} catch(UnknownHostException uhe) {
  uhe.printStackTrace();
} catch(IOException e) {
   e.printStackTrace();
}
```

If you are programming a server, open a socket like this:

```
public static final int PortNumber = 4000;
ServerSocket MyService = null;
try {
  MyService = new ServerSocket(PortNumber);
} catch(IOException ioe) {
   ioe.printStackTrace();
}
```

When you are implementing a server, you also need to create a socket object from the ServerSocket in order to listen for and accept connections from clients. This is done as follows:

```
Socket serviceSocket = null;
try {
  serviceSocket = MyService.accept();
} catch(IOException iex) {
   iex.printStackTrace();
}
```

Creating an input stream   To create an input stream on the client side, you can use the BufferedReader class (in JDK1.1 and above) to receive a response from the server. This is done as follows:

```
BufferedReader is = null;
try {
  is = new BufferedReader(new InputStreamReader(MyClient.getInputStream());
} catch(IOException ioe) {
   ioe.printStackTrace();
}
```

NOTE   If you are using JDK1.0.2, you would create an input stream using the DataInputStream class. This is done as follows:

```
DataInputStream dis = null;
try {
    dis = new DataInputStream(MyClient.getInputStream());
} catch(IOException ioe) {
   ioe.printStackTrace();
}
```

To create an input stream on the server side, you can use the `BufferedReader` to receive input from the client:

```
BufferedReader is = null;
try {
  is = new BufferedReader(new InputStreamReader (serviceClient.getInput-
Stream());
} catch(IOException ioe) {
  ioe.printStackTrace();
}
```

The example provided in section 2.6 shows some of the handy methods provided by the `BufferedReader` class for reading lines of text and Java primitive data types in a portable way.

Creating an output stream   On the client side, you can create an output stream to send data to the server socket using the `DataOutputStream` class. The following code shows how:

```
DataOutputStream os = null;
try {
  os = new DataOutputStream (MyClient.getOutputStream());
} catch(IOException ix) {
  ix.printStackTrace();
}
```

On the server side, you can use the class `DataOutputStream` to send data to the client as follows:

```
DataOutputStream os = null;
try {
  os = new DataOutputStream (serviceClient.getOutputStream());
} catch(IOException ie) {
  ie.printStackTrace();
}
```

Closing sockets   It is important that you always close the input and output streams before closing the sockets. Thus, on the client side, do this:

```
try {
  os.close();
  is.close();
  MyClient.close();
} catch(IOException io) {
  io.printStackTrace();
}
```

And, on the server side, do this:

```
try {
  os.close();
  is.close();
  serviceSocket.close();
} catch(IOException ic) {
  ic.printStackTrace();
}
```

2.5.3 UDP sockets (datagrams)

UDP socket connections are created through the `DatagramSocket` class. A `Datagram-Socket` sends and receives data using packets, which are represented as `DatagramPacket` objects. In order for two programs to talk to each other over a UDP connection, they both have to have `DatagramSocket` connected to a port on their machines. This can be done by creating a `DatagramSocket` object as follows:

```
DatagramSocket connect = new DatagramSocket(5555);
```

In this example we are connecting a UDP socket to a specific port number, 5555, on the local machine. Note that if you are not sure which port to use or you do not care which port will be used, then you can construct the `DatagramSocket` without specifying the port, as follows:

```
DatagramSocket ds = new DatagramSocket();
```

In this case, an unused port on the local machine will be used. You can find out which port has been used by asking the new socket for its port number as follows:

```
int portNumber = ds.getLocalPort();
```

Data is sent over a `DatagramSocket` using `DatagramPacket`, and each `Datagram-Socket` contains a data buffer, the address of the remote host to send the data to, and the port number the server is listening on. Thus, for a client to send a buffer of data to a server listening on port 5555 on machine "purejava," you would write something like this:

```
byte buf[] = {'h', 'e', 'l', 'l', 'o'};
InetAddress address = InetAddress.getByName("purejava");
DatagramPacket packet = new DatagramPacket(buf, buf.length, address, 5555);
ds.send(packet); // See ds above.
```

The remote server can receive the data request from the client as follows:

```
byte buf[] = new byte[256];
DatagramPacket packet = new DatagramPacket(buf, buf.length);
sd.receive(packet);
```

Note that the `DatagramPacket` constructor used in the server's code requires only two arguments: a byte array that contains client-specific data and the length of the byte array. However, when we are constructing a `DatagramPacket` to send over the `DatagramSock-et` as shown above, we have to provide the Internet address and port number of the packet's destination.

Note that in the above examples we did not catch any exceptions. Sending a `Datagram-Packet`, for example, may generate an `IOException` if the network transmission fails for some reason.

2.5.4 Multicast sockets

In addition to the `Socket` and `DatagramSocket` classes, the `java.net` package includes a class called `MulticastSocket`. A `MulticastSocket` is a `DatagramSocket` with additional capabilities for joining groups of other multicast hosts on the Internet. This type of socket is used on the client side to listen for packets that the server broadcasts to multiple clients.

A multicast group is identified by a class D (those in the range 224.0.0.1 to 239.255.255.254, inclusive) IP address. Broadcasting packets to multiple recipients is analogous to radio and television broadcasting. A practical use of multicast IP is for broadcasting audio and video over the Internet. For more information on the multicast backbone (MBONE), see http://www.mbone.com.

A process that wants to listen on the multicast address creates a `MulticastSocket` and then joins the multicast session by calling the `joinGroup()` method. For example, to join a group and send the group a greeting, we would write something like the following:

```
byte msg[] = { 'h', 'i', ' ', 't', 'h', 'e', 'r', 'e' };
InetAddress group = InetAddress.getByName("229.2.56.29");
MulticastSocket ms = new MulticastSocket(6666);
ms.joinGroup();
DatagramPacket greetings = new DatagramPacket(msg, msg.length, group,
6666);
ms.send(greetings);
```

Once the connection to the multicast session is established, a client can read data being broadcasted on the channel as follows:

```
byte buf[] = new byte[1024];
DatagramPacket data = new DatagramPacket(buf, buf.length);
ms.receive(data);
```

Once the broadcast is over, or when we want to stop listening, we can disconnect by leaving the group using the `leaveGroup()` method:

```
ms.leaveGroup(group);
```

If you are thinking of using multicast IP, be aware that it is based on UDP. Therefore, it is not reliable and there is a possibility of losing some data along the way.

2.6 GREETINGS SERVER EXAMPLE

Now, let's look at the development of a simple client/server application. This application also explains the idea of what a protocol is throug the development of a very simpleminded protocol.

In this simple client/server application, the server starts listening on a predetermined port number, and it waits for a client to connect. When the client runs, it will ask the user for a keyword to be sent to the server. If the user types in the right keyword—"Greetings"—then the server will send the message "….and salutations…." back to the client. Otherwise, the server sends the message "Sorry, you don't speak my protocol."

Before listing the Java source code for both the client and the server, here is a sample run. Note that the symbol & starts the server in the background on Unix systems.

```
% java SimpleServer &
SimpleServer Started . . . .
```

```
% java SimpleClient
Please input a keyword: hello
Got from the server: Sorry, you don't speak my protocol.
```

Here is another run with the right keyword:

```
% java SimpleServer &
SimpleServer Started . . . .
% java SimpleClient
Please input a keyword: Greetings
Got from the server: ....and salutations....
```

2.6.1   The server program

The server program in this application is really simple. All it does is create an object of
ServerSocket, and an object of Socket to accept the client's connections, as well as an
input stream through which to read messages from the client and an output stream
through which to send responses back to the connected client. The server program is
shown in example 2.1. Notice that we have chosen to run the server on port number
5000, which is greater than 1023. Port numbers between 0 and 1023 are reserved for services run by system administrators.

Example 2.1: simpleServer.java

```java
import java.io.*;
import java.net.*;
/**
 * @(#) SimpleServer.java
 */
public class SimpleServer {
  public final static int TESTPORT = 5000;
  public static void main(String args[]) {
    // Declaration section:
    // Declare a server socket and a client socket for the server.
    // Declare an input stream and an output stream.
    ServerSocket checkServer = null;
    String line;
    BufferedReader is = null;
    DataOutputStream os = null;
    Socket clientSocket = null;

    // Try to open a server socket on port TESTPORT.
    // Note that you can't choose a port less than 1023 if you are not
    // privileged users (root)
    try {
      checkServer = new ServerSocket(TESTPORT);
      System.out.println("SimpleServer started. . . .");
    } catch (IOException e) {
      System.out.println(e);
    }
    // Create a socket object from the ServerSocket to listen and
    // accept connections.
```

```
      // Open input and output streams.
      try {
        clientSocket = checkServer.accept();
        is = new BufferedReader(new InputStreamReader
                               (clientSocket.getInputStream()));
         os = new DataOutputStream (clientSocket.getOutputStream());
      } catch(Exception ei) {
         ei.printStackTrace();
      }
      // Receive the client's message and check if it contains "Greetings".
      try {
        line=is.readLine();
        System.out.println("we received: "+line);
        if (line.compareTo("Greetings") == 0) {
          os.writeBytes("...and salutations...");
        } else {
           os.writeBytes("Sorry, you don't speak my protocol");
        }
      } catch (IOException e) {
         System.out.println(e);
      }
      // Close the input/output streams and the connection.
      try {
        os.close();
        is.close();
        clientSocket.close();
      } catch(IOException ic) {
         ic.printStackTrace();
      }
    }
  }
}
```

2.6.2   The client program

The client program is shown in example 2.2. The client program is simple as well: it opens a socket connection to port 5000, where the server program is running. It uses the output stream, dos, to send messages to the server, and the input stream, dis, to read incoming messages (replies) from the server.

Example 2.2: simpleClient.java

```
import java.io.*;
import java.net.*;
/**
 * @(#) SimpleClient.java
 */
public class SimpleClient {
   public final static int REMOTE_PORT = 5000;
   public static void main(String argv[]) throws Exception {
     Socket cl = null, cl2=null;
     BufferedReader is = null;
     DataOutputStream os = null;
```

```
BufferedReader stdin = new BufferedReader(new InputStreamReader
    System.in));
String userInput = null;
String output = null;
// Open a connection to the greetings server on port 5000.
try {
 cl = new Socket("machine name",REMOTE_PORT);
 is = new BufferedReader (new InputStreamReader(cl.getInputStream()));
 os = new DataOutputStream(cl.getOutputStream());
} catch(UnknownHostException e1) {
    System.out.println("Unknown Host: "+e1);
} catch (IOException e2) {
    System.out.println("Erorr io: "+e2);
}
// Get input from the user and send it to the greetings server.
try {
    System.out.print("Please input a keyword:");
    userInput = stdin.readLine();
    os.writeBytes(userInput+"\n");
} catch (IOException ex) {
    System.out.println("error writing to server."+ex);
}
// Receive a reply from the greetings server.
try {
    output = is.readLine();
    System.out.println("Got from server: "+output);
 } catch(IOException e) {
    e.printStackTrace();
}
// Close the input stream, output stream, and connection.
try {
  is.close();
  os.close();
  cl.close();
} catch (IOException x) {
    System.out.println("Error writing...."+x);
}
    }
}
```

2.6.3 What is missing?

If you run the server and client programs shown above, you will notice that the client can only make one connection to the server. If you try to run the client again, you will get the error message "Connection refused" because the server is not running. As a matter of fact, the server program shown above dies right after it satisfies the request of one client. That was the intention of this simple server program. In the next chapter, we will discuss the development of multithreaded servers, which are servers that run continuously and are capable of serving multiple clients' requests simultaneously.

2.7   RESOLVING INTERNET ADDRESSES

It is easier for us humans to remember symbolic names rather than a bunch of numbers. For example, it is easier to memorize the string *leo.scs.carleton.ca* rather than the number *134.117.5.3*.

In this section, I'll show you how to translate symbolic names into Internet addresses and vice versa using the `InetAddress` class from the `java.net` package. The `InetAddress` class provides some useful methods that can help us in resolving Internet addresses.

To get the IP address of the network you are running on, use the `getLocalHost()` and `getAddress()` methods of the class `InetAddress` in the `java.net` package. The method `getLocalHost()` returns an `InetAddress` object, and `getAddress()` returns an array of four bytes.

When writing a network-based application, you may need to know the symbolic name (hostname) or the IP address of the machine the application is going to run on. If you are running the application on your machine and you know the symbolic or IP address of your machine, you may hard-code the machine name (for example, `String localHost = "machine-name"`). However, if your application is going to run on different machines, then having the `localHost` hard-coded is not a good idea. It is better to have your program automatically figures out the hostname or IP address of the machine it is running on.

2.7.1   Example: GetName

The source code shown in example 2.3 shows how you would find the symbolic name of the machine you are working on.

`InetAddress` is a class in the `java.net` package. In example 2.3, we a have `host` of type `InetAddress`; the assignment `host = InetAddress.getLocalHost()` returns to an `InetAddress`. For example, if my host name is "leo" and its IP address is "134.117.5.3", then the variable `host` would have the value "leo/134.117.5.3". However, since we are only interested in the symbolic name, we can use the method `getHostName()` to print the machine name "leo".

Example 2.3: GetName.java

```
import java.net.*;
/**
 *   @(#) GetName.java
 */
public class GetName {
   public static void main(String argv[]) throws Exception {
      InetAddress host = null;
      host = InetAddress.getLocalHost();
      System.out.println(host.getHostName());
   }
}
```

2.7.2   Example: GetIP

Internet addresses are in digit format, and they are normally called IP addresses. The example shown above returns the machine name (hostname). But if you want to return the IP number, such as 134.117.5.3, you could modify the example so that it would return the IP number of the local host you are working on, as shown in example 2.4.

The method `getAddress()` returns a byte array of four bytes. For example, if your IP address is 134.117.5.3, then the byte array `ip` defined in example 2.4 would have the following values:

```
ip[0] = 134
ip[1] = 117
ip[2] = 5
ip[3] = 3
```

Example 2.4: GetIP.java

```java
import java.net.*;
/**
 *  @(#)GetIP.java
 */
public class GetIP {
    public static void main(String argv[]) throws Exception {
        InetAddress host = null;
        host = InetAddress.getLocalHost();
        byte ip[] = host.getAddress();
        for (int i=0; i<ip.length; i++) {
            if (i > 0) System.out.print(".");
            System.out.print(ip[i] & 0xff);
        }
        System.out.println();
    }
}
```

As you learned in section 1.2.4, all computers on the Internet have addresses. Each computer has a unique IP address and a name that identifies it. But why do we need addresses? Addresses are important since they help us identify the location of persistence resources, and they support routing as well.

2.7.3   Example: NsLookup

There is a huge number of names and IP addresses on the Internet, so a naming service is needed to map each name to an IP address. This service is known as a DNS. An example of a naming service (a sophisticated DNS client) is the nslookup utility found on Unix systems. Using nslookup, you can find the hostname for an IP address or the IP address for a hostname. It is a very useful utility. The source code in example 2.5 is a simple utility that allows us to find the IP address for any accessible hostname on the Internet.

Example 2.5: NsLookup.Java

```java
import java.net.*;
/**
```

```
 *  @(#) NsLookup.java
 * /
public class NsLookup {
   public static void main(String argv[]) {
      if (argv.length == 0) {
        System.out.println("Usage: java NsLookup <hostname>");
        System.exit(0);
      }
      String host = argv[0];
      InetAddress address = null;
      try {
        address = InetAddress.getByName(host);
      } catch(UnknownHostException e) {
        System.out.println("Unknown host");
        System.exit(0);
      }
      byte[] ip = address.getAddress();
      for (int i=0; i<ip.length; i++) {
        if (i > 0) System.out.print(".");
        System.out.print((ip[i]) & 0xff);
      }
      System.out.println();
   }
}
```

2.7.4   Example: IPtoName

Writing a utility to convert IP addresses to symbolic names was not an easy task in JDK1.0.2 due to a bug in the method getHostName() in the InetAddress class. However, this bug has been fixed in JDK1.1, so the code in example 2.6 should work with JDK1.1 and above.

Example 2.6: IPtoName.java

```
import java.net.*;
/**
 *  @(#) IPtoName.java
 */
public class IPtoName {
 public static void main(String argv[]) {
   if (argv.length == 0) {
     System.out.println("Usage: java IPtoName <IP address>");
     System.exit(0);
   }
   String host = argv[0];
   InetAddress address = null;
   try {
     address = InetAddress.getByName(host);
   } catch (UnknownHostException e) {
     System.out.println("invalid IP--malformed IP");
     System.exit(0);
   }
```

```
        System.out.println(address.getHostName());
    }
}
```

2.8   *SUMMARY*

- Sockets provide a mechanism for processes to communicate across a network, similar to Unix pipes. A socket is the endpoint of a pipe that connects two processes. Unlike regular Unix pipes, the two processes connected by sockets need not be running on the same machine.
- There are three types of sockets: SOCK_STREAM, SOCK_DGRAM, and SOCK_RAW. Java has support for the first two types. For security reasons Java does not support the SOCK_RAW type. SOCK_STREAM sockets are used in connection-oriented communications such as TCP, and SOCK_DGRAM sockets are used in connectionless communications such as UDP.
- TCP is a connection-oriented network communication protocol which ensures that a number of aspects of interprocess communication happen reliably. These aspects include detecting and correcting errors introduced by noise on the network, ensuring that the data the receiver sees is the data that was actually sent, and ensuring that data packets arrive at the receiver in the order in which they were sent.
- UDP is not connection-oriented; using UDP, a program can multicast data simultaneously to many applications. UDP also introduces fewer overheads than TCP, but UDP cannot guarantee reliable transmission of data or that a receiver gets packets in the order in which they were sent.
- In Java, programs create TCP socket connections by calling upon the Socket class. There are four basic steps to programming a client or a server using the Socket class: opening a socket, creating a data input stream, creating a data output stream, and closing the socket(s).

CHAPTER 3

Programming clients and servers

For a server to be useful in a distributed application, it must be able to serve multiple clients' requests simultaneously. Threads provide an easy way to implement this capability.

Threads are processes that run simultaneously in the same address space. They provide a way to write a program that performs multiple tasks simultaneously. The program can then take advantage of computers with multiple CPUs.

In this chapter, to demonstrate multithreading, we'll write some clients for common Internet services, such as a mail (SMTP) client, a finger client, and a ping application.

3.1 PROGRAMMING CLIENTS FOR EXISTING SERVICES

Network programming in Java is seamless and easily done. As we discussed in chapter 2, the java.net package contains useful high-level classes that provide access to TCP, UDP, IP addresses, and various other networking mechanisms. When you are programming clients, TCP connections are created using the Socket class. Once a connection has been set up, you obtain streams to and from the server application, and communicate through the streams' interfaces.

A protocol must exist between servers and clients. As we discussed in chapter 1, a protocol is simply a language, or a set of commands, through which clients and servers communicate with each other. This means that in order to write a client for an existing service, we must understand the underlying protocol. We will discuss the protocols being used as we write new clients.

In this chapter, we will write a number of useful client applications that interact with existing services. We will develop three applications: a *mail* (SMTP) client, a *finger* client, and a *ping* application.

3.1.1 SMTP client

SMTP, which stands for Simple Mail Transfer Protocol, is a protocol that is widely used in the Internet for sending mail messages. The **SMTP** service uses TCP and runs on port 25. The SMTP protocol is not very complicated, but there are a few commands that you need to know in order to understand how it works. As a demonstration, the following is the output of a Telnet session to port 25 on a hypothetical machine that runs an SMTP server. The commands we entered are in **bold** face. The rest of the text is what the system displays. For more information on SMTP, please refer to the specifications in RFC 822/823. Good coverage of many Internet protocols can be found in *Internet System Handbook* by Daniel C. Lynch and Marshall T. Rose (Addison-Wesley, 1993).

```
% telnet MailMachine.com 25
Trying 138.119.1.2...
Connected to MailMachine.com.
Escape character is '^]'.
220 MailMachine.com Sendmail 5.x/SMI-SVR4 ready at Sun, 3 Jan 1999 15:11:04
- 0400
HELO
250 MailMachine.com Hello  (hostname), pleased to meet you
MAIL From: dejavu@acm.org
250 dejavu@acm.org... Sender ok
RCPT To: dejavu@acm.org
250 dejavu@acm.org... Recipient ok
DATA
354 Enter mail, end with "." on a line by itself
From: dejavu@acm.org
Subject: testing
Hi there,
        We are testing the SMTP protocol.
bye.
.
250 Ok
QUIT
221 MailMachine.com closing connection
Connection closed by foreign host.
%
```

As you can see from the output above, you need to know a number of commands in order to implement an SMTP client program. Once you know the SMTP commands, implementing an SMTP client program is a matter of opening a socket connection to port 25 and sending those commands, along with the message to be sent. The source code in example 3.1 shows a simple SMTP mail client.

Example 3.1: smtpClient.java

```java
import java.io.*;
import java.net.*;
/**
 * @(#)smtpClient.java
 */
public class smtpClient {
    public static void main(String[] args) {
        Socket smtpSocket = null;
        DataOutputStream os = null;
        BufferedReader is = null;
        try {
            smtpSocket = new Socket("MailMachine.com", 25);
            os = new DataOutputStream(smtpSocket.getOutputStream());
            is = new BufferedReader(new InputStreamReader (smtpSocket.
                getInputStream()));
        } catch (UnknownHostException e) {
         System.err.println("Don't know host: hostname");
        } catch (IOException e) {
            System.err.println("Couldn't get I/O to");
        }
        // If everything has been initialized, we want to write some data to
        // the socket we have opened a connection to on port 25.
        if (smtpSocket != null && os != null &&is != null) {
          try {
            // The capital string before each colon has a
            // special meaning to SMTP. You may want to read
            // the SMTP specification, RFC1822/1823.
            os.writeBytes("HELO\n");
            os.writeBytes("MAIL From: dejavu@acm.org");
            os.writeBytes("RCPT To:dejavu@acm.org\n");
            os.writeBytes("DATA\n");
            os.writeBytes("From: dejavu@acm.org\n");
            os.writeBytes("Subject: testing\n");
            os.writeBytes("Hi there\n"); // Message body
            os.writeBytes("\n.\n");
            os.writeBytes("QUIT");
            // Keep reading from/to the socket until we receive the "OK"
            //    from SMTP. Once we receive that, we want to break.
            String responseLine;
            while ((responseLine = is.readLine()) != null) {
              System.out.println("Server: " +responseLine);
              if (responseLine.indexOf("Ok") != -1) {
                    break;
                }
            }
            // Clean up:
```

```
            os.close();
            is.close();
            smtpSocket.close();
        } catch (UnknownHostException e) {
         System.err.println("Trying to connect to unknown host: " +e);
        } catch (IOException e) {
            System.err.println("IOException:   " + e);
        }
      }
    }
}
```

3.1.2   Finger client

Finger is an Internet service used to determine which users are currently logged into a particu-lar computer. It can also be used to find out more about an individual user. The finger proto-col is defined in RFC 1288.

The finger service uses TCP and runs on port 79. When someone invokes the finger client, he usually supplies the identifier of a user. For example:

finger userID@MachineName.domain

Or, to find out all the users on a given machine, we omit the userID portion:

finger @MachineName.domain

When the finger client program is invoked, it contacts the finger server on the remote machine by opening a socket connection to port 79 and sending a string containing one of the above commands without the word *finger*.

The source code in example 3.2 shows a simple finger client program.

Example 3.2: Finger.java

```
import java.io.*;
import java.net.*;
/**
 * @(#)Finger.java
 */
public class Finger {
   static String host = null;
   static String user = null;
   public static String localHost() throws Exception {
      InetAddress host = null;
      host = InetAddress.getLocalHost();
      return host.getHostName();
   }
   public static void parse(String str) throws Exception {
     int position = 0;
     while (position != -1) {
        position = str.indexOf('@', position);
        if (position != -1) {
           host = str.substring(position+1);
```

```
            host.trim();
            user = str.substring(0,position);
            user.trim();
            position++;
          } else {
            user = str;
            host = localHost();
          }
      }
  }
  // Just in case we forgot to catch all exceptions, our main()
  // throws an exception. This way, we handle exceptions at once.
  public static void main(String argv[]) throws Exception{
      Socket fingerSocket = null;
      DataOutputStream os = null;
      BufferedReader is = null;
      if (argv.length == 1) {
        parse(argv[0]);
      } else {
        host = localHost();
        user ="@"+host;
      }
      try {
        fingerSocket = new Socket(host, 79);
        os = new DataOutputStream(fingerSocket.getOutputStream());
        is = new BufferedReader (new
        InputStreamReader(fingerSocket.getInputStream()));
      } catch (UnknownHostException e) {
        System.err.println("Couldn't get I/O for the connection to:
               "+host);
      }
      if (fingerSocket != null && os != null && is != null) {
        try {
          os.writeBytes(user);
          os.writeBytes("\n");
          String responseLine;
          while ((responseLine = is.readLine()) != null) {
            System.out.println(responseLine);
          }
          os.close();
          is.close();
          fingerSocket.close();
        } catch (UnknownHostException e) {
          System.err.println("Trying to connect to unknown host: " + e);
        } catch (IOException e) {
          System.err.println("IOException:  " + e);
        }
      )
    }
  }
```

3.1.3   Ping client

Ping, which stands for Packet InterNet Groper, is a program found on Unix systems. Its purpose is to check for reachability of remote hosts by sending them an Internet Control Message Protocol (ICMP) *echo* request and waiting for a reply. The ICMP, which was initially designed to allow routers to report the cause of delivery errors, allows routers and hosts to send error or control messages to other routers and hosts.

Ping is implemented on Unix systems by sending an ICMP echo request to a remote host and waiting for a reply; if the reply contains exactly the same data that was sent in the request, then the remote host is reachable. On the other hand, if the router gateway cannot deliver the echo request, it sends an unreachable message (with an error code) back to the host. The error code can be one of the integer values shown in table 3.1.

Table 3.1   ICMP error codes

Value	What it means
0	Network unreachable
1	Host unreachable
2	Protocol unreachable
3	Port unreachable
4	Fragmentation needed (dividing a datagram into packets)
5	Source route failed

Unfortunately, for security reasons, Java does not have support for ICMP packets. ICMP packets can be created via a socket with the SOCK_RAW type, but Java only supports SOCK_STREAM (TCP) and SOCK_DGRAM (UDP) sockets. It is also important to note that the ICMP protocol requires all programs using it to be run as *root* or be *setuid* to root; however, the TCP and UDP protocols do not require that special privilege.

A simple ping application, however, can still be developed using either the TCP or UDP protocol. If ping was to be developed using UDP, then you could approach it by sending a packet to the remote host's *echo* server (running on port 7). If the echo's reply contains the same data that was sent in the sending packet then the host is considered reachable. As I mentioned in chapter 2, however, UDP is not a reliable protocol, so the packet you send/receive may not be received/sent in the same order it was sent/received or the packet could even be lost. Remember, though, that one advantage of using UDP is that it is a connectionless protocol (unlike TCP where a connection must be opened and closed), so there is no communication overhead when using UDP.

Using TCP, the ping utility can be developed as follows: we first attempt to establish a connection to the remote host echo's port number (again, port 7). If the connection is successfully established, the remote host is considered reachable, and we close the connection. We do not need to send any data to the echo server. Example 3.3 shows a simple ping implementation of this technique.

Example 3.3: Ping.java

```java
import java.io.*;
import java.net.*;
/**
 * @(#)Ping.java
 */
public class Ping {
    public final static int ECHO_PORT = 7;
    public static void main(String argv[]) {
        if (argv.length != 1) {
          System.out.println("Usage: java ping hostname");
          System.exit(0);
        }
        if (alive(argv[0])) {
          System.out.println(argv[0] + " is alive");
        } else {
        System.out.println("No response from " +argv[0]+ ". Host is down or
              doesn't exist.");
        }
    }
    // Check for aliveness through ECHO.
    public static boolean alive(String host) {
        Socket pingSocket = null;
         try {
           pingSocket = new Socket(host, ECHO_PORT);
         } catch (UnknownHostException e) {
            System.err.println("UnknownHostException: " +e);
         } catch (IOException io) {
            System.out.println("IOException: " + io);
         }
         if (pingSocket != null) {
           try {
             pingSocket.close();
           } catch (IOException e) {
              System.err.println("IOException: " + e);
           }
           return true;
         } else {
           return false;
         }
    }
}
```

3.2 PROGRAMMING WITH THREADS

A program with a single flow of control is called a *sequential* program. At any one time in such a program, the computer is executing at a single point. On the other hand, a program with multiple points of execution is called a *concurrent* program. As you can see in figure 3.1, a sequential program has four parts to it: (1) *source code*, (2) *global data*, (3) *heap*, and (4) *stack*.

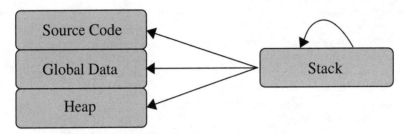

Figure 3.1 A sequential program

The *source code* is the statements and expressions of the program translated into machine language. The *global data* holds the *static* variables of the program, which are usually declared at the top level of the program. The *heap* is the storage that is used by the *new* operator when allocating new objects, and the *stack* is the storage that holds all local variables, method arguments, and other information.

Figure 3.2 shows a multithreaded program with two threads. As you can see, the structure is the same as figure 3.1, except that each thread has its own stack because each thread could call a different set of methods in a completely different order. However, all threads share the same source code, global data, and heap storage. Thus, if a thread makes a change to a local variable, other threads will not be affected since those variables are on the thread's own stack.

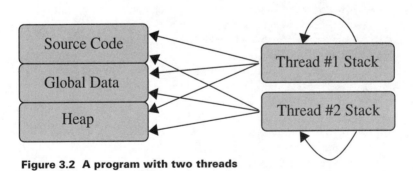

Figure 3.2 A program with two threads

3.2.1 What is a thread?

The term *thread* is derived from the phrase *thread of execution* in operating systems. At any instant in time within a single thread, there is a single point of execution. Using multiple threads in a program means the program has multiple points of execution at any given instant.

Threads can create other threads and kill them. Newly created threads will run in the same address space, which allows them to share data.

While threads give the illusion that two or more events are occurring at the same time, your computer (assuming it has only one CPU) can execute only one thread at any given time. The illusion that threads are executing simultaneously is the result of the rapid switch from one thread to another. Each thread executes for a short period of time, then it passes control to the next thread. However, a computer with multiple CPUs will be executing multiple threads concurrently.

Threads are not a new idea; they have been around for quite some time. However, only few programmers have used them since using them effectively can be a complex task. Fortunately, Java has incorporated threads as part of the language. Java not only made using threads easy, but it also made them effective and productive.

3.2.2 The benefits of threads

You'll see many benefits when you use threads. First of all, they give your program the ability to perform multiple tasks simultaneously. They also provide a way to take advantage of computers with multiple CPUs. Here's an example of how multiple tasks are done simultaneously. Suppose we want to read a line of text from the user via the keyboard. The program will pause until a line of text is entered. This is quite all right if the program has nothing else to do. But if the program needs to do some background work, such as drawing or animating images, then we are wasting CPU time (as it will be idle) until a line of text is available. This background work can be accomplished with threads while the program is waiting for the user's input.

Other benefits of threads include increased application throughput, application responsiveness, and the ability to use the system's resources efficiently.

3.2.3 Example: creating and starting threads

The code in example 3.4 is a simple example that creates and starts two threads. Do not worry about the details now; we will discuss them in the next section.

Example 3.4: MyThread.java

```
/**
 * @(#)MyThread.java
 */
class MyThread extends Thread {
    public MyThread(String name) {
        super(name);
    }
    public void run() {
        for (int i=0; i<3; i++) {
            System.out.println(getName() + ":" + i);
            try {
                Thread.sleep(500);
            } catch(InterruptedException e) {
                e.printStackTrace();
            }
```

```
        }
    }
    public static void main(String argv[]) {
        MyThread t1 = new MyThread("ReadFromSocket");
        MyThread t2 = new MyThread("ReadFromKeyboard");
        t1.start();
        t2.start();
    }
}
```

This example shows a program with two threads: one for reading from a network socket and one for reading from a keyboard. Both threads will run parallel to each other. I ran the code in example 3.4, and I received the following output:

```
ReadingFromSocket:0
ReadingFromKeyboard:0
ReadingFromSocket:1
ReadingFromKeyboard:1
ReadingFromSocket:2
ReadingFromKeyboard:2
```

> **NOTE** If you run the code yourself, do not be surprised if you get an output that looks a bit different, since threads are machine dependent. The order in which the threads will run is not guaranteed. Please see section 3.2.7 for a discussion on scheduling and priorities.

3.2.4 Creating and starting a thread

There are two ways to create a thread in Java. The first way is to create an object from a custom class (such as MyThread) that extends the Thread class as shown above. The MyThread class must override the run() method of the Thread class by providing an implementation for it as shown in example 3.4.

It is important to note that instantiating the MyThread class (for example, MyThread t1 = new MyThread("read");) will not start the object t1 executing as a thread. You must call the thread's start() method in order to start the thread executing. Once the start() method is called, it will in turn call the run() method; that is where all the actions that are to be performed by the thread should be placed.

This method of creating a thread has a drawback—you must extend the Thread class. Since Java does not support multiple inheritance, you cannot write a multithreaded applet since you need to extend both the Applet and the Thread classes, which is not allowed in Java. For this reason, Java gives you another way of creating a thread.

The other way to create a thread in Java is through the use of an interface. The Java interface that is used for creating threads is the Runnable interface. It has the following definition:

```
package java.lang;
public interface Runnable {
    public abstract void run();
}
```

PROGRAMMING CLIENTS AND SERVERS

The only method that this interface defines is the run() method. It is declared abstract, meaning that the implementor of this interface must provide an implementation for the run() method. Using this interface, we can implement our earlier example, as shown in example 3.5.

Example 3.5: MyThread2.java

```
/**
 * @(#)MyThread2.java
 */
class MyThread2 implements Runnable {
    public void run() {
        for (int i=0; i<3; i++) {
            System.out.println(Thread.currentThread().getName() + ":"+i);
            try {
              Thread.sleep(500);
            } catch(InterruptedException e) {
              e.printStackTrace();
            }
        }
    }
    public static void main(String argv[]) {
        MyThread2 s = new MyThread2();
        MyThread2 k = new MyThread2();
        Thread t1 = new Thread(s, "ReadFromSocket");
        Thread t2 = new Thread(k, "ReadFromKeyboard");
        t1.start();
        t2.start();
    }
}
```

When you are creating a thread using the Runnable interface, you have to give a reference to the class that implements the Runnable interface, which is MyThread in this example. Now a thread can be created by calling the Thread class, or a subclass of it, with a target of a Runnable object:

```
MyThread x = new MyThread();
Thread t1 = new Thread(x, "ReadFromSocket");
t1.start();
```

When the thread starts executing, it will call the run() method in the corresponding class that implements the Runnable interface.

Both methods of creating and starting a thread are identical. The main difference is that the class that implements the Runnable interface has access only to the run() method, and not to all the handy methods provided by the Thread class. But as I mentioned earlier, there is a good reason for having the Runnable interface, since Java does not support multiple inheritance directly.

3.2.5 Putting a thread to sleep

Imagine you have a drawing method that runs in a separate thread, and you want to control how fast the thread draws an object. This can be done by briefly *suspending* the thread each time the thread is about to draw an object. You may pause a thread for a specific period of time by putting it to sleep using the sleep() method. The argument to sleep specifies the number of milliseconds for which you want the thread to sleep. Note that the sleep method throws an exception (InterruptedException) and you should catch that exception. As an example, the following code segment puts a thread to sleep for one second:

```
public void run() {
    // More code goes here.
    try {
        Thread.sleep(1000);
    } catch(InterruptedException e) {
        e.printStackTrace();
    }
    // More code goes here.
}
```

3.2.6 Controlling threads

As you learned in section 3.2.4, the start() method is used to bring a newly created thread to life. The Thread class has three methods that allow you to control a thread's execution: stop(), suspend(), and resume(). These methods operate on the current thread object, so they take no arguments. As the name suggests, the stop() method is used to stop and destroy a thread. The suspend() and resume() methods are used to arbitrarily pause and then restart the execution of a thread. These methods are very simple to use. To suspend a thread, use MyThread.suspend(); you can later resume execution of the thread by calling the resume() method MyThread.resume(). Note that suspend() and resume() have been deprecated in Java 2. Another pair of methods, to coordinate threads, is notify() and wait().

3.2.7 Changing thread priority

Threads will normally be competing for processor time. If you wish to give a thread an advantage over other threads, you will need to change its priority. Priorities range from 1 to 10, where 1 is a low priority and 10 is a high priority. The Thread class defines three constants that can be used to select a common priority: MIN_PRIORITY (equal to 1), NORM_PRIORITY (equal to 5), and MAX_PRIORITY (equal to 10). When a thread is first created, it inherits a priority from its parent thread, which is normally 5, the NORM_PRIORITY.

You can get a thread priority by using the getPriority() method, and you can change a thread's priority by calling the setPriority() method, which takes an integer argument that must be greater than 0 and less than or equal to 10. If you pass an argument less than 1 or greater than 10, an IllegalArgumentException will be thrown at run time.

A good example of where you might want to give priorities to different threads would be a multithreaded client that has two threads—a reader and a writer. The reader reads from the server and writes to the console, and the writer reads from the console and writes to the server. In such a case, there might be a problem with shared access to the console. To prevent this, you will have to give the reader a higher priority than the writer. However, if a thread has a high priority, it may not allow other threads to receive processor time. Such a thread is called a *selfish* thread. A nicer thread would sleep for a while or yield so that other threads can run. This can be accomplished using the `yield()` method, which gives other threads the opportunity to run.

3.2.8   Synchronization

Data sharing is one pitfall you may encounter when using threads. If two or more threads have shared access (read and write) to a variable, then you need to take care to coordinate and synchronize data access. As an example, suppose that Alice and Bob are sharing a checkbook. If they are not careful, the checks they write might exceed the balance. The code segment below demonstrates this:

```
int balance;
boolean withdraw(int amt){
    if (balance - amt >= 0) {
      balance = balance - amt;
      return true;
    }
    return false;
}
```

Table 3.2 shows a scenario of what might happen if Alice and Bob are simultaneously executing this code segment.

Table 3.2   Alice and Bob's banking problems

Alice	Bob	Balance
if (80 – 50 >=0)		80
	if (80 – 50 >= 0)	80
Balance = Balance – 50		30
	Balance = Balance – 50	-20

The balance could become negative if Bob and Alice are withdrawing money simultaneously. This withdrawal method needs to be *synchronized* so that only one thread can execute the code at any given time. Providing mutual exclusion (that is, preventing simultaneous access to a shared resource) can be done using the `synchronized` access specifier or `synchronized` block of code. The code segment below demonstrates the use of the synchronized access specifier.

```
int balance;
synchronized boolean withdraw(int amt) {
    if (balance - amt >= 0) {
      balance = balance - amt;
      return true;
    }
```

```
    return false;
}
```

The code segment above can be executed only by one thread at any one time. Note that the `synchronized` word does not affect objects. It just coordinates the sharing of data.

The code below, which uses the `synchronized` block of code, has the same effect as the example above.

```
int balance;
boolean withdraw(int amt) {
    synchronized(this) {
        if (balance - amount >= 0) {
            balance = balance - amt;
            return true;
        }
        return false;
    }
}
```

3.3 *PROGRAMMING NEW SERVICES AND CLIENTS*

In chapter 2, we developed a simple client/server application—the greetings server. One limitation that existed in that application was its inability to serve multiple clients simultaneously. In this section, after the short tutorial on threads programming we just went through, we are ready to program some interesting multithreaded server applications—servers that are capable of serving multiple clients simultaneously. Figure 3.3 shows the sequence of operations for setting up communication between a client and a multithreaded server.

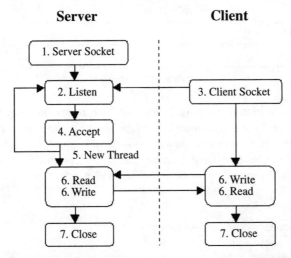

Figure 3.3   Client-socket communication with a multithreaded server

Modifying the greetings server to handle multiple clients' requests simultaneously is very simple, so I will leave it to you as an exercise. In the next section, we will look at an arithmetic client/server application.

3.3.1 Example: arithmetic client/server

The application we will look at is a math application. In this distributed application, the client will send two arrays of integers to the arithmetic server. The arithmetic server will then add the two arrays and return the result (as an array) to the client. The client will then iterate through the resulting array and print its elements.

Reading/writing arrays to streams   The Java API does not include methods for writing an array of integers to a socket, so the first thing we need to do is to write a new class with a method capable of doing just that. There is also no method for reading an array of integers from a socket. So our new class, ArrayIO, has two methods: one for reading an array of integers from a socket, and one for writing an array of integers to a socket. The complete source code is shown in example 3.6.

Example 3.6: ArrayIO.java

```java
import java.io.*;
/**
 * @(#)ArrayIO.java
 */
class ArrayIO {
  public ArrayIO() {
  }
  /**
   * Write an array of integers to a socket.
   */
  public void writeArray(DataOutputStream out, int arr[])
        throws Exception {
    for (int i=0; i<arr.length; i++) {
      out.write(arr[i]);
    }
  }
  /**
   * Read an array of integers from a socket.
   */
  public int[] readArray(BufferedReader br) throws Exception {
    int c[] = new int[10];
    for (int h=0; h<10; h++) {
      try {
        c[h] = (int) br.read();
      } catch(IOException il) {
        il.printStackTrace();
      }
    }
    return c;
  }
}
```

Both the client and server will use the `ArrayIO` class for reading and writing arrays of integers to sockets. Once a client sends two arrays of integers to the server, the server will read them and call a method that adds the two arrays together. In order to add two arrays of integers, we need a simple class—let's call it `ArrayMath`—to do just that. The source code for the `ArrayMath` class is shown in example 3.7.

Example 3.7: ArrayMath.java

```java
import java.io.*;
/**
 * @(#)ArrayMath.java
 */
class ArrayMath {
   public ArrayMath() {
   }


   /**
    * A simple method to add two arrays of integers
    */
   public int[] addArray(int a[], int b[]) {
      int result[] = new int[10];
      for (int s=0; s<result.length; s++) {
        result[s] = a[s] + b[s];
      }
      return result;
   }
}
```

Using the `ArrayIO` and `ArrayMath` classes, we can now develop our client/server application.

The arithmetic client   The code for the client is very simple. All it does is open a socket connection, an input stream, and an output stream. Once this is done, the client uses the method `writeArray()` from the `ArrayIO` class to send two arrays of integers to the server. Then it waits for the server to send the result as an array. Once the client receives the array, the client iterates through the array and prints each element in it. After that, it closes the I/O streams and the socket. The source code for the arithmetic client is shown in example 3.8.

Example 3.8: Client.java

```java
import java.io.*;
import java.net.*;
/**
 * @(#)Client.java
 */
public class Client {
   public final static int REMOTE_PORT = 3333;
   static int a[] = {1, 2, 3, 4, 5, 6, 7, 8, 9, 10};
   static int b[] = {5, 5, 5, 5, 5, 5, 5, 5, 5, 5};

   public static void main(String argv[]) throws Exception {
```

```
        Socket cl = null, cl2=null;
        BufferedReader is = null;
        DataOutputStream os = null;
        ArrayIO aio = new ArrayIO();
        try {
            cl = new Socket("hostname",REMOTE_PORT);
            is = new BufferedReader(new InputStreamReader(cl.getInputStream()));
            os = new DataOutputStream(cl.getOutputStream());
        } catch(UnknownHostException e1) {
            System.out.println("Unknown Host: "+e1);
        } catch (IOException e2) {
            System.out.println("Erorr io: "+e2);
        }
        try {
            aio.writeArray(os, a);
            aio.writeArray(os, b);
        } catch (IOException ex) {
            System.out.println("error writing to server..."+ex);
        }
        // Receive results from the math server.
        int result[] = new int[10];
        try {
            result = aio.readArray(is);
        } catch(Exception e) {
            e.printStackTrace();
        }
        System.out.println("The sum of the two arrays: ");
        for (int j=0; j<result.length; j++) {
            System.out.print(result[j]+" ");
        }
        System.out.println("");
        // Close the input stream, output stream, and connection.
        try {
            is.close();
            os.close();
            cl.close();
        } catch (IOException x) {
            System.out.println("Error writing...."+x);
        }
    }
}
```

The arithmetic server   Programming the arithmetic server is not as hard as you may expect. You do want it to be able to serve multiple simultaneous client requests—it has to be a multithreaded server. But with the help of the tutorial on threads programming earlier in this chapter, you know that you just need to subclass (or inherit from) the Thread class and implement the run() method—that is actually where all the actions to be performed by the server go. However, the thread will not start executing until the start() method is called, which will, in turn, call the run() method. If you look at the server code in example 3.9, you will see that all the actions are being performed in the run() method of the Connects class.

In this run() method, we actually read two arrays from the client socket and add them together, then we send the resulting array back to the client.

Example 3.9: Server.java

```java
/**
 * @(#)Server.java
 */
import java.io.*;
import java.net.*;
import java.util.*;

public class Server extends Thread {
    public static final int MATH_PORT = 3333;
    protected ServerSocket listen;
    // Constructor.
    public Server() {
        try {
          listen = new ServerSocket(MATH_PORT);
        } catch(IOException ex) {
          System.out.println("Exception..."+ex);
        }
        this.start();
    }
    // Multithreading -- create a new connection for each request
    public void run() {
        try {
          while(true) {
             Socket client = listen.accept();
             Connects cc = new Connects(client);
          }
        } catch(IOException e) {
          System.out.println("Exception..."+e);
        }
    }

    // Main program.
    public static void main(String argv[]) throws IOException {
        new Server();
    }
}

class Connects extends Thread {
    Socket client;
    BufferedReader is;
    DataOutputStream os;
    ArrayIO aio = new ArrayIO();
    ArrayMath am = new ArrayMath();
    public Connects(Socket s) { // Constructor
        client = s;
        try {
          is = new BufferedReader(new InputStreamReader(client
```

```
                getInputStream())); 
            os = new DataOutputStream(client.getOutputStream());
        } catch (IOException e) {
          try {
            client.close();
          } catch (IOException ex) {
            System.out.println("Error getting socket streams:"+ex);
          }
          return;
        }
        this.start(); // Thread starts here
      }
      public void run() {
        int a1[] = new int[10];
        int a2[] = new int[10];
        try {
          a1 = aio.readArray(is);
          a2 = aio.readArray(is);
        } catch(Exception ioe) {
         ioe.printStackTrace();
        }
        int r[] = new int[10];
        r = am.addArray(a1, a2);
        try {
         aio.writeArray(os, r);
        } catch(Exception e) {
            e.printStackTrace();
        }
      }
    }
}
```

3.4   SUMMARY

- Knowing a service's communication protocol enables you to code a Java client for that service quite easily. To write a client, you need to know the commands the service expects to receive, the format in which it expects to receive them, and the data that your client should expect in reply.
- A program with a single flow of control is called a sequential program. A program with multiple, simultaneous flows of control is called a concurrent, or multithreaded, program. A multithreaded program has four parts: source code, global data, heap, and stack.
- Threads can create other threads and kill them. Newly created threads run in the same address space, allowing them to share data, but each thread has its own stack. As shown by our arithmetic server, threads give your program the ability to perform multiple tasks simultaneously, and they give your program a way to take advantage of computers with multiple CPUs.
- Java has built-in support for threads via the Thread class, which we used in the arithmetic server to respond to multiple clients' requests simultaneously.

C H A P T E R   4

Sockets in real-world applications

Web browsers communicate with HyperText Transfer Protocol (HTTP) servers to request services, which are normally information resources such as Hypertext Markup Language (HTML) documents and images. When a resource is found, it is sent to the browser, which will display it according to the HTML tags. A simple HTTP server is relatively easy to implement.

Security should be a major concern if you allow outside clients (such as web browsers) to access your server. In this chapter, to demonstrate Java's security features, we'll start by implementing a simpleminded but secure HTTP server. This server grants browsers access to web pages without giving Internet surfers access to information that you would like to protect, such as users' data files or the system password file (/etc/passwd).

JDBC is a Java API for database connectivity. It allows you to execute SQL statements from any relational database. JDBC makes it unnecessary to develop a separate program to acess relational databases from different vendors. I'll explain more about JDBC in this chapter.

You'll also learn about proxy servers in this chapter—what they are, how they work, and how to implement them. Finally, you'll learn about JDBC, a Java API that enables you to execute SQL statements on relational databases throughout a network without regard for the vendor of the database.

4.1 DEVELOPING A MULTITHREADED HTTP SERVER

HTTP is an application-level protocol; an implementation of it is called an HTTP server or a web server. Web browsers communicate with an HTTP server and submit requests for a service. This service is normally an information resource (such as a document or an image). The server receives the request, tries to locate the specified resource, and sends it to the browser if it is found. HTTP supports several request methods, such as GET, POST, and HEAD. To keep things simple, we will only implement the GET method so that our server will be able to serve only documents and images.

Here are two sample GET requests:

```
GET http://hostname.domain/doc.html HTTP/1.0
GET /doc.html HTTP/1.0
```

If you would like to experiment with the GET command, then telnet to port 80 (where a standard HTTP server is normally running) on a machine that runs an HTTP server. Once you're there, type some commands similar to the two lines above, and see what you will get—it should be a bunch of HTML text.

When using a web browser—Netscape, for example—you might have noticed that when you're giving it a URL of the form http://hostname.domain/, it will try to load the document index.html, which is usually in the root directory. (This, of course, depends on the server configuration.)

Our HTTP program will consist of two classes: httpd and Connect. The httpd class will have the main() method and it will call the Connect class. The Connect class will handle the communications; it initializes streams for communication, and its run() method will handle all the communications with the client and will provide the service to the client. The two classes look as follows:

```
public class httpd extends Thread {
   public static void main() {
      new httpd();
   }
}

class Connect extends Thread {
   // Implementation goes here.
}
```

Let's look at the Connect class in more detail. It extends (inherits from) the Thread class. As I pointed out in the threads tutorial in chapter 3, once you inherit the Thread class, you should override the run() method with your own. Remember, the run() method of the Connect class handles all the communications with the client and serves the client. In other words, the run() method will receive the request line from the client and it will try to see if it can perform the services the client is asking for. Thus, the run() method would look like this:

SOCKETS IN REAL-WORLD APPLICATIONS

```
public void run() {
    try {
        String request = is.readLine();
        System.out.println( "Request: "+request );
        StringTokenizer st = new StringTokenizer( request );
        if ( (st.countTokens() >= 2) && st.nextToken().equals("GET") ) {
            if ( (request = st.nextToken()).startsWith("/") )
                request = request.substring( 1 );
            if ( request.endsWith("/") || request.equals("") )
                request = request + "index.html";
            File f = new File(request);
            shipDocument(os, f);
        } else {
            os.writeBytes( "400 Bad Request" );
        }
        client.close();
    } catch ( IOException e ) {
        System.out.println( "I/O error " + e );
    } catch (Exception ex) {
        System.out.println("Exception: "+ex);
    }
}
```

When the run() method is called, it will not take effect, meaning the thread will remain idle until you call its start() method. A good place to put the start() method in is the constructor of the Connect class. But before you call the start() method, you should initialize streams for communication. The Connect class with the constructor would look like this:

```
class Connect extends Thread {
    Socket client;
    DataInputStream is;
    DataOutputStream os;

    public Connect(Socket s) { // Constructor
        client = s;
        try {
            is = new DataInputStream(client.getInputStream());
            os = new DataOutputStream(client.getOutputStream());
        } catch (IOException e) {
            try {
                client.close();
            } catch (IOException ex) {
                System.out.println("Error while getting socket streams:"+ex);
            }
            return;
            this.start(); // Thread starts here. Start() will call run().
        }

    public void run() {
        // The code from above goes here.
    }
```

```
public static void shipDocument(DataoutputStream out, File f) {
  try {
    DataInputStream in = new DataInputStream(new FileInputStream(f));
    int len = (int) f.length();
    byte buf[] = new byte[len];
    in.readFully(buf);
    out.writeBytes("HTTP/1.0 200 OK\r\n");
    out.writeBytes("Content-Length: " + buf.length +"\r\n");
    out.writeBytes("Content-Type: text\html\r\n\r\n");
    //out.write(buf, 0, len);
    out.write(buf);
    out.flush();
    in.close();
  } catch(FileNotFoundException e) {
     out.writeBytes("404 Not Found");
  } catch(IOException ex) {
     System.out.println("Error writing…."+ex);
  }
 }
}
```

Notice that the shipDocument includes some of the required HTTP response header information, such as Content-Length and Content-Type: text/html. The Content-Type here is text/html, meaning that this HTTP server is able to serve only text and HTML documents. If you request an image (for example, one in .gif format) the browser will display the image as scrambled text. To handle images, you need to specify the Content-Type of the document. For example, if a requested file has a .gif extension, then the Content-Type must be image/gif. Likewise, if the extension is .jpg or .jpeg, the Content-Type must be image/jpg and image/jpeg, respectively. For more information on content types, please refer to the HTTP specification at http://www.w3C.org.

Now, let's look at the httpd class. The httpd class is inheriting from the Thread class as well, so we need to override the run() method.

As I mentioned earlier, the httpd object is a thread, and its run() method loops forever as it listens for clients' requests. Our implementation of run() looks as follows:

```
public void run() {
   try {
      while(true) {
        Socket client = listen.accept();
        Connect cc = new Connect(client);
      }
   } catch(IOException e) {
      System.out.println("Exception..."+e);
   }
}
```

Notice that the run() method is making a new instance of the Connect class. This happens because the run() method loops forever, and each time a client connects, the ServerSocket creates a new Socket and the server creates a new thread. The Socket is created in the Connect class.

Again, in order to start the thread, you need to call the start() method, and a good place for that is in the constructor of the httpd() class. Before you call the start() method, however, you should create a ServerSocket object. The httpd class would look as follows:

```
public class httpd {
    public static void final int HTTP_PORT = 8080;
    protected ServerSocket listen;

    public httpd() {
        try {
          listen = new ServerSocket(HTTP_PORT);
        } catch(IOException ex) {
          System.out.pritnln("Exception..."+ex);
        }
        this.start();
    }

    public void run() {
        // Insert the code for run() from above.
    }

    public static void main(string argv[]) throws IOException {
      new httpd();
    }
}
```

Our httpd server supports multithreading and is able to serve multiple web pages simultaneously. Try to compile the httpd.java file, then run the server and see how it works.

4.2 SECURITY IN HTTP

Is the simple HTTP server I developed above secure? The answer is certainly no. If you are up to some experimentation, try to fetch some documents that the server should not be allowed to get. For example, on my Unix workstation, I ran the server above to see if I could get the password file (which is normally located at /etc/passwd). I constructed the following URL and passed it to Netscape: http://myHostName:8080/../../../../../etc/passwd. The server was able to satisfy the request and Netscape displayed the password file on the screen. Notice that the number of ".." I use depends on how far I am from the root directory, and the countdown starts from the directory where I ran the HTTP server.

In a standard HTTP server, you certainly don't want people to be able to fetch documents that they are not allowed to access. In other words, you would want the server to have access only to a certain area of the file system, not the whole thing. Fortunately, Java allows you to create secure environments. Java provides the SecurityManager class that you can inherit from to create a secure environment for your application. Ideally, in this example, you would want to prevent people from using ".." in their URLs. In order to create a secure environment for our HTTP server, create a customized security manager by inheriting from the Security-Manager and overriding some of its methods. The SecurityManager class has various methods, including checkAccess(), checkRead(), checkWrite(), and checkConnect(). Just as an example, you would want to disallow people from reading files they should not have read access to. Thus, your new SecurityManager can be constructed as follows:

```
class OurHttpSecurityManager extends SecurityManager {
    public void checkAccess(Thread g) { };
    . . . .
    // Here are the methods we want to override.

    public void checkRead(String filename){
       if (filename.indexOf("..") != -1) {
         throw new SecurityException("Not enough privileges to read: "+file-
name+");
       }
    }
}
```

This is a very simple security manager. Now that it's written, it's time to install it in your HTTP server. Installing it is easy; simply add a line in the main() body of the program as follows:

```
        System.setSecurityManager(new OurHttpdSecurityManager());
```

The OurHttpSecurityManager class shown in this example throws a security exception once a user tries to read a file he does not have access to. Therefore, you need to catch that security exception. This new catch has to be added to the shipDocument method. Your new shipDocument method would then look like this:

```
public static void shipDocument(DataOutputStream out, File f) {
  try {
    . . . .
    // Everything is the same as in the ShipDocument example earlier.
    . . . .
  } catch (FileNotFoundException e1) {
    out.writeBytes("404 Not Found");
  } catch (SecurityException e3) {
    out.writeBytes("403 Forbidden");
  }
}
```

4.3 PROXY SERVERS

Proxy servers represent a common approach for providing Internet access through corporate firewalls. Think of a firewall as a secretary to a set of computers. In order for an outsider to access any of those computers, he has to get permission from the secretary. Figure 4.1 shows where a proxy server may fit in a corporate network.

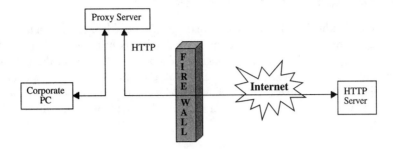

Figure 4.1 A proxy server in a network

The primary goal of a proxy server is to create a single access and control point to the Internet; it will allow people within the company network to access the Internet, but it will prevent outsiders from accessing the company's internal networks.

4.3.1 How proxy servers work

A proxy server's main function is to receive a request from a web browser, perform that request, and return the results to the browser. Keep in mind that the request might be performed after some authorization checks are run.

To better understand what is actually happening, imagine you request the following URL through a web browser:

```
http://www.somesite.com/home.html
```

Assuming that there is a proxy, the browser will send your request to a proxy server (such as proxy.somecompany.com), asking for:

```
GET http://www.somesite.com/home.html
```

The proxy server proxy.somecompany.com will then contact www.somesite.com with this request:

```
GET /home.html
```

4.3.2 Advantages of proxy servers

There are several advantages to this indirect approach of accessing the web, including these benefits:

- All external accesses can be forced to go through the proxy, which therefore creates a single access and control point. A proxy server will have to run on a fast machine in order to be able to process all the requests quickly and keep clients happy.
- Requests for certain sites can be restricted or banned, thus providing a safer Internet environment for children.
- All HTML documents being transferred can be logged along with the IP address of the requesting machine. Any disputes can then be solved quickly.
- Only the IP address of the proxy will be known to outsiders, thereby preventing attackers from knowing all the IP addresses of corporate machines.

4.4 DATABASE ACCESS VIA SOCKETS

With the introduction of Java, many developers were quickly interested in using Java to access databases. This was especially true for those developers using lightweight database engines such as mSQL from Hughes Technologies to connect databases with the web. To satisfy the increased interest, a package for accessing mSQL databases from Java was developed. The package is called MsqlJava, and it allows developers to perform mSQL queries in Java. Via MsqJava, a connection to an mSQL database can be established using the following segment of code:

```
private sycnhronized void connDB() {
    Msql msql;
    try {
      msql = new Msql();
      msql.Connect("myHostName", "myUserName");
      msql.SelectDB("myDataBase");
    } catch (MsqlException e) {
        e.printStackTrace();
    }
}
```

Once a connection to a database has been established, queries can be performed. For example, to insert a new record (one that does not already exist) in a database, code similar to the following can be used.

```
String r[];
try {
    MsqlResult res = msql.Query("select * from tableName");
    if ((r=res.FetchRow)) == null) {
      msql.Query("INSERT INTO database (field1, field2) VALUES (val1,
val2)");
    } else {
        System.out.println("The record is already in the database");
    }
} catch (MsqlException e) {
    e.printStackTrace();
}
```

While we are not really using sockets here, the MsqlJava package itself is using them to connect to the mSQL database server.

The increased interest in accessing databases from Java has led JavaSoft to the development of JDBC, which is a package that provides a smart and portable method for accessing databases.

4.5 JDBC EXPLAINED

JDBC is a Java API for database connectivity; it is part of the Java API from JavaSoft. JDBC is not an acronym, though people often think it stands for *Java DataBase Connectivity*. JDBC provides an API in the `java.sql` package that makes it possible to develop database applications using Java. Figure 4.2 shows the general architecture of JDBC.

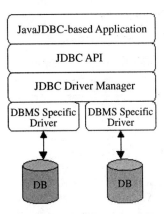

Figure 4.2 The general architecture of JDBC

Using JDBC, a developer could execute SQL statements from any relational database. The best part of JDBC is that it is not necessary to develop a separate program to access databases from different vendors. A Java application built on top of the JDBC API goes through three different phases:

1 Opening a connection to a database.

2 Creating a statement object through which it passes SQL statements to the underlying DBMS.

3 Retrieving the results.

NOTE   The JDBC examples in this section have been produced using JDK1.1, an mSQL server, and an mSQL JDBC driver from Imaginary (http://www.imaginary.com/Java).

4.5.1   The JDBC Security Model

JDBC follows the standard applet security model:

- It assumes that unsigned applets are untrustworthy.
- Untrusted applets are not allowed to access local databases.
- Untrusted applets are only allowed to open a database connection back to the server they were downloaded from.

Applications and trusted applets have no connection restrictions.

4.5.2   The JDBC DriverManager

The topmost class in the java.sql hierarchy is the DriverManager class. As the name suggests, the DriverManager keeps track of driver information. When a driver is loaded, it registers with the DriverManager. When a Java application (built on top of JDBC) opens a connection, the DriverManager selects the driver that suits that application depending on the JDBC URL. The JDBC URL takes the following form:

```
jdbc:<subprotocol><subname>
```

This URL has three parts: jdbc, subprotocol, and subname. The first part, jdbc, is the protocol, and it is always jdbc in a JDBC URL. The second part is the subprotocol, which is usually the driver of the database connectivity mechanism. The third part, the subname, identifies the database.

Suppose we have the following JDBC URL:

```
jdbc:msql://machine-name.com:port#/testDB
```

This URL says that the protocol is jdbc. The subprotocol is msql, which is the driver that works with the mSQL server. The subname //machine-name.com:port#/testDB identifies the database. In this case, machine-name.com is the machine name that has the mSQL server, port# is the port number on which the server is listening, and testDB is the name of a database.

When a driver developer develops a new driver for a particular RDBMS, the developer should register the driver name as a subprotocol with Sun. Then when the DriverManager presents this name to its list of registered drivers, the driver for which this subprotocol name is reserved should recognize it and establish a connection to the database it identifies.

4.5.3   Anatomy of a JDBC application

Implementing a JDBC application involves a number of steps. I will explain each one in this section. Figure 4.3 shows the architecture of a typical JDBC application.

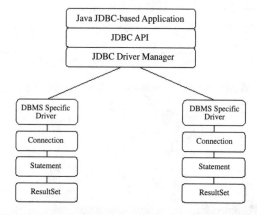

Figure 4.3 Architecture of a typical JDBC application

Notice that the application in figure 4.3 is making connections to more than one JDBC driver.

To simplify the development of JDBC applications, follow these steps when accessing a relational database using JDBC.

1 *Select a driver.* As I mentioned earlier, the `DriverManager` manages a set of drivers, and it is the responsibility of the `DriverManager` to select the driver that can handle your connection. Thus, the first step in creating a JDBC application is to call the method `Class.forName`. The call to `Class.forName` will explicitly load the driver class. For example, the following segment of code loads the class `com.imaginary.sql.msql.MsqlDriver`:

```
Class.forName("com.imaginary.sql.msql.MsqlDriver");
```

2 *Decide which URL to use.* Here's an example using the rules of the previous section:

```
String url="jdbc:msql://machine-name.com:port#/testDB";
```

3 *Establish a connection.* Once a driver has been loaded and registered with the `Driver-Manager`, it is available for establishing a connection with a database. A request for a connection is made through a call to the method `DriverManager.getConnection`. The fragment of code to establish a connection looks like this:

```
Connection con = DriverManager.getConnection(url, "ID", "Pass");
```

4 *Create a statement object.* Once a connection to a database has been established, it can be used to send SQL statements to the database. An instance of `Statement` can be created as follows:

```
Statement stmt = con.createStatement();
```

Now the SQL statements to be sent to the database are supplied as an argument to a method that is executing the `Statement` instance. The code may look like this:

```
ResultSet rs = stmt.executeQuery("Select * from tableName");
```

The result of `executeQuery` will produce a single result set—a set of rows and columns in the form of a matrix, for example.

NOTE   `Statement` provides three different methods for executing SQL statements: `executeQuery`, `executeUpdate`, and `execute`.

The method `executeQuery` is mostly used with the `SELECT` statement, and `executeUpdate` is used to execute SQL statements such as `INSERT`, `UP-DATE`, `DELETE`, `CREATE TABLE`, and `DROP TABLE`. The execute method is used when a statement may return more than one `ResultSet` object. This might happen when executing a stored procedure, for example.

---

5 *Access the result.* Once the code in step 4 has been executed, the `ResultSet` object, `rs`, contains all of the rows which satisfied the condition in the SQL statement. The `Result.next` method is used to move to the next row of `rs`. Access to the data in the rows can be obtained through the various methods of `ResultSet.get`. For example, suppose we have a table called `emps` that contains records with fields called name, age, `salary`, and `kids`. If the query `SELECT * from emps` were executed, the following fragment of code shows how to get the results:

```
ResultSet rs = stmt.executeQuery("select * from emps");
```

```
while (rs.next()) {
    String f1 = rs.getString(1);
    int    f2 = rs.getInt(2);
    float  f3 = getFloat(3);
    int    f4 = getInt(4);
    System.out.println("We got the following results: ");
    System.out.println(f1, f2, f3, f4);
}
```

rs.getString(1) refers to the first column, and rs.getInt(2) refers to the second column, and so on. However, note that we could just as well use rs.get-String("name") and rs.getInt("kids") instead of rs.getString(1) and rs.getInt(4), respectively, since the numbers refer to the corresponding columns.

6 *Close the connection.* Once you have executed the SQL statements and have received your results, it is time to close the connection. It can be done this way:

```
stmt.close();
con.close();
```

4.5.4   A persistent storage for Java objects

A *persistent storage* is a nonvolatile place for storing the *state* of objects. Depending on the application you are writing, you may sometimes need your objects to exist even when the application that created them shuts down. For example, imagine writing an application that keeps track of employee records. The kind of information you might want to keep track of may include an employee's name, age, and salary. This can be done using a Java program as shown in example 4.1.

Example 4.1: Employee.java

```
import java.io.*;
/**
 * @(#)Employee.java
 */
public class Employee {
    String name;
    int age;
    int salary;

    public Employee(String name, int age, int salary) {
        this.name = name;
        this.age = age;
        this.salary = salary;
    }

    public static void print(Employee emp) {
        System.out.println("-----------------------------");
        System.out.println(emp.name+" Record:");
        System.out.println("Name: "+emp.name);
        System.out.println("Age: "+emp.age);
        System.out.println("Salary: "+emp.salary);
```

```
    }

    public static void main(String argv[]) {
        Employee emily = new Employee("E. Jordan", 27, 35000);
        Employee john = new Employee("J. McDonald", 30, 39000);

        // Print Emily's information.
        print(emily);
    }
}
```

When you run the employee program, the objects emily and john will be created. When the program exists, their state will be destroyed. However, if you have a persistent storage, you could then have persistent objects with lifetimes longer than that of the program which created them. One way to achieve persistence in Java is though JDBC. ObjectStore PSE, Jeevan, and Java object serialization represent alternative approaches to achieve persistence. In chapter 5, you will learn how object serialization can be used for persistence.

Now, let's see how to develop a persistent storage for your employees using JDBC. Using mSQL, I have created a database called "employees" and a table in that database called "employee." The employee table is shown in table 4.1.

Table 4.1 Employee table

Name	Age	Salary
E. Jordan	27	35000
J. McDonald	30	39000

The source code in example 4.2 shows how to fetch all the rows from the employee table using JDBC.

Example 4.2: Emp.java

```
import java.sql.*;
/**
 * @(#)Emp.java
 */
class Emp {
    public static void main(String argv[]) {
        try {
            Class.forName("com.imaginary.sql.msql.MsqlDriver");
            String url = "jdbc:msql://machine-name.com/port#/employees";
            Connection con = DriverManager.getConnection(url, "qusay", "");
            Statement stmt = con.createStatement();
            ResultSet rs = stmt.executeQuery("SELECT * from employee");
            System.out.println("The Results we got are:");
            while(rs.next()) {
                String str = rs.getString(1);
                int f1 = rs.getInt(2);
                float f2 = rs.getFloat(3);
```

```
                System.out.println(" Name= " + str);
                System.out.println(" Age= " + f1);
                System.out.println(" Salary= " + f2);
            }
            stmt.close();
            con.close();
        } catch( Exception e ) {
            System.out.println(e.getMessage());
            e.printStackTrace();
        }
    }
}
```

The following is a sample run of the code in example 4.2.

```
% java Emp
The Results we got are:
Name= E. Jordan
Age= 27
Salary= 35000.0
Name= J. McDonald
Age= 30
Salary= 39000.0
```

Now, let us look at an example of how to update the database. The source code in example 4.3 inserts a new record into the employee table.

Example 4.3: UpdateEmp.java

```java
import java.sql.*;
/**
 * @(#)UpdateEmp.java
 */
class UpdateEmp {
    public static void main(String argv[]) {
        if (argv.length != 3) {
            System.err.println("Usage: java UpdateEmp [name] [age] [salary]");
            return;
        }
        try {
            Class.forName("com.imaginary.sql.msql.MsqlDriver");
            String url = "jdbc:msql://machine-name.com:port#/employees";
            Connection con = DriverManager.getConnection(url, "qusay", "");
            Statement stmt = con.createStatement();
            stmt.executeUpdate("INSERT INTO employee (name, age, salary) " +
        "VALUES(" + "'" + argv[0] + "'" + ", " + argv[1] + ", "+argv[2] +")");
            System.out.println("Insert Succeeded.");
            stmt.close();
            con.close();
        } catch( Exception e ) {
            System.out.println(e.getMessage());
            e.printStackTrace();
        }
```

```
        }
    }
```

The following is a sample run of the code in example 4.3.

```
% java UpEmp "L. Johnson" 41 49000.00
```

Now, if you run the employee program again in example 4.2, you will be able to see the record you added to the database.

```
% java Emp
The Results we got are:
Name= E. Jordan
Age= 27
Salary= 35000.0
Name= J. McDonald
Age= 30
Salary= 39000.0
Name= L. Johnson
Age= 41
Salary= 49000.0
```

4.6   SUMMARY

- Information on the world wide web is sent mainly through the HTTP, which is an application-level protocol through which web browsers submit requests for services. The HTTP protocol supports several request methods, such as GET, POST, and HEAD. In this chapter, we implemented the GET method, which is used to retrieve the requested information.
- We implemented a simpleminded multithreaded HTTP server. I pointed out some of the security issues and showed you how to solve them by devising a security policy and implementing it by inheriting from the SecurityManager class.
- Proxy servers are commonly used to provide Internet access through corporate firewalls. A web proxy server creates a single access and control point to the Internet.
- JDBC is a Java API for database connectivity. JDBC allows a developer to access relational databases from different vendors in a portable way.

CHAPTER 5

Advanced sockets programming

The distributed applications we have developed so far sent only data streams over sockets. What if you want to transfer full-blown objects over the wire? Object serialization is a technique by which a program can save the state of objects to a file and later on read them back into memory or send an object over the network.

In this chapter, you'll learn how object serialization can be used to send object over sockets and implement persistency for Java objects. Then we'll discuss authenticity—methods, such as digital signatures, for determining whether a message really originated from the client that the message claims it came from.

5.1   OBJECT SERIALIZATION

Object serialization is a mechanism used extensively in RMI, as you will see in part II of this book. However, it is also useful in any program that wants to save the state of objects to a file and read those objects later to reconstruct the state of the program, or to send an object over the network using low-level sockets.

In object serialization, the object to be worked with is a Java object that must implement the java.io.Serializable interface—if it doesn't, it can't be used with object serialization.

Note that the `Serializable` interface does not have any methods. It is merely used to inform the JVM that you want the object to be serialized.

Besides an object, you also need an I/O stream. To use object serialization for saving objects, you must create an instance of an `ObjectOutputStream`, which is a subclass of `FilterOutputStream`. As an example, the following code segment shows how to save a serialized string to a file:

```
FileOutputStream fos = new FileOutputStream("str.out");
ObjectOutputStream oos = new ObjectOutputStream(fos);
oos.writeObject("this string is being saved");
```

The `writeObject` method is used to save an object to the output stream. This method can be called any number of times to save any number of objects. However, the object passed to `writeObject` must implement the `Serializable` interface.

Reading the objects you have saved is trivial. The following example shows how to read the serialized string object you saved above.

```
FileInputStream fis = new FileInputStream("str.out");
ObjectInputStream ois = new ObjectInputStream(fis);
Object o = ois.readObject();
```

As with `writeObject`, `readObject` can be called any number of times to read any number of objects from the input stream. When you are reading objects from a stream, you must know what type of objects are expected in the stream. This means that programs that serialize objects should be kept in sync with programs that deserialize objects.

5.1.1   Object serialization and persistence

In this section we will revisit the problem of object persistence that we discussed in chapter 4 in regards to keeping track of employees' data. We will see how object serialization can provide us with a persistent storage.

First, let's modify our `Employee` class (developed in example 4.1) to include object serialization. We first need to have our class implement the `Serializable` interface to inform the JVM of our intention of serializing objects. Notice that I have modified the `print()` method a bit. The new `Employee` class is shown in example 5.1.

Example 5.1: Employee.java

```java
import java.io.*;
/**
 * @(#)Employee.java
 * A serialized class to keep track of employees
 */
public class Employee implements Serializable {
    String name;
    int age;
    int salary;

    public Employee(String name, int age, int salary) {
        this.name = name;
        this.age = age;
```

```
        this.salary = salary;
    }

    public void print() {
        System.out.println("Record for: "+name);
        System.out.println("Name: "+name);
        System.out.println("Age: "+age);
        System.out.println("Salary: "+salary);
    }
}
```

The class in example 5.1 does some initialization through a constructor and provides a method for printing an employee's records.

Now we can develop a new class that creates instances, or objects, of Employee and serializes them by saving their states in a file we'll call db. Example 5.2 shows this new class.

Example 5.2: SaveEmp.java

```
import java.io.*;
/**
 * @(#)SaveEmp.java
 * This class creates some instances of the Employee
 * class and serializes them by saving their states to
 * a file.
 */
public class SaveEmp {
    public static void main(String argv[]) throws Exception {
        // Create some objects.
        Employee emily = new Employee("E. Jordan", 27, 35000);
        Employee john = new Employee("J. McDonald",290, 39000);
        // Serialize the objects emily and john.
        FileOutputStream fos = new FileOutputStream("db");
        ObjectOutputStream oos = new ObjectOutputStream(fos);
        oos.writeObject(emily);
        oos.writeObject(john);
        oos.flush();
    }
}
```

Running example 5.2 creates two objects, emily and john, and serializes them by saving their states to a file called db.

Now we can write a new class that deserializes the objects emily and john and prints their records. The new class is shown in example 5.3.

Example 5.3: ReadEmp.java

```
import java.io.*;
/**
 * @(#)ReadEmp.java
 * This class deserializes the objects emily and john by reconstructing
 * their states, which are saved in a file.
 */
```

```
public class ReadEmp {
    public static void main(String argv[]) throws Exception{
        // Deserialize the objects emily and john.
        FileInputStream fis = new FileInputStream("db");
        ObjectInputStream ois = new ObjectInputStream(fis);
        Employee emily = (Employee) ois.readObject();
        Employee john = (Employee) ois.readObject();
        // Print the records after reconstructing the states.
        emily.print();
        john.print();
    }
}
```

Compile and run the code in example 5.4 to see how the program will reconstruct the state of the objects emily and john, and how it prints their data.

5.1.2   Security in object serialization

To see the important benefit of the **Serializable** interface, let us consider the following code:

```
public class PasswordFile implements Serializable {
    private String passwd;
    . . . .
}
```

If we serialize this object, we will end up writing the password to the file, among other data, and anyone will be able to read the password. This happens because object serialization has access to all instance variables, including private, within a serializable class.

There are two ways to serialize an object without exposing any sensitive data to the world. The first is to mark any sensitive data fields as transient. The passwd above can now be written as:

```
                    private transient String passwd;
```

At the time serialization happens, the JVM will skip over any fields that are declared transient. However, if you want to serialize the transient data with the rest of the object, you must override the writeObject and readObject methods, in which you can control what data is sent and how it is stored.

The second way for dealing with sensitive data is to implement the Externalizable interface, which is a subclass of the Serializable interface. This interface has two methods that a class must implement: the writeExternal and readExternal methods.

5.1.3   Controlling the serialization

So far, serialization has been performed automatically using ObjectInputStream, ObjectOutputStream, writeObject, and readObject. However, there are situations, as you saw earlier with the PasswordFile, where you might want to have control over which fields are serialized and which are not. In addition to the Serializable interface we have used, the java.io package includes another interface: Externalizable. This interface is to be used when you want to define an object that has a complete control over serialization (such as the encoding used to send data).

The `Externalizable` interface, which is a subclass of `Serializable`, has two methods that an `Externalizable` object must implement. The two methods are `writeExternal` and `readExternal`, and they have the following signatures:

```
public void writeExternal(ObjectOutput) throws IOException
```

```
public void readExternal(ObjectInput) throws IOException
```

Implementing these methods is not a complicated process. It really depends on how you want to encode the information encapsulated in an object. For example, you may want to use some cryptographic routines to encode the data. When implementing the `writeExternal` method, you must manually write each field of data that you want to save to the `ObjectOutput`. The implementation of `readExternal` is just undoing what `writeExternal` did.

As an example, let me show you how the `PasswordFile` class can be serialized to protect the `passwd` field from being read by the world by implementing the `Externalizable` interface. As I mentioned above, the first step is to implement the `writeExternal` method. Here is a sample implementation:

```
public void writeExternal(ObjectOutput objout) throws IOException {
    // Some other code goes here.

    // Write the field.
    objout.writeObject(passwd);

    // Do other things.
}
```

Now we need to decode the object from the `ObjectInput` in the `readExternal` method, which can be implemented as follows:

```
public void readExternal(ObjectInput objin) throws IOException, ClassNot-
FoundException {
    // Read the field.
    this.passwd = (String) objin.readObject();
    // Do other things.
}
```

5.1.4   Versioning serialized objects

If you write a useful piece of software, then most likely you will be the one providing maintenance for it. Maintenance may include bug fixes and adding new features. Every time you have a new version of your classes, you will have to think about backward compatibility. As an example, if we have a serialized object and you want to remove an instance variable or add a new one, what would be the effect if you want to reserialize or deserialize?

The object serialization mechanism uses an identifier to keep track of all classes. This identifier is called the `serialVersionUID`, and it is computed from the structure of the class to form a unique 64-bit value identifier. The JDK comes with a program called serialver that can be used to find out if a class is serializable and that can get its `serialVersionUID`. If you invoke the program with –show, it puts up a simple user interface as the one shown in figure 5.1.

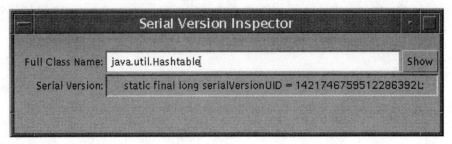

Figure 5.1 The serialVersionUID **for java.util.Hashtable**

To find out if a class is serializable and to determine its serialVersionUID, enter its full class name in the input text field and click the Show button. If the class is serializable, you will get a serialVersionUID value. Figure 5.1 shows the serialVersionUID for java. util.Hashtable. Once you get this value, you can include it in subsequent versions of the class to indicate that the new version of the class is compatible with the version identified by the serialVersionUID. This can be done by declaring the following in your version class:

```
Static final long serialVersionUID = 1421746759512286392L;
```

Note that the value computed by serialver is fixed for all compatible classes.

5.2 OBJECTS OVER SOCKETS

The classes included in the java.net package contain methods for reading/writing (or exchanging) primitive data types between client and server processes. As you saw in chapter 3 when we developed the arithmetic server, we had to write our own methods to read and write arrays of integers to sockets since no methods are provided for such operations. A good question at that time would be whether we can transfer objects over sockets. The answer is definitely yes. With the object serialization API, it is possible to write objects over sockets.

5.2.1 Sending objects on the wire

If you are already familiar with distributed object technology, you may ask why we are using sockets for this. Why not use a distributed object system (such as RMI) for this purpose? If you would like to send objects over sockets while avoiding the overhead of using a distributed object system, then using sockets and object serialization is the way to go.

In this section I will show you how to send objects over sockets using the example we developed in chapter 3—the arithmetic server. As a reminder of what that server does, the client sends two arrays of integers to the server, which then adds up the arrays and returns the result back to the client.

Developing a serializable class   We need a class that would serve as an interface for the client and server. This class will define two methods: one for setting the array and one for displaying the result. Example 5.4 shows the MathObj class.

Example 5.4: MathObj.java

```
import java.io.*;
import java.util.*;
/**
 * @(#)MathObj.java
 */
public class MathObj implements Serializable {
   private int x[] = null;
   public MathObj(){
   }

   public int[] set(int msg[]){
      x = msg;
      return x;
   }

   public int[] out() {
      return x;
   }
}
```

The most important thing to note about the MathObj class is that it implements the Serializable interface. Again, the Serializable interface does not have any methods—it is merely used to let the JVM know that you want to allow the object to be serialized. The methods defined in the MathObj class are simple enough. The set() method takes an array of integers and returns an array of integers. The out() method is used to display the sum of the two arrays.

Implementing the server   The server is a simple normal server that waits for a connection. When a connection is made, it reads an object from the client. Reading an object is done by invoking the readObject() method of the InputObjectStream. Notice how the server creates objects of type MathObj. Example 5.5 shows the complete source code for the server class.

Example 5.5: ArithServer.java

```
import java.io.*;
import java.net.*;
import java.util.*;
/**
 * @(#)ArithServer.java
 * This example shows how to use object serialization to send and receive
 * objects over sockets.
 */
public class ArithServer {
   /**
```

```
 * Create the server socket and use its stream to receive serialized
 * objects.
 */
public static void main(String args[]) {
    ServerSocket ser = null;
    Socket soc = null;
    MathObj x = null;
    MathObj y = null;
    int z1[] = new int[5];
    int z2[] = new int[5];
    int result[] = new int[5];
    try {
        ser = new ServerSocket(4343);
        /**
         * This will wait for a connection to be made to this socket.
         */
        soc = ser.accept();
        InputStream o = soc.getInputStream();
        ObjectInput s1 = new ObjectInputStream(o);
        OutputStream o2 = soc.getOutputStream();
        ObjectOutput s2 = new ObjectOutputStream(o2);
        x = (MathObj) s1.readObject();
        y = (MathObj) s1.readObject();
        z1 = x.out();
        z2 = y.out();
        for(int i=0; i<z1.length; i++) {
         System.out.println(z1[i]);
        }
        for(int i=0; i<z2.length; i++) {
            System.out.println(z2[i]);
        }
        for(int p=0; p<z1.length; p++) {
         result[p] = z1[p] + z2[p];
        }
        for(int p1=0; p1<result.length; p1++) {
            System.out.println(result[p1]);
        }
        MathObj myM = new MathObj();
        myM.set(result);
        s2.writeObject(myM);
        s2.flush();
        s1.close();
        s2.close();
    } catch (Exception e) {
        e.printStackTrace();
        System.out.println(e.getMessage());
    }
}
}
```

Implementing the client The client program is, again, a simple client. This client defines
two arrays and uses the MathObj class's methods to write them to the server. It simply defines

two `MathObj` objects and uses the `set()` method to define the two arrays. It then writes the two instances of `MathObj` to the server as objects using `writeObject`. The client source code is shown in example 5.6.

Example 5.6: ArithClient.java

```java
import java.io.*;
import java.util.*;
import java.net.*;
/**
* @(#)ArithClient.java
 */
public class ArithClient {
    public static void main(String args[]) {
        int a[] = {4, 4, 4, 4, 4};
        int b[] = {2, 2, 2, 2, 2};

        try {
            // Create a socket.
            Socket soc = new Socket(InetAddress.getLocalHost(), 4343);
            OutputStream o = soc.getOutputStream();
            ObjectOutput s = new ObjectOutputStream(o);
            InputStream in = soc.getInputStream();
            ObjectInput s2 = new ObjectInputStream(in);
            MathObj a1 = new MathObj();
            MathObj a2 = new MathObj();
            MathObj res = null;
            int arr[] = new int[5];

            a1.set(a);
            a2.set(b);
            s.writeObject(a1);
            s.writeObject(a2);
            s.flush();

            res = (MathObj) s2.readObject();
            arr = res.out();
            for(int i=0; i<arr.length; i++) {
            System.out.println(arr[i]);
        }
            s.close();
            s2.close();
        } catch (Exception e) {
            System.out.println(e.getMessage());
        }
    }
}
```

5.3   DIGITALLY SIGNED MESSAGES

The proliferation of world-wide computer networks has led to communication channels protection issues. Communication channels are accessible to eavesdroppers, and the only way to enforce protection of those channels is to apply cryptography. Cryptography is used to protect information to which illegal access is possible.

5.3.1   The java.security package

The Java security API lets developers incorporate low-level and high-level security functionality into their applications. It provides APIs for digital signatures, message digests, key management, and access control lists. Right now, we are only concerned with digital signatures and how to use them to authenticate messages over sockets.

5.3.2   Digital signatures

In real life, it is easy to differentiate between originals and copies. For example, it's easy to tell the difference between a handwritten note and a photocopy of it. In the digital world, however, the task of differentiating between originals and copies is almost impossible because all information is represented as bits. For example, imagine that you, as a client, send a bank transaction to a server, but before your message reaches the server, someone along the wire modifies it so that the reply from the server would go back to him. In the digital world, we need a mechanism by which one party can send a "signed" message to another party so that the receiver can verify the true identity of the sender.

A digital signature establishes sender authenticity. It is analogous to an ordinary written signature in these ways:

- It must be able to identify the author, data, and time of the signature.
- It must be verifiable by third parties to resolve disputes.

For digital signatures to be of practical use, they must have the following properties:

- Easy to produce.
- Easy to recognize and verify.
- Computationally infeasible to forge.

An example of a digital signature is the digital signature algorithm (DSA), which is supported by the security API in JDK 1.1 and above. Digital signatures can be implemented using a simple scheme provided by public-key cryptosystems in which each party has a pair of keys (one is public and the other is private), as opposed to just one private key as in single- or private-key cryptosystems. The interfaces that provide for generating and using digital signatures in JDK1.1 include `KeyGenerator`, `KeyPairGenerator`, and `Signature`, to name a few.

5.3.3   Example: signing a file over sockets

The example presented in this section is a client/server application where the client reads a file, generates a pair of keys, signs the contents of the file, and sends an object over the network to a server. The object contains the public key generated by the client, the signature, and the contents of the file. The server receives the object and verifies that the signature is correct.

In this example, three pieces of code need to be developed: a signed object, a client application, and a server application. Let's look at each separately.

Step 1: Developing a signed object In order to send objects over sockets, we have to use object serialization. Therefore, we need to serialize our signed object. This can be done easily by having our signed object implement the Serializable interface. As mentioned earlier, the Serializable interface does not have any methods, so there are no methods to override. Example 5.7 shows the implementation of a SignedObject.

Example 5.7: SignedObject.java

```
import java.io.*;
import java.security.*;
/**
 * @(#)SignedObject.java
 */
public class SignedObject implements Serializable {
   byte b[];
   byte sig[];
   PublicKey pub;

   // Constructor
   public SignedObject(byte b[], byte sig[], PublicKey pub) {
     this.b = b;
     this.sig = sig;
     this.pub = pub;
   }
}
```

The first thing to note from example 5.7 is the second import statement:

```
import java.security.*;
```

The methods for signing data are contained in the java.security package, so we are importing everything from that package. Also, note that the SignedObject will carry three things: the contents of a file from the client, a signature, and a public key. PublicKey is actually a methodless interface used for type safety and identification for public keys. A public key is really a number associated with an entity (such as an individual or an organization), and everyone who wants to have trusted interactions with that entity should know of it.

Step 2: Developing a client application The client in this example has four tasks to perform:

- Read the contents of a file, which are given to it as an argument on the command line.
- Generate a pair of keys (public and private) using the security API.
- Sign the contents of the file.
- Send an object containing the above three items across the network to the server.

These steps can be followed easily from looking at the client's code that is shown in example 5.8.

Example 5.8: Client.java

```java
import java.io.*;
import java.net.*;
import java.security.*;
/**
 * @(#)Client.java
 */
public class Client {
    public static void main(String argv[]) {
        Socket s = null;
        ObjectOutputStream os = null;

        try {
          s = new Socket("purejava", 4000);
          os = new ObjectOutputStream(s.getOutputStream());
         System.out.println("Generating keys...this may take a few minutes");
          // Generate public and private keys.
          KeyPairGenerator kgen = KeyPairGenerator.getInstance("DSA");
          kgen.initialize(256);
          KeyPair kpair = kgen.generateKeyPair();

          // Generate a signature.
          System.out.println("Generating Signature....");
          Signature sig = Signature.getInstance("SHA/DSA");
          PublicKey pub = kpair.getPublic();
          PrivateKey priv = kpair.getPrivate();
          sig.initSign(priv);

          // Read a file and compute a signature.
          FileInputStream fis = new FileInputStream(argv[0]);
          byte arr[] = new byte[fis.available()];
          fis.read(arr);
          sig.update(arr);

          // Send the SignedObject on the wire.
          SignedObject obj = new SignedObject(arr, sig.sign(), pub);
          os.writeObject(obj);

          // Close streams.
          fis.close();
          os.close();
          s.close();
        } catch (Exception e) {
          e.printStackTrace();
        }
    }
}
```

The two most important things that are accomplished in example 5.8 are generating the public and private keys and signing the data file.

In order to generate a digital signature, we must generate the public and private keys using the `KeyPairGenerator` class. In example 5.8, we are generating a public and private key pair for the algorithm named DSA, which has a length of 256 bits. The next step is to initialize the pair of keys. This is done using the `initialize()` method of the `KeyPairGenerator` class. The argument to the `initialize()` method is the strength of the key in bits. In our example we are generating keys of length 256 bits. Please remember that the longer a key is, the more secure it is. We are using 256 bits in this example so that the computer will generate the keys in a matter of seconds. Longer key lengths require more CPU power to generate the keys. Stronger and more secure keys can be initialized more securely using this line:

```
kgen.initialize(1024, new SecureRandom());
```

In this case, the `initialize()` method takes two arguments: the strength and the source of randomness. The source of randomness must be an instance of the `SecureRandom` class; to keep things simple, we are using an empty constructor of the `SecureRandom` class. In this case, it will automatically generate a "seed" value required for the random number generator.

The next and final step in generating the pair of keys is to use the `KeyPair` class as follows, and as shown in example 5.8:

```
KeyPair pair = kgen.generateKeyPair();
```

At this point we are ready to sign the data:

As shown in example 5.8, a digital signature is created using an instance of the `Signature` class. To sign the data, however, involves four steps:

1 *Getting a signature object.*   To get a signature object for generating signatures using the DSA algorithm, we use the following fragment of code, as shown in example 5.8:

```
Signature sig = Signature.getInstance("SHA/DSA");
```

2 *Initializing the signature object.*   Before a signature object can be used for signing, it must be initialized. The initialization is done using the `initSign` method of the `Signature` class. This method takes an instance of `PrivateKey` as an argument. This is done as follows (also shown in example 5.8):

```
PrivateKey priv = kpair.getPrivate();
sig.initSign(priv)
```

3 *Providing the data to be signed to the signature object.*   This is done by reading the data (a file in our case) to be signed into an array of bytes and then supplying it to the signature object by calling the `update` method of the `Signature` class as shown in example 5.8.

4 *Generating the signature and sending it over the wire.*   The last step is to generate the digital signature for the data, and, of course, send it over the wire. In example 5.8, this is shown as follows:

```
SignedObject obj = new SignedObject(arr, sig.sign(), pub);
os.writeObject(obj); // Write the signed object to the output stream.
```

Step 3: Developing a server application   A server would have to run forever listening for client's requests. In this case, however, the server will also need to read an object from the client and verify that the signature is valid. The server code is shown in example 5.9. The server here does not inherit from the Thread class, as discussed in chapter 3; instead, it implements the Runnable interface. This is another way of implementing multithreaded servers, as we discussed in chapter 3.

Example 5.9: Server.java

```java
import java.io.*;
import java.net.*;
import java.security.*;
/**
 * @(#)Server.java
 */
public class Server implements Cloneable, Runnable {
    ServerSocket service = null;
    Socket clientSocket = null;
    ObjectInputStream ois = null;
    Thread worker = null;
    KeyPairGenerator kgen;
    KeyPair kpair;

    public static void main(String argv[]) throws IOException {
        Server serv = new Server();
        serv.startServer();
    }

    public synchronized void startServer() throws IOException {
        if (worker == null) {
            service = new ServerSocket(4000);
            worker = new Thread(this);
            worker.start();
        }
    }

    public void run() {
        Socket client = null;
        if (service != null) { // Original or clone?
          while(true) {
             try {
               client = service.accept();
               Server newServer = (Server) clone();
               newServer.service = null;
               newServer.clientSocket = client;
               newServer.worker = new Thread(newServer);
               newServer.worker.start();
             } catch(IOException e) {
```

```
                e.printStackTrace();
            } catch(CloneNotSupportedException e) {
                e.printStackTrace();
            }
        }
    } else {
        perform(clientSocket);
    }
}

private void perform(Socket client) {
    try {
        ois = new ObjectInputStream(clientSocket.getInputStream());
        // Read object from client.
        SignedObject obj = (SignedObject) ois.readObject();
        // Generate object's signature.
        Signature sig = Signature.getInstance("SHA/DSA");
        sig.initVerify(obj.pub);
        sig.update(obj.b);

        // Verify the signature.
        boolean valid = sig.verify(obj.sig);
        if (valid) {
            System.out.println("Signature is valid");
        } else {
            System.out.println("Signature is not valid...spy!");
        }
    } catch(Exception e) {
        e.printStackTrace();
    }

    // Close streams and connection.
    try {
        ois.close();
        clientSocket.close();
    } catch(IOException ex) {
        ex.printStackTrace();
    }
}
}
```

Besides listening for connections, the server program in this example will have to receive the signed object and verify if the signature is valid. To verify the authenticity of the signature, we need the data, the signature, and the public key corresponding to the private key used to sign the data.

To start the verification process, just as with signature generation, we need to create an instance of the Signature class:

```
Signature sig = Signature.getInstance("SHA/DSA");
```

The next step is to initialize the signature object with the public key:

```
sig.initVerify(obj.pub); // Please refer to example 5.8.
```

Then we'll use the update() method to provide the signed data to the signature that we want to verify:

```
sig.update(obj.b);
```

And finally, we can verify the signature and report the result:

```
boolean valid = sig.verify(obj.sig);
if (valid) {
  System.out.println("Signature is valid");
} else {
    System.out.println("Signature is not valid");
}
```

In this client/server example, the flag valid should be true if we are verifying the signature we generated. If someone was spying over the network and managed to modify the signature, then the flag would be false.

5.4 SUMMARY

- Object serialization is a mechanism that can be used in any application that needs to save the state of objects to a file and read them back into memory later on, or to send an object over the network using low-level sockets.
- For a Java object to be serialized it must implement the java.io.Serializable interface. This interface merely informs the JVM that you want the object to be serialized.
- DSA is a way of generating a digital signature, which makes it possible for a message receiver to verify the claimed identity of the message sender. DSA is supported in JDK1.1 in the java.security package.

C H A P T E R   6

Case study: a global compute engine

A number of ongoing research projects are working to turn the world wide web into a super-computer. In this chapter, we'll discuss the design and implementation of a global web-based compute engine suitable for implementation in Java.

I'll start off by presenting an overview of the web and its computing models. I'll give you an overview of a design for a simple global web-based compute engine, and show you why CGI is no good for implementing such a system. Then I'll describe a client/server-based architecture of the system and show you how it can be implemented in Java. Along the way, you'll learn about some advanced Java features such as security managers and class loaders.

As a sidenote before we begin, here is what Tim Berners-Lee, director of the World Wide Web Consortium, had to say about web-based global computing:

"The vision of the World-Wide Web as a global computing platform is one aspect driving the evolution of the Web, perhaps the aspect most appropriate for a 50th anniversary look ahead."("World-Wide Computer," *Communications of the ACM*, Feb 1997).

6.1 INTRODUCTION

The world wide web, or web for short, has been very successful in doing what it was designed for—serving as a network-based hypermedia *information system*. The simplicity of creating documents for the web and the ease of navigating the web are some of the key concepts behind its success.

The current model of the web, however, has limited support for computing. The web's current computing models of the web include *server-side* computing using Common Gateway Interface (CGI) or server-side scripts, and *client-side* computing using scripted HTML files (using JavaScript) and applets. But these computing models are limited, since they were designed for processing information dynamically.

The existing computing models, however, suggest that the web has the potential of becoming a general purpose distributed computing system, since an extension to the web's functionality to include global compute engines (to which users will be able to upload code) is possible.

6.2 GLOBAL WEB-BASED COMPUTING

Global computing in this sense means that local code is to be executed globally. If you have a large program that requires a sophisticated computer processor and you do not own one, then it should be possible for you to send that code to a global compute engine that will execute the program and send you the results.

In this section we will discuss why there is a need for global computing and why it should be web based.

6.2.1 Why global computing?

Ted Lewis of the Naval Postgraduate School contends:

"The limits of parallelism seem to block further advances in processor performance beyond the next 10,0002 years. But a third alternative leads to the concept of an uncoordinated, globally distributed, parallel megacomputer. Such computers already exist in the form of asynchronous nodes on the Internet, but they have yet to be used to their fullest extent." ("The Next 10,0002 Years: Part I & II," *Communications of the ACM*, April 1996).

In computational-intensive programs, there is always a need for more computing power and better performance. Having a global computing system in those situations would solve many problems related to performance, fault tolerance, and resource limitation. One major advantage of such a system would be the ability to use as many idle (and perhaps faster) machines on the Internet as possible to solve large and complex problems. One example of such a problem is the RSA129 factoring project where more than 1600 machines were used to factor an integer 129 digits long (see http://www.rsa.com).

6.2.2 Why web-based computing?

The web, so far, has been widely used as a global *information resource* system. When a user visits a web site, generally all he sees is information (both static and dynamic), forms to fill in, and animated images.

The current simplified computing model of the web allows the user to execute server-side programs using CGI scripts. In addition, it allows the user to download and execute server-side miniprograms (applets) on his machine. In this case, when the user requests a web page that contains an applet, the applet migrates to the client's machine and gets executed there.

The purpose of this chapter is to show you how to build a simple compute engine on top of the web using Java; we will also discuss some advanced Java topics including class loaders and security managers. This idea represents an evolutionary process when you look at the following advantages of choosing the web as the base on which to build our global compute engine. First, the great success of the web gives users an opportunity to extend its concepts by including *computing resources*, thus extending its services. Second, users are already familiar with the web, its interface, and how to use it, thus providing them with an already-familiar user interface, which makes the system commonly usable.

6.2.3   Issues to consider

In order to extend the web's functionality with general distributed computing power by building a global compute engine, various issues need to be considered.

A New URL   A Uniform Resource Locator (URL) is a unique identifier that gives information for locating a resource on the Internet. Existing URLs fail to address computing resources. It is therefore necessary to develop a new URL specification that is capable of handling and identifying computing resources on the Internet. We will not discuss this topic any further, as it is a complicated issue and requires the development of a new protocol. If you are interested in this area, you may want to take a look at the new Service Location Protocol that is being developed at Sun Microsystems (see http://www.srvloc.org).

Communication   A number of issues need to be considered when clients are communicating with a global compute engine. Here are two of them:

- *Scheduling*   In case of a high demand on the currently available computing resources, a scheduling mechanism that regulates and schedules requests is needed.
- *Security*   Security is a major concern in every distributed computing system. With a global compute engine, clients will be able to upload code to remote machines on which the code will be executed. However, this introduces some security risks and concerns. For example, a client's code may contain some malicious instructions to delete files from the compute engine machine's file system. In order to provide a remedy, a security policy needs to be devised and implemented to protect the compute engine's file system. Java provides a nice way of implementing a security policy through a custom security manager, as you will see in section 6.6.2.

6.3   *WHY NOT CGI?*

The file-upload feature, which is an extension of HTML that allows information providers to express file upload requests, can be used to develop a simplified version of the global compute engine. In this version, clients will be able to upload their program files to remote machines and have them executed as shown in figure 6.1. Using CGI and the file-upload feature has a number of advantages and disadvantages. These are outlined in the following sections.

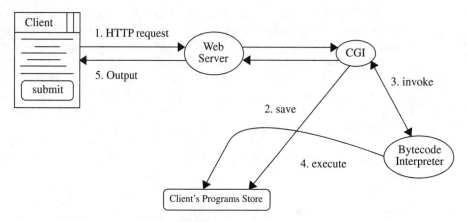

Figure 6.1 A simple compute engine using CGI

6.3.1   Advantages

The advantages of using CGI-based file-upload to implement a simple global compute engine include the following:

- *Simplicity*   The main advantage of using CGI file-upload is the simplicity of implementing a system in which only one CGI script is needed to handle uploading the file and collecting the output.
- *Ease of use*   From the user's point of view, this feature is all point-and-click. When the user is presented with an HTML form, he needs only to click a button to get a dialog box with a view of his local disk. From there, he can choose the file to be uploaded for remote execution.

6.3.2   Disadvantages

Despite the simplicity and ease of using CGI file-upload, there are some disadvantages as well as limitations in using it to implement a global compute engine.

- *Incompatibility*   A number of web browsers are available to the user. However, not all browsers are compatible with each other, since they do not all implement the same features.
- *Space inefficiency*   Uploading the whole file to the server's machine is a waste of bandwidth. In addition, the file has to be saved on the server's machine, thus taking up valuable space.
- *Inconvenience*   If the client's program consists of multiple files, then the client is required to upload all the files to the server's machine.
- *Limited input/output*   CGI was developed for the purpose of form-based information processing. Once the user fills out the form and submits it, there are not many interactions between the user and the script interpreting the form. However, in our case, when a program runs, it may need some input from the user, so more interactions are

required. This I/O limitation represents a problem when CGI is used to carry out real computations.

6.4   THE CLIENT/SERVER MODEL

For the system to be efficient, the client should not have to upload all the program files to the server's machine. With the help of dynamic code loading, the client sends a URL specifying the location of the code to be executed. The server will, in turn, fetch the code from the URL and load it dynamically (on-the-fly). Once the code has been successfully loaded dynamically, the server will collect the results and send them back to the client. Dynamic code loading via class loaders is one of the neat features built in into Java.

Implementing a global compute engine using dynamic code loading requires, in addition to the web server process, another server process and a client application. The client program can be one of two things: a dynamic applet or a CGI script that the browser calls from the web server to generate a form for the user to fill out. On the other hand, the server program, which is really the compute engine itself, is responsible for getting the client's request, executing the program, and sending the results back to the client.

6.5   SECURITY ISSUES

There are some security risks associated with executing code over the network. In this section we'll examine the risks associated with dynamic code loading. We will not discuss the risks associated with using CGI file-upload, since I won't be showing you the implementation of this simple model.

If the global compute engine loads arbitrary classes into the system through a class loader mechanism, the compute engine's integrity will be at risk due to the power of the class loader mechanism. Therefore, to be sure that an untrusted code cannot perform any malicious actions such as deleting files, the compute engine should run in a restricted environment: a *sandbox*. An extensible security model needs to be developed to protect the host's file system from potential malicious code from the client.

The extensible security model will not allow the client's code to perform any harmful actions, including the following, which are considered to be security risks:

- Reading from or writing to files on the compute engine's host.
- Deleting files from the compute engine's host.
- Executing system commands such as `rm` or `del`.
- Creating or listing files or directories.
- Making the compute engine quit.
- Loading a new security manager.
- Loading a new class loader.

6.6   IMPLEMENTATION DETAILS

The CGI file-upload implementation is trivial, so we won't discuss its implementation here. Instead, we will discuss the implementation of the compute engine (server), the client, the class loader, and the security manager.

6.6.1   The class loader

Classes are introduced into the Java environment when they are referenced by name in a class that is already running. The first class that gets executed is the one with the main(String argv[]) method in it, declared as static. Once the main class is running, future attempts at loading classes are carried out by the class loader.

Normally, the JVM loads classes from the directory defined by the CLASSPATH environment variable on the local file system. However, the compute engine has to be capable of dynamically loading classes off the network. In order to do this, we need to implement a class loader, which is an innovative idea in the Java environment. We will call our class loader Net-ClassLoader. This class loader is a subclass of ClassLoader, which is defined in the java.lang package with extended functionality:

```
public class NetClassLoader extends ClassLoader {
     // Implementation details go here.
}
```

The only method that must be implemented by the NetClassLoader is the abstract loadClass method that does the following:

- Verifies the class name.
- Checks to see if the requested class has already been loaded.
- Checks to see if the class is a system class.
- Defines the class for the JVM.
- Resolves the class (see below).
- Returns the class to the loader.

The loadClass method has the following signature:

```
public synchronized Class loadClass(String className,
 boolean resolveIt) throws ClassNotFoundException {
}
```

The variable className, which is of type String, will contain the URL of the class to be loaded. Therefore, this variable must have a valid URL (such as http://www.scs.carleton.ca/~qusay/sampleClass.class). If other classes happen to be referenced by sampleClass.class, then the class loader should be able to load them as well. This is actually done through the variable resolveIt, which is a flag that, when set to true, tells the class loader that classes referenced by this class name should be loaded as well.

One hidden issue when working with class loaders in JDK1.02 is the inability to cast an object that was created from a loaded class into its original class. The object to be returned needs to be casted. This issue can be solved in JDK1.1 and above by using the reflection API.

To demonstrate this hidden issue, let's look at a typical use of the NetClassLoader we are developing, which follows this form:

```
NetClassLoader ncl = new NetClassLoader();
Object o;
Class c;
c = ncl.loadClass("someClass");
o = c.newInstance();
((someInterface) o).someClassMethod();
```

We cannot cast o to someClass because only the loader knows the new class it has loaded. This presents a glitch in the global compute engine—the engine will not be able to run just any class without any modifications. However, this is a limitation in JDK1.0.2. For example, in order for the applet class loader embedded in Netscape or the Applet Viewer to load applets, the developer has to extend the Applet class first. The same idea can be applied in the compute engine—there has to be an abstract class or an interface that clients must extend in order for their classes to be loaded by the compute engine. We will use an interface that every client must implement. Our interface definition is shown in example 6.1.

Example 6.1: Compute.java

```
/**
 * @(#)Compute.java
 */
public interface Compute {
    void run();
}
```

Now, if a client wants to use our compute engine, he must implement the interface above by providing an implementation to the run() method. A simple example may look as follows:

```
public class Example implements Compute {
    public void run() {
        System.out.println("This is a sample test.");
    }
}
```

The complete source code for NetClassLoader is shown in example 6.2.

Example 6.2: NetClassLoader.java

```
import java.io.*;
import java.net.*;
import java.util.*;
/**
 * @(#)NetClassLoader.java
 */
public class NetClassLoader extends ClassLoader {
  private Hashtable classes = new Hashtable();

  // Constructor
  public NetClassLoader() {
  }
  /**
   * Loads a class with the specified name and returns it.
   */
  public Class loadClass(String className) throws ClassNotFoundException {
      return (loadClass(className, true));
  }
```

```
/**
 * This method is called by the loadClass above.
 */
public synchronized Class loadClass(String className, boolean resolveIt)
   throws ClassNotFoundException {
   Class result;
   byte  classData[];
   result = (Class) classes.get(className);
   if (result==null) {
     try {
       result = findSystemClass(className);
       if (result!=null) classes.put(className,result);
     } catch(Exception e) {
     }
   }
   if (result==null) {
     classData = null;
     if (0==className.indexOf("http://")) {
       classData = loadnet(className);
     }
     if (classData!=null) {
       result = defineClass(classData, 0, classData.length);
       if (resolveIt) resolveClass(result);
       if (result!=null) {
         classes.put(className, result);
       }
     }
   }
   return(result);
}
// . . . .
// The loadNet method belongs here. It is shown in example 6.3.
// . . . .
}
```

In example 6.2, notice that the loadClass method invokes the loadNet method. The loadNet method has the following signature:

```
private byte[] loadNet(String className) {
   // Implementation details go here.
}
```

This method is actually responsible for fetching a class, off the network, of the given className and returning it to the loader as an array of bytes. Then, in turn, the class loader will load it dynamically. The loadNet method is shown in example 6.3.

Example 6.3: loadNet

```
/**
 * Loads a class with the specified name off the network.
 */
```

```
private byte[] loadnet(String name) {
    URL url=null;
    DataInputStream dis=null;
    URLConnection urlc=null;
    byte data[];
    int filesize;
    System.out.println("Loading "+name+" from the network");
    try {
     url = new URL(name);
    } catch(MalformedURLException e) {
     System.out.println("NetClassLoader: "+e);
    }
    try {
     urlc = url.openConnection();
     dis = new DataInputStream(urlc.getInputStream());
    } catch(Exception e) {
     System.out.println("NetClassLoader: can not open URL "+e);
    }
    filesize = urlc.getContentLength();
    data = new byte[filesize];
    try {
     dis.readFully(data);
    } catch(IOException i) {
     System.out.println("NetClassLoader: could not read: "+name);
    }
    if (data==null) System.out.println("DATA = NULL");
    return(data);
}
```

6.6.2   The security policy

With the global compute engine, clients will be able to run their programs on remote machines. The use of this facility potentially adds a new security vulnerability. To protect the global compute engine's host file system, an extensible security model that consists of two layers is developed.

The first layer comes from the Java run-time system itself. The second layer is based on the java.lang.SecurityManager class, which allows developers to implement their own custom security managers.

Layer I: Safety provided by Java   The first layer in our security model is provided by the Java language run-time system. This layer provides the necessary features to limit the likelihood of unintentionally flawed programs and it provides a simple secure execution environment that consists of the following sublayers:

- The Java compiler.
- The Java bytecode interpreter.
- A mechanism for dynamically loading and checking libraries at runtime.
- An automated garbage collector.

Layer II: Custom security manager   In Layer I, the built-in Java safety ensures that the Java system is not subverted by invalid code. However, that layer is not able to protect against malicious code. For example, imagine that a client is aware of a file with the name *sensitive.txt* that exists on the compute engine's host file system. The client may write a piece of malicious code to delete that file; it may look something like this:

```
public class Del implements Compute {
  public void run(String str) {
    File f  = new File("path to sensitive.txt");
    if ((f.delete() == true) {
      System.out.println("File:"+f+"has been deleted.");
    } else {
       System.out.println("Operation is not allowed");
    }
  }
}
```

This is the kind of malicious code that Layer I cannot protect the compute engine's host file system against. However, given that Java code will adhere to the restrictions imposed by the Java run-time system, we can devise our own security policy at the application level. This will allow us to state what sort of instructions a Java program can and cannot follow; this is accomplished by implementing and installing a security manager.

The SecurityManager class, which is part of the java.lang package, provides the necessary mechanism for creating a custom security manager that defines tasks that an application can and cannot do.

To understand how it helps, the following code segment demonstrates how the Java interpreter's security manager works:

```
public boolean OP(Type arg) {
    SecurityManager sm = System.getSecurityManager();
    if (sm != null) {
      sm.checkOP(arg);
    }
}
```

This shows that when a public method call invokes the system security manager, the system determines whether the operation OP is allowed. This means if a security manager is installed by an application, operations will be checked before they are performed.

The security policy for the global compute engine states that a client's code, when loaded dynamically, should not be allowed to perform certain actions, including those listed here:

- Reading from (or writing to) files on the compute engine's host system.
- Creating files or directories on the compute engine's host system.
- Deleting files or directories on the compute engine's host system.
- Executing commands such as rm or del.
- Making the Java interpreter exit.
- Checking for the existence of a file.
- Creating a ClassLoader object.
- Creating a SecurityManager object.
- Manipulating threads other than its own.

A sample security manager source program is shown in example 6.4. Be aware that the code implements only part of the security policy for the compute engine. We disallow the client's code from deleting files and quitting the JVM. The rest is left for you to implement as an exercise.

Example 6.4: RunnerSecurityManager.java

```java
import java.io.*;
import java.util.*;
/**
 * @(#)RunnerSecurityManager.java
 */
class RunnerSecurityManager extends SecurityManager {
    private boolean silent = true;
    private boolean checkDelete = true;
    private boolean checkExit = true;

    // Constructor
    RunnerSecurityManager() {
        System.out.println("RunnerSecurityManager started");
    }
    /**
     * The following operations are allowed. This is just hypothetical
     * though.
     * More restricted access should be imposed when working with
     * class loaders.
     */
    public void checkConnect(String host, int port) { };
    public void checkCreateClassLoader() { };
    public void checkAccess(Thread g) { };
    public void checkListen(int port) { };
    public void checkLink(String lib) { };
    public void checkPropertyAccess(String key) { };
    public void checkAccept(String host, int port) { };
    public void checkAccess(ThreadGroup g) { };
    public void checkExec(String cmd) { };
    /**
     * Check to see if a file with the specified filename can be deleted.
     */
    public void checkDelete(String file) {
        if(checkDelete) {
            throw new SecurityException("Sorry, not allowed to delete "+file);
        } else if(!silent) {
            System.out.println("RunnerSecurityManager FILE="+file+" :
                checkDelete");
        }
    }
    /**
     * Check to see if the system has exited the Java Virtual Machine.
     */
    public void checkExit(int status) {
```

```
        if(checkExit) {
          throw new SecurityException("Sorry, checkExit "+status);
        } else if(!silent) {
            System.out.println("RunnerSecurityManager STATUS="+status+" :
                checkExit");
        }
    }
  }
)
```

6.6.3   The compute engine

The source code for the compute engine is shown in example 6.5. As you can see, the first thing we do in the main program is install the customized security manager RunnerSecurityManager by creating an instance of it and registering it using the instruction System.setSecurityManager(RSM), where RSM is an instance of RunnerSecurity Manager.

The call to the ComputeEngine() constructor initializes the ComputeEngine by having it listen on a port number (5000 in this case). It then starts the thread by calling its start() method, which in turn calls the run() method that creates an instance of the Connect class (example 6.6) and initializes the compute engine to accept connections from clients.

Example 6.5: ComputeEngine.java

```java
import java.io.*;
import java.net.*;
import java.util.*;
/**
 * @(#)ComputeEngine.java
 */
public class ComputeEngine extends Thread {
    public static final int EXEC_PORT = 5000;
    protected ServerSocket listen;

    // Constructor
    public ComputeEngine() {
        try {
          listen = new ServerSocket(EXEC_PORT);
        } catch (IOException e) {
         System.out.println("Error in creating server socket: "+e);
        }
        System.out.println("Exec server listening on port: "+EXEC_PORT);
        this.start();
    }
    /**
     * Accepts a new connection in a separate thread of execution.
     */
    public void run() {
        try {
          while(true) {
              Socket cl = listen.accept();
              Connect cc = new Connect(cl);
          }
        } catch(IOException ex) {
```

```
            System.out.println("Error listening for connections: "+ex);
        }
    }
    /**
     * This is where execution starts. Set our custom security
     * manager, and create an instance of the compute engine.
     */
    public static void main(String argv[]) {
        RunnerSecurityManager RSM;
        try {
            RSM = new RunnerSecurityManager();
            System.setSecurityManager(RSM);
        } catch (SecurityException se) {
            System.out.println("RunnerSecurityManager already running");
        }
        new ComputeEngine();
    }
}
```

In example 6.5, notice that we are using a TCP-based network connection in order to achieve reliability in communication between clients and the compute engine. The compute engine uses the ServerSocket class to accept connections from clients. Whenever a client connects to the port number the compute engine is listening on, the ServerSocket allocates a new Socket object, which is connected to some new port, for the client to communicate through. At this point, the server goes back to listen for more requests.

The compute engine is a multithreaded server capable of serving multiple clients. What makes the compute engine multithreaded is the fact that the server object itself is a thread. Its run() method loops forever as it listens for connections from clients. Whenever a client connects, the compute engine creates a new Socket and a new thread to handle the communication over the Socket. The newly created thread is an instance of the Connect class, which is shown in example 6.6.

Example 6.6: Connect.java

```
import java.io.*;
import java.net.*;
/**
 * @(#)Connect.java
 */
class Connect extends Thread {
    Socket client;
    // BufferedReader is;
    DataInputStream is;
    PrintStream os;
    /**
     * Creates input and output streams and makes the input stream ready to
     * receive information from the client.
     */
    public Connect(Socket s) { // Constructor
        client = s;
        try {
```

```
        is = new DataInputStream(client.getInputStream());
        os = new PrintStream(client.getOutputStream());
    } catch (IOException e) {
     System.out.println("Error...."+e);
    }
    this.start();
}
/**
 * Reads information from the client and creates an instance of our
 * custom network class loader.
 */
public void run() {
    String url = null;
    try {
      url = is.readUTF();
    } catch (IOException es) {
        System.out.println("Error writing..."+es);
    }
    String className = url;
    // Redirect the output stream to the client socket.
    System.setOut(os);
    // Use the NetClassLoader.
    NetClassLoader sc = new NetClassLoader();
    try {
      Object o;
      o = (sc.loadClass(className, true)).newInstance();
      ((Compute) o).run();
    } catch (Exception cne) {
        System.out.println("Error...."+cne);
    }
    // Close the input and output streams and the connection to the
    // client.
    try {
      is.close();
      os.close();
      client.close();
    } catch (IOException xx) {
        System.out.println("Error closing..."+xx);
    }
  }
}
```

6.6.4   Command-line client

The client program is really simple in this case. All it does is open a connection to the ComputeEngine server and pass a URL of the class to be loaded. Then it receives the results from the ComputeEngine and displays them on the console. The source code in example 6.7 shows the client program. Our client here is a command-line-based client. However, a GUI-based client can be also implemented. Furthermore, the client to the compute engine can be implemented either as a CGI script or an applet. I chose to implement it as a command-line client for simplicity and demonstration ease.

Example 6.7: ComputeClient.java

```java
import java.io.*;
import java.net.*;
/**
 * @(#)ComputeClient.java
 */
public class ComputeClient {
    public final static int REMOTE_PORT = 5000;;
    /**
     * This is the main program of the client.
     */
    public static void main(String argv[]) throws Exception {
        String host = argv[0];
        String url = argv[1];
        Socket cl = null, cl2=null;
        BufferedReader is = null;
        DataOutputStream os = null;
        // Open the connection to the compute engine on port 5000.
        try {
          cl = new Socket(host,REMOTE_PORT);
          is = new BufferedReader(new InputStreamReader
              (cl.getInputStream()));
          os = new DataOutputStream(cl.getOutputStream());
           System.out.println("Connection is fine...");
        } catch(UnknownHostException e1) {
          System.out.println("Unknown Host: "+e1);
        } catch (IOException e2) {
          System.out.println("Erorr io: "+e2);
        }
        // Write the URL to the compute engine.
        try {
          os.writeUTF(url);
        } catch (IOException ex) {
          System.out.println("error writing to server..."+ex);
        }
        // Receive results from the compute engine.
        String outline;
        try {
         while((outline = is.readLine()) != null) {
          System.out.println("Remote: "+outline);
          }
        } catch (IOException cx) {
           System.out.println("Error: "+cx);
        }
        // Close the input stream, output stream, and connection.
        try {
          is.close();
          os.close();
```

```
        cl.close();
    } catch (IOException x) {
      System.out.println("Error writing...."+x);
    }
  }
}
```

6.7 OTHER ISSUES

There are many interesting issues related to web-based global computing that need to be exploited. The following sections provide some highlights.

6.7.1 Searching for computing resources

Search engines on the web have greatly simplified the task of the web surfer by allowing him to search for information on a particular topic by typing in a keyword. We need a similar tool for the compute engine so that users would not have to memorize the name or IP address of a remote compute engine. Instead, users should be able to search for compute engines just as they search for information. Such a tool should also be able to show information about a compute engine's load and other characteristics.

6.7.2 Broker

A more efficient search approach (as opposed to the search engine) is a broker. The broker keeps track of all compute engines that run on remote hosts. Thus, if a user wants to use a remote compute engine, all he has to do is contact the broker by telling it what kind of compute engine is needed and for how long.

A broker can be developed that keeps track of a database as shown in figure 6.2, so whenever a compute engine is started, it will automatically contact the broker and register itself by giving information to the broker. Such information may include what processor the compute engine is running on, when it is available, and how long it is available for.

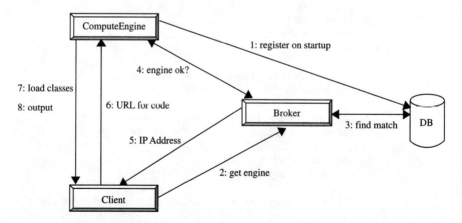

Figure 6.2 Broker-based searching

In the future, if the idea of this global compute engine becomes popular, it may be necessary to have a broker for each time zone or country.

6.8   SUMMARY

- The web has been very successful at what it was designed to be—a network-based hypermedia information system. The current model of the web, however, has limited support for compute resources. The current computing models of the web include server-side computing usingCGI scripts, and client-side computing using scripted HTML files (using JavaScript) and applets. These models, however, are limited since they were mainly designed for processing information dynamically.
- CGI is not suited for implementing a web-based compute engine for a number of reasons, most notably because of its limited I/O mechanisms.
- Our simple client/server computer engine loads classes over the network as needed, using a custom network class loader. We made our custom loader by extending Java's Class-Loader.
- Loading arbitrary classes across the network raises some security issues. To provide a remedy, we devised an extensible security policy and implemented a custom security manager by extending Java's SecurityManager.

RMI

C H A P T E R   7

Overview of RMI

Remote method invocation (RMI) is an alternative approach for developing distributed applications. As we have seen throughout part I, developing distributed applications using sockets involves designing an application-level protocol. RMI, however, abstracts the interface between the client and server to a local procedure call. Therefore, when you use RMI, you don't need to choose or design a protocol.

RMI objects can communicate with one another if they are all implemented in Java. If Java is your language of choice, then RMI provides an ideal system for building distributed applications.

This chapter gives you an overview of RMI, including its three layers and some of its most valuable features, such as distributed garbage collection and convenient access to streams.

7.1   INTRODUCTION TO RMI

Developing distributed applications using low-level sockets involves the design of a *protocol*. As you learned in chapter 1, a protocol is a set of commands (or a language) agreed upon by the client and server through which they will be able to carry on a beneficial conversation. Designing such a protocol is both hard and error-prone. One issue, for example, is *deadlock*.

In a deadlock, processes never finish executing. Such processes may be holding system resources and thus preventing other processes from accessing these resources.

Java's RMI is an alternative to low-level sockets. A remote method invocation is a form of the RPC that is available on other systems. Instead of creating and instantiating objects on local machines, you create some of the objects on other (possibly remote) machines, and you communicate with those objects as you normally would with local objects. In other words, in RMI, communication interfaces are abstracted to the level of a local procedure call. Therefore, there is no need for a protocol, and distributed applications can be developed more easily.

Unlike CORBA, as you will see in part III, your objects can only communicate with one another if they are all implemented in Java. If Java is your language of choice (and it's a very attractive one), then RMI could be your best communication alternative for creating distributed applications.

7.2   WHAT IS RMI?

RMI is a core package of the JDK1.1 (and above) that can be used to develop distributed applications. It enables software developers to write distributed applications in which the methods of remote objects can be invoked from other JVMs, which could possibly be running on different hosts. RMI is very similar to, but easier to use than, the RPC mechanism found on other systems; the programmer has the illusion of calling a local method from a local class file, when in fact all the arguments are shipped to the remote target and interpreted, and the results are sent back to the callers. Figure 7.1 illustrates the difference between local and remote method invocation.

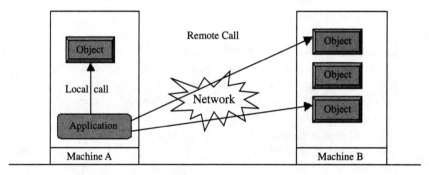

Figure 7.1 Local vs. remote method invocation

The simplicity of creating distributed applications using RMI is quite appealing to software developers who are interested in distributed objects technology.

The features supported by RMI are those that are most valuable for building distributed applications, including these:

- Transparent invocations.
- Distributed garbage collection.
- Convenient access to streams.

OVERVIEW OF RMI

Remote invocations are transparent since they are identical to local ones; thus, their method signatures are identical as well.

7.3 THE GOALS OF RMI

The RMI specification (see http://java.sun.com/products/jdk/rmi/index.html lists these goals of the RMI package:

- Support seamless remote invocations on objects in different Java virtual machines.
- Support callbacks from servers to clients.
- Integrate the distributed object model into the Java language in a natural way while retaining most of the Java language's object semantics.
- Make differences between the distributed object model and the local Java object model apparent.
- Make writing reliable distributed applications as simple as possible.
- Preserve the safety provided by the Java run-time environment.

In addition to these key goals, the RMI system aims to be flexible and extensible. The goals of RMI also included extensibility to provide:

- Varying remote invocation mechanisms such as *unicast* and *multicast*.
- Capability of supporting multiple transports.
- Distributed garbage collection.

7.4 THE RMI SYSTEM ARCHITECTURE

The RMI system is built in three layers: the *stub/skeleton* layer, the *remote reference* layer, and the *transport* layer, as shown in figure 7.2.

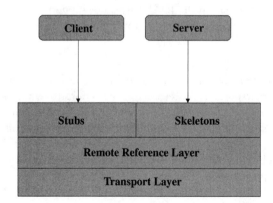

Figure 7.2 RMI system architecture

Each layer is built using a specific interface and is defined by a specific protocol. Therefore, each layer is independent of the others and can be replaced by an alternate implementation without affecting the other layers in the system. For example, the current transport layer in the RMI system is TCP-based, but a transport layer based on UDP could be substituted.

Transporting an object from one address space to another is done transparently through the use of *object serialization*.

7.4.1   The stub/skeleton layer

The stub/skeleton layer is the interface between the application layer and the rest of the system. When a server application is developed, stubs and skeletons are generated using the RMI's *rmic* compiler, which generates proxy classes (to act as placeholders) from the server's bytecodes. The stub/skeleton layer transmits data to the remote reference layer via the abstraction of marshal streams, which use object serialization. Therefore, this layer does not deal with the specifics of any transport.

A client-side stub for a remote object is responsible for many tasks: initiating remote calls, marshaling arguments to be sent, informing the remote reference layer that the call should be invoked, unmarshaling the return value (or exception), and informing the remote reference layer that the call is complete. A server-side skeleton, on the other hand, is responsible for unmarshaling incoming arguments from the client, calling the actual remote object implementation, and marshaling the return value (or exception) onto the stream for transport back to the client.

7.4.2   The remote reference layer

The remote reference layer is a middle layer between the stub/skeleton layer and the transport layer. This layer is responsible for providing the ability to support varying remote reference or invocation protocols independent of the client stubs and server skeletons. The unicast protocol, for example, may provide point-to-point invocation, and a multicast protocol may provide invocation to replicated groups of objects. Other protocols may deal with specific replication strategies or persistent references to the remote object, such as enabling remote object activation. However, not all of these features are supported in some versions of the RMI system. For example, the RMI system in the JDK1.1 does not support object activation, but the RMI system in Java 2 does support activation, as you will see in chapter 10.

7.4.3   The transport layer

The transport layer is a low-level layer that ships marshal streams between different address spaces. The transport layer is responsible for setting up connections to remote address spaces, managing connections, listening for incoming calls, maintaining a table of remote objects that reside in the same address space, setting up a connection for an incoming call, and locating the dispatcher for the target of the remote call and passing the connection to this dispatcher.

In this layer, remote object references are represented by an object identifier and an endpoint. This representation is called a *live reference*. Given a live reference for a remote object, the object identifier looks up which objects should be the target of the remote call, and the endpoint sets up a connection to the address space in which the remote object resides. As I mentioned earlier, the RMI system uses a TCP-based transport, but since the transport layer supports multiple transports per address space, it is possible to use a UDP-based transport. Therefore, both TCP and UDP can be supported in the same address space or virtual machine.

7.5   HOW RMI WORKS

When a client invokes an object implementation from the server, as shown in figure 7.2, the three layers of RMI come in to play. The most important layer to the programmer is the stub/skeleton layer. RMI comes with an rmic compiler that generates stubs and skeletons from user-defined remote interfaces. Basically, stubs are client proxies and skeletons are server-side entities. Stubs will allow clients to communicate with the other layers of the system. This is, of course, done automatically as you will have to inherit from RMI classes. You will then be able to use some of the helper functions available in RMI.

So, first, an invocation will pass through the stub/skeleton layer, which serves as an interface between an application and the rest of the RMI system. Its sole purpose is to transfer data to the remote reference layer through marshal streams. This is actually where object serialization comes in to play—it enables Java objects to be transmitted between different address spaces.

Once the data has passed through the stub/skeleton layer, it will go through the remote reference layer, which carries out the semantics of the invocation and transmits data to the transport layer using connection-oriented streams such as TCP. This means that it is the responsibility of the remote reference layer to determine the nature of the object and whether it resides on a local machine or a remote machine across the network. The remote reference layer also determines whether the object can be instantiated and started automatically, or if it must be declared and initialized beforehand.

Finally, the data will arrive at the transport layer, which is responsible for setting up connections and managing those connections.

7.6   DISTRIBUTED GARBAGE COLLECTION

When stand-alone applications are developed using Java, objects that are no longer referenced by any client are automatically deleted. This is a desirable feature when developing distributed applications. The RMI system provides a distributed garbage collector that automatically deletes remote objects that are no longer referenced by any client. RMI uses a reference-counting garbage collection algorithm which allows the RMI system to keep track of all live references within each virtual machine. When a live reference enters a virtual machine, its reference count is incremented. As live references become unreferenced, the reference count is decremented. When the reference count reaches zero, there are no live references, so objects can then be garbage collected. However, note that since objects are allowed to be passed around the network, the RMI system keeps track of virtual machine identifiers as well so that the RMI garbage collector first ensures that objects are only collected when there are no local or remote references to them. Also, as long as a local reference to a remote object exists, it cannot be garbage collected, since it can be passed in remote calls or returned to clients. Passing a remote object adds the identifier to the referenced set for the virtual machine to which it was passed.

7.7   *RMI* AND THE *OSI* REFERENCE MODEL

The OSI Reference Model defines a framework that consists of seven layers of network communicaiton, as discussed in chapter 1. Figure 7.3 shows how RMI can be described by this model.

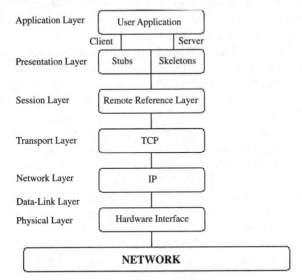

Figure 7.3 RMI within the OSI model

The user's application is at the top layer. It uses a data representation scheme to transparently communicate with remote objects. Notice how the RMI system itself consists of three layers: the stub/skeleton layer, the remote reference layer, and the transport layer, as you learned about earlier in this chapter.

7.8   *SECURITY*

Security is a major concern in every distributed application, and distributed applications built using RMI are no exception. While RMI appears to be a straightforward method for creating distributed applications, there are a number of security issues that you should be aware of when developing mission-critical systems in RMI.

- RMI uses a simple approach to creating the connection between the client and the server. Objects are serialized and transmitted over the network in plain text. They are not encrypted, so anyone monitoring the network traffic could read all the data being transmitted.
- There is no authentication; a client just requests an object (stub), and the server supplies it. Subsequent communication is assumed to be from the same client.
- There is no access control to the objects.
- There are no security checks on the RMI registry itself; any caller is allowed to make requests.

- Stubs are assumed to be matched to skeletons; however, programs could be constructed to simulate RMI network calls, while allowing any data to be placed in the requests.
- There is no version control between stubs and skeletons. Therefore, it is possible for a client to use a down-level stub to access a more recent skeleton, breaking release-to-release binary compatibility.

In chapter 9, you will learn how some of these security risks can be handled by signing remote objects. And in chapter 10, when we talk about new RMI features in Java 2, we will discuss product versioning APIs that can be used to specify how the packages of a system should evolve so that the goal of an open scalable distributed system can be achieved.

7.9   SUMMARY

- Developing distributed applications using sockets involves the design of a protocol, but this can cause errors. Protocol design can be avoided using RMI. RMI is a form of RPC that is available on other systems. In RMI, communication interfaces are abstracted to the level of a local procedure call. Therefore, there is no need for designing a protocol.
- The RMI system is built in three layers: the stub/skeleton layer, the remote reference layer, and the transport layer. Each layer is built using a specific interface and is defined by a specific protocol. Each layer is independent of the others and can be replaced by an alternative implementation without affecting the other layers in the system.
- The stub/skeleton layer is responsible for transferring data to the remote reference layer through marshal streams. This is where object serialization comes in to play—it enables Java objects to be transmitted between different address spaces.
- The remote reference layer is responsible for providing the ability to support varying remote reference or invocation protocols independent of the client stubs and server skeletons.
- The transport layer is responsible for setting up connections to remote address spaces, managing connections, listening for incoming calls, maintaining a table of remote objects that reside in the same address space, setting up connections for incoming calls, and locating the dispatcher for the target of the remote call and passing the connection to this dispatcher.
- The features supported by RMI are those that are most valuable for building distributed applications, namely transparent invocations, distributed garbage collections, and convenient access to streams.

C H A P T E R   8

Getting Started with RMI

Unlike sockets, RMI does not require an application-level protocol. But with no protocol, how do a client and server know how to communicate? In RMI, all information about a server's services is provided in a remote interface definition, in the form of method signatures. By looking at the interface definition, a programmer can tell what methods a server can perform, including what data they receive and what data they send in response.

A remote interface definition specifies the characteristics of the methods provided by a server that are visible to clients. These characteristics include methods' signatures. A programmer of a client should be able to tell what methods the server is providing and how to invoke them simply by looking at that remote interface. Clients obtain references to remote objects through the RMI registry, which is a simple naming service.

In this chapter, we apply the concepts introduced in chapter 7 by walking through the development of an RMI-based application. You'll learn how to define and implement an interface to a server, plus how to use the RMI registry, which is a simple naming service through which clients obtain references to remote objects.

8.1 ANATOMY OF AN RMI-BASED APPLICATION

Building a distributed application using RMI involves six steps. These steps should be implemented in the order shown; however, steps 2 and 3 can be interchanged.

1 Define a remote interface.

2 Implement the remote interface and the server.

3 Develop a client (an application or an applet) that uses the remote interface.

4 Generate stubs and skeletons.

5 Start the RMI registry.

6 Run the server and the client.

Let's examine each step through the development of a distributed application. The featured application is the arithmetic server that we developed, using sockets, in chapter 3. Given two arrays of integers and an operation to perform (such as add, subtract, or multiply), the arithmetic server will perform the requested operation on the two arrays and return the resulting array to the client. For the sake of simplicity, we will only discuss the *add* operation. As an exercise, you can modify the application by adding more related methods of your choice.

The first step is to define a remote interface. When designing an interface, think about the methods (operations) that should be supported and the parameters that each method should take.

8.1.1 Defining a remote interface

A remote interface definition specifies those characteristics of the methods provided by a server that are visible to the server's clients. The characteristics include the names of the methods and the types of their parameters; together these create method signatures. By looking at a remote interface, the programmer of a client will be able to tell what methods the server provides and how to call them.

Note that any remote method invocation may fail because it may not be able to connect to a server, perhaps because the server is down or it is overloaded. Thus, remote method invocations must be able to report error messages. RMI handles this using *exception handling*.

To indicate that an object in an interface is actually a remote object, the object must implement a remote interface. A remote interface has the following characteristics:

- The remote interface must be declared public. Otherwise, clients will not be able to load remote objects which implement that remote interface.
- The remote interface extends the interface java.rmi.Remote. This is done to fulfill the requirement for making the object a remote one.
- Each method declared in the remote interface must declare java.rmi.RemoteException in its throws clause.

The remote interface for the arithmetic server we are using is shown in example 8.1. Notice how the characteristics listed above are implemented. The interface contains just one method, add, which returns an array of integers to the caller.

Example 8.1: Arith.java

```
/**
 * @(#) Arith.java
 */
public interface Arith extends java.rmi.Remote {
```

```
    int[] add(int a[], int b[]) throws java.rmi.RemoteException;
}
```

Now we can compile our remote interface:

% javac Arith.java

8.1.2   Implementing the remote interface

The second step in the development cycle of a distributed application using RMI is implementing the remote interface defined in step 1. This is done by writing a class that implements the above interface. The implementation class needs to do the following:

- Specify the remote interface being implemented.
- Define the constructor for the remote object.
- Implement the methods that can be invoked remotely.
- Create an instance of the security manager and install it.
- Create one (or more) instance(s) of a remote object.
- Register one (or more) remote object(s) with the RMI registry.

To illustrate these steps, the implementation of the remote interface for the arithmetic server is shown in example 8.2. The sections that follow the example explain the code in details.

Example 8.2: ArithImpl.java

```java
import java.rmi.*;
import java.rmi.server.UnicastRemoteObject;
/**
 * @(#) ArithImpl.java
 */
public class ArithImpl extends UnicastRemoteObject implements Arith {
    private String objectName;

    public ArithImpl(String s) throws Remote Exception {
        super();
        objectName = s;
    }

    public int[] add(int a[], int b[]) {
        int c[] = new int[10];
        for (int i=0; i<10; i++) {
            c[i] = a[i] + b[i];
        }
        return c;
    }

    public static void main(String argv[]) {
        RMISecurityManager sm = new RMISecurityManager();
        System.setSecurityManager(sm);
        try {
            ArithImpl obj = new ArithImpl("ArithServer");
            Naming.rebind("//hostname/ArithServer", obj);
```

```
                System.out.println("ArithServer bound in registry");
        } catch (Exception e) {
            System.out.println("ArithImpl error: "+ e.getMessage());
            e.printStackTrace();
        }
    }
}
```

The implementation can now be compiled using the javac compiler:

% javac ArithImpl.java

Specifying the remote interface   The implementation class for the arithmetic server is
ArithImpl, which is shown in example 8.2. It extends the java.rmi.server.Unicas-
tRemoteObject class. Extending this class indicates that the ArithImpl class is used to create a single, nonreplicated, remote object that uses RMI's default socket-based transport for
communication. In chapter 9, you will learn how to implement factories for creating objects.

Defining a remote object constructor   A constructor basically initializes variables of
each newly created instance of a class. In Java, by default, a constructor is provided for
you.

The constructor for the ArithImpl class initializes the private string variable objectName with the name of the remote object. There are two things to note about the
ArithImpl constructor:

- The constructor throws java.rmi.RemoteException for the reasons explained above.
- The super method of the constructor of java.rmi.server.UnicastRemoteObject
  exports the remote object by listening for incoming calls to the remote object on an
  anonymous port number. Note that the call to the super method is actually provided by
  default, but it was called here to remind you that Java constructs the superclass before the
  subclass.

Providing implementation for remote methods   In our example, we only have one
remote method, the add operation. The implementation class provides implementation for
this method. In the add method, the arguments to the remote method are two arrays of type
int, and the return value is an array of type int as well. However, note that arguments to, or
return values from, remote methods can be of any Java type. They can be objects if those
objects implement the java.io.Serializable interface.

As mentioned in chapter 7, local objects are passed by copy, and remote objects are passed
by reference. This reference is actually a reference to a stub, or a client-side proxy, for the remote object.

While the ArithImpl class does not define any methods not specified in the remote interface, it is possible that an implementation class defines methods that are not defined in the
remote interface. These methods, however, would be utility methods for use by the implementation class itself, and they cannot be invoked from remote clients.

Creating a security manager and installing it   The main() method in example 8.2
creates an instance of the RMISecurityManager and installs it. This is a must; if it's not
done, no class loading for RMI classes is allowed. The purpose of the method is to protect the

host from malicious code sent from the client. If you do not want to use the default security manager RMISecurityManager you can define and customize your own. For more information on security managers, please refer to chapters 4 and 6.

Creating instances of remote objects   The following line, which is found in example 8.2, creates an instance of the remote object. Once the instance is created, the server is ready to listen for clients' requests.

```
ArithImpl obj = new ArithImpl("ArithServer");
```

Registering remote objects with the RMI registry   In order for a client to be able to invoke a method on a remote object, the client must first obtain a reference to the remote object. A client obtains such a reference from a registry. Therefore, a remote object must be registered in the RMI registry. A naming convention is thus needed for registering and looking up objects by name. The RMI system provides a solution with its URL-based registry that allows you to bind objects in the form //host/objectName, where objectName is a simple name.

From example 8.2, the line

```
Naming.rebind("//hostname/ArithServer", obj);
```

registers the remote object with the RMI registry. Once it is registered, clients can look up the object by name, obtain a reference to it, and remotely invoke methods on it.

If you want to run the code in example 8.2, you will need to replace hostname with a hostname on which the server will run. Also, note the following about the arguments to rebind:

- If the hostname is omitted from the URL, the host defaults to the current host.
- The RMI registry, by default, will run on port 1099. However, a port number can be supplied in the URL—for example, //purejava:4000/ArithServer where 4000 is the port number. This will be necessary only if the server creates a registry on a port other than the default.

8.1.3   Developing a client that uses the remote interface

In this step, we'll develop a client that remotely invokes any of the remote interface methods. In this case, we only have one method: add. Example 8.3 shows a sample implementation of a client that uses the add method of the remote interface.

Example 8.3: ArithApp.java

```
/**
 * @(#) ArithApp.java
 */
import java.rmi.*;
import java.net.*;

public class ArithApp {
    public static void main(String argv[]) {
        int a[] = {1, 2, 3, 4, 5, 6, 7, 8, 9, 10};
        int b[] = {1, 2, 3, 4, 5, 6, 7, 8, 9, 10};
```

```
      int result[] = new int[10];

      try {
        Arith obj = (Arith)Naming.lookup("//hostName/ArithServer");
        result = obj.add(a, b);
      } catch (Exception e) {
        System.out.println("ArithApp: "+e.getMessage());
        e.printStackTrace();
      }
      System.out.print("The sum = ");
      for (int i=0; i<result.length; i++) {
        System.out.print(result[i] + "     ");
      }
      System.out.println();
    }
  }
```

The client code can now be compiled:

```
% javac ArithApp.java
```

As you can see in example 8.3, the client must first get a reference to the ArithServer from the server's registry. This is done within the try { } construct. Once a reference is obtained, the client remotely invokes the method add on arrays a and b, and stores the return value (an array of integers) in a new array and then iterates through that array, displaying the final result.

8.1.4 Generating stubs and skeletons

Once all the code is written, we are ready to generate the stubs and skeletons. Stubs and skeletons are determined and dynamically loaded as needed at run time. The stubs and skeletons are used to connect the client and server together as shown in figure 8.1.

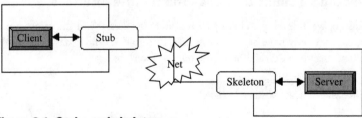

Figure 8.1 Stubs and skeletons

RMI stubs and skeletons are generated easily using the rmic compiler, which is of the form:

```
% rmic <options> <classname>
```

For our arithmetic example, stubs and skeletons can be generated this way:

```
% rmic ArithImpl
```

This command will generate two files: ArithImpl_Skel.class and ArithImpl_Stub.class. The ArithImpl_Skel.class file is a server skeleton, and the ArithImpl_Stub.class file is a client proxy or stub.

Table 8.1 shows the valid optional arguments to the rmic compiler, and it gives a description of each.

Table 8.1 Command-line rmic optional argument list

Argument	Meaning
-keep	Do not delete intermediate generated source files.
-keepgenerated	Same as "-keep".
-show	Use graphics user interface to rmic.
-v1.1	Create stubs/skeletons for JDK1.1 stub protocol version.
-v1.2	Create stubs/skeletons for Java 2 stub protocol version.
-vcompat	Create stubs/skeletons for both JDK1.1 and Java 2 (default).
-g	Generate debugging info.
-depend	Recompile out-of-date files recursively.
-nowarn	Do not generate any warnings at compile time.
-verbose	Output messages about what the compiler is doing.
-classpath <path>	Specify where to find input source and class files.
-d <directory>	Specify where to place generated class files.
-J <runtime flag>	Pass the argument to the Java interpreter.

8.1.5   Starting the RMI registry

The RMI registry is a naming service that allows clients to obtain a reference to a remote object, as shown in figure 8.2. Think of the RMI registry as a manager for RMI remote object references.

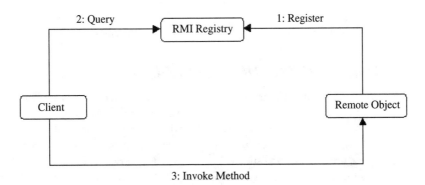

Figure 8.2 The RMI registry manages RMI references

Therefore, before the server and the client are run, the RMI registry must be started. The RMI registry can be started in a Unix environment as follows:

```
% rmiregistry &
```

NOTE   In Windows95 or Windows NT, use the commands start rmiregistry or javaw rmiregistry to start the RMI registry.

This will, by default, run the RMI registry and start it listening on port 1099. If you wish to start the RMI registry on a different port number, you need to specify the port number on this command line:

```
% rmiregistry 3000 &
```

This will start the registry to listen to port 3000. If you start the RMI registry on a port number other than the default, you will have to specify the port number when binding an object. So instead of writing

```
Naming.rebind("//hosname//ArithServer", obj);
```

you will need to write

```
Naming.rebind('hostname//ArithServer:portNumber", obj);
```

where portNumber is the port number on which the RMI registry is listening.

8.1.6   Running the server and the client

Once the RMI registry is running and everything else is in place, we can fire up our server and client applications. The server can be started as follows:

```
% java ArithImpl &
```

And, similarly, the client application can be started using the Java interpreter:

```
% java ArithApp
```

This last step will display the following output:

```
The sum = 2    4    6    8    10    12    14    16    18    20
```

This is the sum of the two arrays provided by the client.

8.2   WORKING WITH THE RMI REGISTRY

A registry is a simple naming service that maps names to remote objects. The RMI system uses the java.rmi.registry.Registry interface and the java.rmi.registry.LocateRegistry class to provide a service for retrieving and registering objects by simple names.

The java.rmi.registry.Registry interface provides methods for lookup, binding, rebinding, unbinding, and listing the contents of a registry. In this section, I will show you how to use some of these methods to remove objects from, and add objects to, the RMI registry.

8.2.1   Removing an object from the registry

To remove an object from the RMI registry, first list the objects in the registry, then check to see whether the object you want to remove is available in the registry. If it is, invoke the unbind() method on it. The following code segment shows how an object can be removed from the registry.

```
String rmiObject[];
PrintStream out = System.out;
try {
    rmiObjects = Naming.list("rmi://hostname");
} catch (RemoteException e) {
    System.out.println("Couldn't locate registry");
} catch (MalformedURLException ex) {
    ex.printStackTrace();
} catch (UnknownHostException) {
}

for (int i=0; i<rmiObjects.length(); i++) {
    // If object is found
    if(rmiObject[i].equals("myObject")) {
        System.out.println("Object is in registry");
    }
}

String u = "rmi://hostname/MyObject";
try {
    Naming.unbind(u);
} catch (NotBoundException e) {
} catch (RemoteException e2) {
} catch (MalformedURLException e3) {
} catch (UnknownHostException e4) {
}
```

Note that an application can only remove an object that is bound to the registry which is running on the same machine as the application invoking the unbind() call. This prevents servers on other machines from replacing objects in your registry.

8.2.2   Rebinding an object to the registry

To rebind an object to the RMI registry, first locate the RMI registry, then use the rebind() method to rebind the object. The following code shows how to rebind an object to the RMI registry.

```
Registry reg;

try {
    reg = java.rmi.registry.LocateRegistry.createregistry(5000);
} catch(RemoteException e) {
    e.printStackTrace();
}
```

```
try {
   reg.rebind("myObject", Remote);
} catch(RemoteException re) {
} catch(AccessException ae) {
}
```

8.3   RMI VS. SOCKETS

In this section, we will compare the arithmetic server we developed in this chapter to the same application we developed using sockets in chapter 3.

In comparing both implementations, notice that the RMI version is simpler and we had to write less code. In the sockets version, we had to write some additional methods for reading and writing arrays of integers to sockets. However, this was not a concern in the case of RMI. In the case of the socket-based arithmetic server, we did not really have to worry about the design of a protocol; however, in bigger and more sophisticated applications, the design of a protocol would be necessary when developing such applications using sockets. But in the case of RMI, no protocol is necessary, as remote invocations are similar to local ones.

As you learned in chapter 5, where we developed the arithmetic server using sockets and object serialization, it is possible to transfer objects over sockets. Therefore, if you do not wish to use RMI since the use of it involves some overhead, then you can use sockets and object serialization facilities to transfer objects over sockets.

8.4   SUMMARY

- Developing distributed applications with RMI is far easier than programming them using sockets. When you're programming with RMI, there is no need to design an application-level protocol. RMI takes care of all the nitty gritty communication details.

- The task of creating an RMI-based application involves six simple steps:
  Defining a remote interface.
  Implementing the remote interface.
  Developing a client.
  Generating stubs and skeletons.
  Starting the naming service.
  Running the server and the client.

C H A P T E R   9

Advanced RMI programming

An RMI client cannot start up an RMI server and create instances of it if that server implements the UnicastRemoteInterface. If you want to enable your clients to do that, you must build a dynamic server by implementing a factory that would create objects and manage them.

Callbacks are often implemented in languages such as C/C++ by passing a function pointer to another function. Since Java does not have pointers, callbacks can be implemented using interfaces. Callbacks are useful in many situations; for example, say you want a client of a stock exchange market server to display the rapidly changing information about stocks as they arrive at the server.

The RMI system lacks some security features such as authentication and access control. The java.security package can be used to build safer RMI-based applications.

In this chapter, we'll cover three advanced topics in RMI programming: implementing a dynamic server with factories, callbacks in a distributed Java application, and improving RMI's security with java.security.

9.1 THE CITY INFORMATION SERVER

In this section we will develop an application called the city information server, and we will modify it in subsequent sections throughout the chapter. Clients of the city information server will provide a city name and get various bits of information about that city. In this application, the server will provide only two methods: one for getting the population and another for getting the temperature. As an exercise, you can add more methods to the server to make it more interesting. You might actually want to consider having RMI talk to a database server that has records of different cities around the world.

In developing this application we will follow the same steps for developing an RMI-based application that were described in great detail in the previous chapter.

9.1.1 Defining a remote interface

The interface for the city information server is shown in example 9.1.

Example 9.1: City.java

```
import java.rmi.*;
/**
 * @(#)City.java
 */
public interface City extends Remote {
    int getPopulation(String cityName) throws RemoteException;
    int getTemperature(String cityName) throws RemoteException;
}
```

The City interface defines two remote methods: getPopulation and getTempera-ture. Both methods take a cityName of type String as an argument and return an int. As a remote interface, the City interface extends the Remote interface, and each of its methods throws a RemoteException.

9.1.2 Implementing the remote interface

Implementing the City interface is a straightforward process, as shown in example 9.2.

Example 9.2: CityImpl.java

```
import java.rmi.*;
import java.rmi.server.UnicastRemoteObject;
/**
 * @(#)CityImpl.java
 */
public class CityImpl extends UnicastRemoteObject implements City {
    private String name;

    public CityImpl(String name) throws RemoteException {
        super();
        this.name = name;
    }
```

```
public int getPopulation(String cityName) throws RemoteException {
   if (cityName.equals("Toronto")) {
      return 10;
   } else if (cityname.equals("Ottawa")) {
      return 2;
   } else {
      return 0;
   }
}

public int getTemperature(String cityName) throws RemoteException {
   // The temperature returned is just for illustration purposes.
   return 1;
}

public static void main(String argv[]) {
   System.setSecurityManager(new RMISecurityManager());
   try {
      CityImpl obj = new CityImpl("CityServer");
      Naming.rebind("//hostname/CityServer", obj);
      System.out.println("CityServer bound in registry");
   } catch (Exception e) {
      e.printStackTrace();
   }
}
}
```

In the main() method in example 9.2, we first install the RMISecurityManager, then we register the remote objects in the RMI registry.

9.1.3 Developing a client

Now we can write a client application that invokes one or more of the methods provided by the City interface. This client application is simple—all we need to do is get a reference to the remote object and invoke one or more of its methods. A sample client application is shown in example 9.3.

Example 9.3: CityApp.java

```
import java.rmi.*;
/**
 * @(#)CityApp.java
 */
public class CityApp {
   public static void main(String argv[]) {
      int pop = 0;
      try {
         City Obj = (City) Naming.lookup("//hostname/CityServer");
         pop = obj.getPopulation("Toronto");
      } catch (Exception e) {
         e.printStackTrace();
      }
```

```
        System.out.println("The population of Toronto is: "+ pop);
    }
}
```

9.1.4 Generating stubs and skeletons

Generating client stubs and server skeletons is easy. The rmi compiler, rmic, can be used to generate the stubs and skeletons with one command:

```
% rmic CityImpl
```

9.1.5 Starting the RMI registry

As I mentioned in the previous chapter, the RMI registry can be started on a Unix system as follows:

```
% rmiregistry &
```

This will start the RMI registry on the default port number 1099. Please refer to the previous chapter for more information on how to start the RMI registry on a different port number.

9.1.6 Running the server and the client

In order to run the application, we first run the server, CityImpl in this case, and then we run the client. This is done the same way you would start any stand-alone Java application using the Java interpreter. This is explained in detail in the previous chapter.

9.2   IMPLEMENTING FACTORIES

In the previous section, we developed an RMI-based application in which the client invokes remote methods of a server. Because the server implements the UnicastRemoteInterface, the client cannot start up the server and create instances of it. To get around this issue, create a dynamic server where clients would be able to start up the server and instantiate objects. A dynamic server can be created by implementing a *factory*. The factory will create, on the fly, a server for your clients. With the factory, you will also be able to create multiple instances of remote objects and have them all interact together. Therefore, a factory would create objects for you and manage them. A factory is really a server just like the one implemented in the previous section; the only difference is that a factory would have just one method responsible for creating objects that will be later used by clients as normal servers.

9.2.1 Defining a factory interface

Rather than having one city information server deal with all requests regarding all cities, which would lead to overloading the server (and perhaps causing a crash), we can instead create a different CityImpl server for each city in a particular country. Using this technique, each city information server would then deal only with requests that are related to that city/country and the server would not get overloaded.

Our job here is to define a factory interface whose implementation would be capable of creating dynamic servers. The factory interface must have just one method that returns an object reference and creates its server. This means that the factory method will take the cityName for which it needs to create a server dynamically as an argument. The factory interface, City-Factory, is defined in example 9.4.

Example 9.4: CityFactory.java

```
import java.rmi.*;
/**
 * @(#)CityFactory.java
 */
public interface CityFactory extends Remote {
    City2Impl getCityServer(String cityName) throws RemoteException;
}
```

Since we are passing the cityName for which a dynamic server should be created, we do not need to pass a cityName for the methods defined in the City interface. When we invoke a method (getPopulation, for example), we already know the city name since the whole server is devoted to that city. The new City interface is shown in example 9.5.

Example 9.5: City2.java

```
import java.rmi.*;
/**
 * @(#)City2.java
 */
public interface City2 extends Remote {
    int getPopulation() throws RMIException;
    int getTemperature() throws RMIException;
}
```

9.2.2 Implementing the City2 interface

The initial City interface was designed to return information when it was given a city name. But the city name is now handled by the factory, so given a city name, the factory will create an information server for that city. Example 9.6 shows the modified CityImpl server.

Example 9.6: City2Impl.java

```
import java.rmi.*;
import java.rmi.server.UnicastRemoteObject;
/**
 * @(#)City2Impl.java
 */
public class City2Impl extends UnicastRemoteObject implements City2 {
    private String cityName;

    public City2Impl() throws RemoteException {
        super();
    }
    public City2Impl(String cityName) throws RemoteException {
        super();
        this.cityName = cityName;
```

```
        }

        public int getPopulation() throws RemoteException {
            if (cityName.equals("Toronto")) {
                return 10;
            } else if (cityname.equals("Ottawa")) {
                return 2;
            } else {
                return 0;
            }
        }

        public int getTemperature() throws RemoteException {
            // Just for illustration.
            return 1;
        }
    }
```

Notice how the constructor for the `City2Impl` sets the city name for which a server should be created. The constructor will be called by the factory's method to instantiate a server for a particular city. Also notice that there is no `main()` method in this version of the server implementation. The `main()` method will be contained in the factory server.

9.2.3   Implementing the CityFactory interface

Implementing the `CityFactory` interface is similar to implementing the `City2Impl` server. In this implementation, the `getCityServer` method will be responsible for instantiating the `City2Impl` and passing back a `City2Impl` object to the client. The implementation of the `CityFactory` interface is shown in example 9.7.

Example 9.7: CityFactoryImpl.java

```java
import java.rmi.*;
import java.rmi.server.UnicastRemoteObject;
/**
 * @(#)CityFactoryImpl.java
 */
public class CityFactoryImpl extends UnicastRemoteObject implements City-
Factory {
    public CityFactoryImpl() throws RemoteException {
        super();
    }

    public City2Impl getCityServer(String cityName) throws RemoteException {
        City2Impl cityServer = new City2Impl(cityName);
        return cityServer;
    }

    public static void main(String argv[]) {
        System.setSecurityManager(new RMISecurityManager());
        try {
```

```
            CityFactoryImpl obj = new CityFactoryImpl();
            Naming.rebind("//hostname/CityFactory", obj);
            System.out.println("CityFactory bound in registry");
        } catch(Exception e) {
          e.printStackTrace();
        }
    }
}
```

Now with this factory, your clients will be able to create different City2Impl servers. If you want to keep track of the servers that are created, you need to create a Vector object to maintain a list of servers.

9.2.4 Invoking the factory

Creating and instantiating a factory is no different than creating and instantiating a normal remote object. We just have to create a factory and use it to create remote objects so that we can invoke their methods. Example 9.8 shows the modified CityApp client, City2App.

Example 9.8: City2App.java

```
import java.rmi.*;
/**
 * @(#)City2App.java
 */
public class City2App {
    public static void main(String argv[]) {
        Remote obj = null;
        CityFactoryImpl cityfactory;
        City2 ottawa = null;
        City2 toronto = null;
        int ottawaPopulation = 0;
        int torontoPopulation = 0;

        try {
          obj = Naming.lookup("//hostname/CityFactory");
        } catch (Exception e) {
          e.printStackTrace();
        }
        if (obj instanceof CityFactoryImpl) {
           cityFactory = (CityFactoryImpl) obj;
        }

        // Create a server for each city.
        try {
          ottawa = new CityFactoryImpl().getCityServer("Ottawa");
          toronto = new CityfactoryImpl().getCityServer("Toronto");
        } catch (RemoteException e) {
          e.printStackTrace();
        }
        // Invoke methods on those servers.
        try {
```

```
      ottawaPopulation = ottawa.getPopulation();
      torontoPopulation = toronto.getPopulation();
    } catch (RemoteException e) {
      e.printStackTrace();
    }
    // Print the results.
    System.out.println("The population of Ottawa is: "+ottawaPopulation);
    System.out.println("The population of Toronto is: "+torontoPopula-
tion);
  }
}
```

9.2.5 Running the factory

To run the whole newly modified city information server, you need to compile all the programs and generate stubs and skeletons for `CityFactoryImpl` and `City2Impl`. Start the RMI registry and the `CityFactoryImpl` server, then start the client. If all goes well, the client will display the results on the screen.

9.3 *IMPLEMENTING CALLBACKS*

A *callback* is a mechanism that is heavily used in many programming environments, especially in GUI construction kits. The Abstract Window Toolkit (AWT) APIs in Java use callbacks heavily. Basically, callbacks are invocations of methods that are defined by a programmer and executed by the application in response to some actions taken by a user at run time.

Callbacks are most familiar to GUI programmers. For example, when a user interacts with a widget, the interface code calls back the computational code in order to respond to the user's action. Therefore, when a user selects an item from a pull-down menu, the interface code for the menu will call back the computational code to invoke the selected item from the menu.

9.3.1 Callbacks in Java

Callbacks are often implemented in other languages such as C/C++ by passing a function pointer to another function. The receiving function uses the function pointer to invoke another function when a particular event occurs. As Java doesn't have pointers, I will show you how to implement callbacks using interfaces.

Callbacks can be implemented in Java using interfaces by simply having an interface and a class that implements that interface; the object's interface methods will be used as callbacks.

9.3.2 Implementing callbacks in   RMI

There are many situations where callbacks might be needed. For example, suppose that a client of a city information server wants to display information about the temperature of a city as it arrives at the server. Or imagine that a client of a stock exchange market server wants to display the rapidly changing information about stocks as it arrives at the server. This kind of dynamic update can be implemented in an RMI application using callbacks.

Creating a callback interface   Since the client wants to update its information as new information arrives at the server, the client will need a method that the server can invoke when new information exists at the server side. Therefore, we need a client callback interface. Figure 9.1 illustrates a server calling back a client.

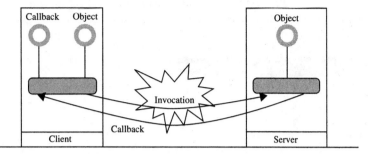

Figure 9.1 A server calling back a client

The client callback interface would have just one method that the city information server can invoke whenever it has some new information. A simple client callback interface is shown in example 9.9.

Example 9.9: Callback.java

```
/**
 * @(#)Callback.java
 */
public interface Callback {
    void tempChanged(String cityName, int temp);
}
```

The Callback interface defines one method, tempChanged, that takes a city name and the new temperature for the city. When this method is invoked (called back by the server), the client will display new temperature information about the city, according to the new information that has arrived at the server.

The city information server, however, will not send an information update to a client without our telling it that we do wish to receive such updates. In order to do that, we have to send the server an object on which it can invoke the callback. This object should be of type Callback. This means that we need to change the City interface to add a new method definition that would register the callback. Example 9.10 shows the City interface with the new changes—we'll call the new interface CallCity.

Example 9.10: CallCity.java

```
import java.rmi.*;
/**
 * @(#)CallCity.java
 */
public interface CallCity extends Remote {
    int getPopulation(String cityName) throws RemoteException;
    int getTemperature(String cityName) throws RemoteException;
```

```
        void register(Callback cb) throws RemoteException;
}
```

Implementing the callback interface   In order for a client to send itself to the server and register for updates, it has to implement the `Callback` interface. Example 9.11 shows the client code with the new modifications.

Example 9.11: CallCityApp.java

```java
import java.rmi.*;
import java.net.*;
/**
 * @(#)CallCityApp.java
 */
public class CallCityApp implements Callback {
  // . . . .
  // Everything is the same as in example 9.3.
  // Replace City with CallCity, however.
  // . . . .

  // Implement the Callback interface.
   public void tempChanged(String cityName, int tmp) {
       System.out.println("Dynamic Update: ");
       System.out.println("CityName: "+cityName);
       System.out.println("Temp: "+tmp);
   }
}
```

   The `CallCityApp` client provides a simple implementation for the `Callback` interface simply by displaying the new information that has been received.

Implementing the register callback method   The city information server will have to be modified so that it implements the new method, `register`, in the `City` interface. Basically, the server will have a list of clients that wish to be called back when new information arrives at the server. The `register` method can be implemented as shown in example 9.12.

Example 9.12: CallCityImpl.java

```java
import java.util.*;
import java.rmi.*;
import java.rmi.server.UnicastRemoteObject;
/**
 * @(#)CallCityImpl.java
 */
public class CallCityImpl extends UnicastRemoteObject implements CallCity {
  Vector list = new Vector();
  // Everything remains the same as in example 9.2.
  // You should, however, replace City with CallCity
  // and CityImpl with CallCityImpl.
  public void register(Callback cb) {
```

```
        list.addElement(cb);
    }
```

Registering a callback   The city information server will have a list of clients that wish to be informed about new information on the server. Therefore, our client needs to register with the server for a callback. To do so, we need to modify our client again to add a method invocation on a remote object. We want to invoke the `register` method from the server so that we can register the client. Example 9.13 shows the new modifications.

Example 9.13: CallCity2App.java

```java
import java.rmi.*;
import java.net.*;
/**
 * @(#)CallCity2App.java
 */
public class CallCity2App implements Callback {
    public static void main(String argv[]) {
        int pop = 0;
        Callback c = (Callback) new CityApp();
        CallCity obj = null;

        try {
          obj = (CallCity)Naming.lookup("//purejava/CallCityImpl");
          pop = obj.getPopulation("Toronto");
        } catch (Exception e) {
            System.out.println("ArithApp exception:"+e.getMessage());
            e.printStackTrace();
        }
        // Register the callback.
         try {
           obj.register(c);
        } catch (RemoteException e) {
          System.out.println("Error: ");
          e.printStackTrace();
        }
    }
    // The implementation of the Callback interface remains the same here.
}
```

Invoking a callback   In order for the server to actually invoke a callback, we need to modify it again by adding a new method through which it would accept the changes that it sends back to the client. This method will take a city name and a temperature, then it will iterate through the list of registered clients that wish to be informed of new changes and invoke that new method on them. A fragment of code of the modified server is shown in example 9.14.

Example 9.14: CallCity2Impl.java

```java
import java.util.*;
import java.rmi.*;
import java.rmi.server.UnicastRemoteObject;
```

```
/**
 * @(#)CallCity2Impl.java
 */
public class CallCity2Impl extends UnicastRemoteObject implements CallCity
{
    // Everything else is the same.
    public void setTemp(String cityName, int tmp) {
        for (int i=0; i<list.size(); i++) {
            Callback cb = (Callback) list.elementAt(i);
            cb.tempChanged(cityName, tmp);
        }
    }
}
```

To make sure that no clients are being added to the list while objects are being notified, you may want to synchronize access to the list by acting upon a temporary copy of the list. The following code shows how such an enhancement can be introduced.

```
Vector temp;
Synchronized (this) {
    temp = (Vector) list.clone();
}
```

Now you would use the new temp copy to iterate through the list.

9.4   SIGNING OBJECTS OVER RMI

RMI is lacking some security features such as authentication and access control. The purpose of this section is not to redesign the RMI system to include security features, but rather to show how the java.security package can be used to build safer RMI-based distributed applications. In this section, I will show you how to sign objects over RMI.

9.4.1   The java.security package

The Java security API lets developers incorporate low-level and high-level security functionality into their applications. It provides APIs for digital signatures, message digests, key management, and access control lists. For a discussion on digital signatures, please refer to chapter 5, section 5.3.

9.4.2   Example

This example is a client/server application where the client reads a file, generates a pair of keys, signs the contents of the file, and sends an object over the network to a server. The object contains the public key generated by the client, the signature, and the contents of the file. The server receives the object and verifies that the signature is correct.

In this example, three pieces of code need to be developed: a signed object, a client application, and a server application. Let's look at each separately.

In order to send objects over sockets, we have to use object serialization, which was discussed in chapter 5. Thus, we have to serialize our signed object. This can be done easily just by having our signed object implement the `Serializable` interface. Notice that the `Serializable` interface does not have any methods, so there are no methods to override. Example 9.15 shows the implementation of a `SignedObject`. As you can see from this example, the `SignedObject` will carry three things: the contents of a file from the client, a signature, and a public key.

Example 9.15: SignedObject.java

```
import java.io.*;
import java.security.*;
import java.rmi.*;
import java.rmi.server.*;
/**
 * @(#)SignedObject.java
 */
public class SignedObject implements Serializable {
    byte b[];
    byte sig[];
    PublicKey pub;

    public SignedObject(byte b[], byte sig[], PublicKey pub) {
        this.b = b;
        this.sig = sig;
        this.pub = pub;
    }
}
```

Now we can define a remote interface. Example 9.16 shows the `SignedInterface`, which is a remote-enabled interface, as it extends the `Remote` interface. The `SignedInterface` defines two methods: `put`, which takes an argument of type `String` and returns a `String`, and `getString`, which takes no arguments and returns a `SignedObject`.

Example 9.16: SignedInterface.java

```
import java.io.*;
import java.security.*;
import java.rmi.*;
import java.rmi.server.*;
/**
 * @(#)SignedInterface.java
 */
interface SignedInterface extends Remote {
    public String put(String str) throws RemoteException;
    public SignedObject getString() throws RemoteException;
}
```

Once the remote interface is defined, we can implement the interface. Example 9.17 shows an implementation for the `SignedInterface`. This example also acts as a server. It accepts the file to be signed as the first argument, and it generates public and private keys as well as signatures. Then it publishes everything with the RMI registry.

Example 9.17: Server.java

```java
import java.io.*;
import java.security.*;
import java.rmi.*;
import java.rmi.server.*;
/**
 * @(#)Server.java
 */
class Server extends UnicastRemoteObject implements SignedInterface {
    SignedObject s;
    String name;
    String str;
    public Server(String name) throws RemoteException {
        super();
        this.name = name;
    }

    public String put(String str) throws RemoteException {
        this.str = str;
        return str;
    }

    public Server(SignedObject s) throws RemoteException {
        super();
        this.s = s;
    }

    public SignedObject getString() throws RemoteException {
        return s;
    }

    public static void main(String argv[]) throws Exception {
        System.out.println("Generating keys...");
        KeyPairGenerator kgen = KeyPairGenerator.getInstance("DSA");
        kgen.initialize(256);
        KeyPair kpair = kgen.generateKeyPair();

        Signature sig = Signature.getInstance("SHA/DSA");
        PublicKey pub = kpair.getPublic();
        PrivateKey priv = kpair.getPrivate();
        sig.initSign(priv);

        FileInputStream fis = new FileInputStream(argv[0]);
        byte arr[] = new byte[fis.available()];
        fis.read(arr);
        sig.update(arr);
        System.setSecurityManager(new RMISecurityManager());
        SignedObject ss = new SignedObject(arr, sig.sign(), pub);
```

```
            System.out.println(pub);
            System.out.println(ss.pub);
            Server sss = new Server(ss);
            Naming.rebind("//localhost/Server", sss);
            System.out.println("Server bound in registry");
        }
    }
```

Now we can develop a client that will talk to the server developed above and get the signed object from it, then check to see whether the signature is valid. Example 9.18 shows the client implementation.

Example 9.18: Client.java

```
import java.io.*;
import java.security.*;
import java.rmi.*;
import java.rmi.server.*;
/**
 * @(#)Client.java
 */
class Client {
    public static void main(String argv[]) throws Exception {
        SignedInterface rs = (SignedInterface)Naming.lookup("//hostname/
Server");
        String out = rs.put("Hello there");
        System.out.println("I got: "+out);

        SignedObject so = rs.getString();
        System.out.println(so.toString());

        Signature sig = Signature.getInstance("SHA/DSA");
        sig.initVerify(so.pub);
        sig.update(so.b);
        System.out.println(so.pub);
        boolean valid = sig.verify(so.sig);
        if (valid) {
          System.out.println("valid signature");
        } else {
          System.out.println("invalid signature");
        }
    )
}
```

9.5   SUMMARY

- A client cannot start up a server and create instances of it if the server implements the UnicastRemoteInterface interface. To enable a client to create multiple instances of a server, implement a remote-object factory.

- A factory is a server that has one method which is responsible only for creating objects that will be used later by clients as normal servers. It also allows you to create multiple instances of remote objects and have them all interact with each other.
- A callback is an invocation of a method that is defined by a programmer and executed by the application in response to actions taken by a user at run time. Callbacks are often implemented in languages such as C/C++ by passing a function pointer to another function. As Java does not have pointers, callbacks can be implemented in Java using interfaces. We can simply have an interface and a class that implements that interface; the object's interface methods are used as callbacks.
- The RMI system lacks some security features such as authentication and access control. The `java.security` package can be used to build safer RMI-based applications. In this chapter, you learned how to use this package to sign objects over RMI.

C H A P T E R   1 0

RMI programming with Java 2

The Socket class in the java.net package comes with pre- and post-processing methods. Sometimes it's necessary to process data before sending it to, or after receiving it from, a socket. Examples of this include encrypting data or compressing data sent over a connection.

Prior to Java 2, there was no way to create secure communication between RMI clients and servers. Java 2 has introduced new RMI features that enable you to write secure RMI applications using Secure Sockets Layer (SSL) sockets.

For a distributed system to be highly available, its object implementations must be active at all times. A naïve implementation would take up too many system resources by keeping all the objects executing and consuming memory at once. One of the enhanced RMI features in Java 2 is object activation, a mechanism for providing persistent references to objects and allowing objects to begin executing on an as-needed basis.

This chapter discusses some of the new and enhanced RMI features that have been introduced in Java 2, which help you develop secure, highly available distributed applications. These include the Socket and RMISocketFactory types, SSL sockets, remote object activation, and product versioning.

10.1 CREATING A CUSTOM SOCKET TYPE

The Socket class, which is part of the java.net package, comes with pre- and post-processing methods; sometimes it is necessary to process data before sending it to, or after receiving it from, a socket. Such cases include encrypting data and compressing data sent over a connection. Java 2 includes the ability to create a custom socket type, which solves the problem.

10.1.1 The mechanics of creating a custom socket type

The development of a custom socket type involves four steps:

1   Extending an appropriate output stream to create an output stream for the socket.

2   Extending an appropriate input stream to create an input stream for the socket.

3   Creating a java.net.Socket subclass, implementing the appropriate constructors, and overriding the getInputStream, getOutputStream, and close methods.

4   Creating a java.net.ServerSocket subclass, implementing the constructor, and overriding the accept method to create a socket of the desired type.

For a good example on how to create a custom Socket type, please refer to the CompressionSocket class provided by JavaSoft in Java 2 (see http://java.sun.com/products/jdk/rmi).

10.2 CREATING A CUSTOM RMISOCKETFACTORY

The default transport protocol being used by RMI is the TCP protocol, which is provided by the java.net.Socket and ServerSocket classes. However, creating and installing a custom RMISocketFactory class allows the RMI transport layer to use a non-TCP transport protocol. Prior to the release of Java 2, it was not possible to create an RMISocketFactory that produced more than one type of socket. But now with Java 2 and the new java.rmi.server. SocketType class, you can create a custom RMISocketFactory that produces the type of socket you want.

10.2.1 A single type of socket

Creating a custom RMISocketFactory that produces a single type of socket is done in four steps:

1   Deciding which type of socket you want to produce. The socket type is usually application-specific. For example, if you are sending sensitive data over the connection, you may want to use a socket that encrypts data. You can either use an off-the-shelf package that encrypts data or you can develop your own custom socket type as outlined above.

2   Extending the RMISocketFactory class by providing new implementations for steps 3 and 4 in this list.

3   Overriding the createSocket method of the RMISocketFactory class.

4   Overriding the createServerSocket method of the RMISocketFactory class.

A hypothetical implementation could look like this:

```
public class myRMISocketFactory extends RMISocketFactory {
    public Socket createSocket(String host, int port) throws IOException {
        mySocketType socket = new mySocketType(host, port);
        return socket;
    }

    public ServerSocket createServerSocket(int port) throws IOException {
        myServerSocket server = new myServerSocket(port);
        return server;
    }
}
```

10.2.2   More than one type of socket

The steps listed in the previous section for creating a custom RMISocketFactory to produce a single type of socket can also be used to create a custom RMISocketFactory that produces more than one type of socket. The only new thing you need to do is find a way to specify which type of socket needs to be returned by createSocket and createServerSocket. The RMISocketFactory class also declares the following methods:

```
public Socket createSocket(String host, int port, SocketType type);
public ServerSocket createServerSocket(String host, int port, SocketType);
```

The additional parameter, SocketType, gives the RMISocketFactory access to methods and data specific to the type of socket being created. The SocketType class has three data members:

```
private String protocol;
private byte[] refData;
private Object serverData;
```

These data members are to be set by the programmer in the body of the constructor of SocketType. The member protocol refers to the name of the protocol a particular socket type is using for communication. The other two members, refData and serverData, may contain any extra data required by the protocol.

10.2.3   Using a custom RMISocketFactory

To use a custom RMISocketFactory in an application, you need to set the socket factory to the custom RMISocketFactory in both the client and the server. This can be done using the setSocketFactory() class method of RMISocketFactory. The setSocketFactory() method has the following signature:

```
public synchronized static void setSocketFactory(RMISocketFactory fac)
```

For example, the following code segment installs an instance of myRMISocket Factory:

```
try {
    RMISocketFactory.setSocketFactory(new myRMISocketFactory());
} catch (IOException e) {
```

```
        e.printStackTrace();
    }
```

If you set a custom RMISocketFactory that produces more than one type of socket, then in addition to the above step, you need a way to tell the RMI system which type of socket to use. If you assume that your server extends UnicastRemoteObject, then notifying the RMI run-time system which socket type to use can be accomplished by creating a remote object constructor that calls the following UnicastRemoteObject constructor:

```
protected UnicastRemoteObject(int port, SocketType socketType)
```

So, if you have the following code for server implementation,

```
public serverImpl(String s) throws RemoteException {
    super();
    name = s;
}
```

it can be modified for a new socket type (for example, mySocket), as follows:

```
public serverImpl(String s) throws RemoteException {
    super(0, new SocketType("mySocket", null, null));
    name = s;
}
```

You will also need to change any references to the old SocketType to the new Socket-Type.

Once the RMISocketFactory is installed, your RMI application will use sockets of the desired type.

10.3   SSL SOCKETS

The RMI enhancements in Java 2 allow developers to use SSL sockets with RMI. Therefore, it is now possible to establish secure communications between RMI clients and servers.

The following example of a custom RMISocketFactory, which produces sockets of type SSLSocket, is borrowed from the new RMI documentation that comes with Java 2.

```
import java.io.*;
import java.net.*;
import java.rmi.server.*;
import java.net.ssl.*;

public class MySSLSocketFactory extends RMISocketfactory {
    public Socket createSocket(String host, int port) throws IOException {
        SSLSocket socket = SSLSocketFactory.getDefault().createSocket(host,
port);
        String ciphers[] = socket.getEnabledCipherSuites();
        socket.setEnabledCipherSuites(ciphers);
        return socket;
    }

    public ServerSocket createServerSocket(int port) throws IOException {
```

```
        SSLServerSocket server = SSLServerSocketFactory.getDefault().create-
Socket(port);
        String ciphers[] = server.getEnabledCipherSuites();
        Server.setEnabledCipherSuites(ciphers);
        return server;
    }
}
```

The SSLSocket class, which is part of the javax.net.ssl package, is distributed with a number of JavaSoft products, including Java WebServer, HotJava, and the JavaServer Toolkit.

A number of SSL implementations can be used with Java. Most SSL implementations use RSA algorithms that must be licensed from RSA (see http://www.rsa.com) if it is to be used in the USA. Some of the available implementations include SSLava Toolkit from Phaos Technologies in the USA, and from outside the USA, J/SSL from Baltimore Technologies and Java Secure Sockets Layer Protocol from JCP Computer Services.

10.4 *REMOTE OBJECT ACTIVATION*

A remote object can either be active or passive. An active remote object is an object that is instantiated in a JVM on some system. On the other hand, a passive remote object is an object that is not yet instantiated in a JVM; however, it can be brought into an active state. The process of transforming an object from a passive state to an active state is called *activation*.

10.4.1 Overview

A distributed object system, which may be composed of thousands of objects, should be highly available. To support this, object implementation would have to be active at all times; however, this is unreasonable because if objects remain active they will be taking up quite a lot of the system's resources. In addition, clients need to be able to store persistent references to objects so that communications among objects can be established after a system crash. Thus, there is a need for a mechanism that can provide persistent references to objects.

One of the RMI-enhanced features that was introduced in Java 2 is object activation, which is a mechanism for providing persistent references to objects and allowing objects to begin executing on an *as-needed* basis. Therefore, if an "activatable" remote object is invoked, the system will instantiate that object in an appropriate JVM if it is not already running. Again, this process is known as *activation*. The RMI system uses lazy activation, which means that activating an object is deferred until the first method invocation by a client on that object. Lazy activation is implemented using a *faulting remote reference*, also known as a *fault block*. Therefore, each remote object's stub contains a faulting remote reference type that contains both a persistent handle (or an activation identifier) and a live reference containing the active remote reference type of the object.

10.4.2 Activation protocol

The activation protocol is composed of several entities: the faulting reference, the activator, an activation group in a JVM, and the remote object being activated. This protocol is used during a remote method invocation when the live reference for a target object is unknown. The activation protocol, normally one per host, supervises activation by playing the following two roles:

1 A database of information that maps activation identifiers to the information necessary to activate an object (such as the object's class and location).

2 A manager of JVMs that starts up JVMs when necessary and forwards requests for object activation to the right activation group in a JVM.

The activation protocol is smart enough not to consult with the group on each activation request. This is done by keeping a cache of the current mapping of activation identifiers to active objects.

How does it work? A faulting reference uses an activation identifier and calls the activator, which is an RMI interface, to activate the object associated with the identifier. The activator looks up the object's activation descriptor, which contains the following information:

- The object's group identifier.
- The object's class name.
- A CodeSource class of the location to load the object's class code from.
- Object-specific initialization data, such as the name of a file containing the object's state.

Now, if the activation group in which the object should reside exists, the activator will forward the activation request to that group; otherwise, the activator initiates a JVM by executing an activation group before forwarding the activation request to it. At this point, the activation group loads the class for the object and instantiates it using a special constructor that takes several arguments, one of which is the activation descriptor that was previously registered.

After an object is finished activating, the activation group sends back a marshaled object reference to the activator, which will record the activation identifier and active reference, and return the live reference to the faulting reference. The faulting reference will then forward method invocations via the live reference to the remote object directly.

The RMI system in Java 2 provides an implementation for the activation system described here. To use activation, you must first run the activation daemon known as rmid.

10.4.3   Creating an activatable remote object

Creating an activatable remote object involves two steps:

1 Registering an activation descriptor for the remote object.

2 Including a special constructor in the object's class which the RMI system will use to construct and activate the remote object.

ActivationDesc is a class that contains the necessary information to activate an object. This activation descriptor can be registered in three different ways:

1 By calling the static register method of the Activatable class.

2 By creating an activatable object via the constructor of the Activatable class that has the CodeSource as its first argument.

3 By exporting an activatable object explicitly by invoking the `Activatable` class's `exportObject` method that takes an `ActivationDesc`, the remote object implementation, and a port number as arguments.

The rest of this section gives you the directions for creating an activatable object via the constructor of the `Activatable` class.

The object implementation class must define a special public constructor that takes two arguments: an activation identifier of type `ActivationID`, and an activation data (`java.rmi.MarshalledObject`) that is given in the activation descriptor during registration. This special constructor will be used by the activation group when it is time to activate an object in the JVM. The `Activatable` class has two forms of constructors:

- `Protected Activatable(java.security.CodeSource source, java.rmi.MarshalledObject data, int port) throws java.rmi.RemoteException;`
- `Protected Activatable(ActivationID id, int port) throws java.rmi.RemoteException;`

The first constructor should be used when you are initially constructing an object to both register and export an activatable object on a specified port. The second constructor should be used to reactivate the object. In both cases, a `RemoteException` will be thrown if an error occurs during registration, export, or reactivation.

Here is an example of a remote object interface and its server implementation, which extends the `Activatable` class.

```
public interface Service extends java.rmi.Remote {
    public void sayHi() throws java.rmi.RemoteException;
}

public class ServiceImpl extends Activatable implements Service {
    // Initial construction, registration, and export.
    public ServiceImpl(CodeSource source, MarshalledObject data) throws
        java.rmi.RemoteException {
        // Register object with activation system, then export it on a
        // random port.
        super(source, data, 0);
    }

    // Activation and export - constructing the object.
    public ServiceImpl(ActivationID id, MarshalledObject data) throws
        java.rmi.RemoteException {
        // Export the object to the RMI run-time.
        super(id, 0);
        // Do some initialization.
    }

    public void sayHi() {
        // Implementation goes here.
    }
}
```

In the example above, the object is not explicitly responsible for exporting itself because the code above extends the `Activatable` class and the constructors of that class take care of exporting the object to the RMI run-time system. However, as you will see in the next example, if an object implementation does not extend the Activatable class, then the implementation must export the object explicitly via a call to one of the Activatable class's exportObject static methods.

Now, we will look at the version where the server does not extend the Activatable class. Here the server object is responsible for exporting itself during initial construction and activation.

```java
public class ServiceImpl extends myClass implements Service {
    // Initial creation constructor.
    public ServiceImpl(CodeSource source, MarshalledObject data) throws
java.rmi.RemoteException {
        // Create an activation descriptor for the object.
        ActivationDesc desc = new ActivationDesc("ServiceImpl", source, data);
        // Register and export the object on an anonymous port.
        Activatable.exportObject(desc, this, 0);
    }

    // Activation constructor.
    public ServiceImpl(ActivationID id, MarshalledObject data) throws
java.rmi.RemoteException {
        // Export the object.
        Activatable.exportObject(id, this, 0);
    }

    public void sayHi() {
        // Implementation goes here.
    }
}
```

But what if you want to register an activation remote object with the activation system without creating the object? The activation system allows you to do this by registering an activation descriptor (an instance of the ActivationDesc class) for the object, which will contain all the necessary information to activate the object when needed. An activation descriptor for the above example, ServiceImpl, can be registered as follows:

```java
Service service;
ActivationDesc desc;
CodeSource source = new CodeSource(http://hostname/source, null);
MarshalledObject data = new MarshalledObject("data");
Desc = new ActivationDesc("ServiceImpl", source, data);
Service = (Service) Activatable.register(desc);
```

The register() method returns a RemoteStub object that can be passed as a parameter in any method call expecting an object that implements the Service interface. The register() call throws the following exceptions: java.rmi.NoSuchGroupException, ActivationException, and java.rmi.RemoteException. This should be handled in your code.

10.5 VERSION CONTROL

The general main idea of version control is that users should no longer complain "If I upgrade, something will break." In distributed systems, product versioning is very important, as many problems can occur when packages evolve and are updated independently.

Prior to the release of Java 2, there was no version control between stubs and skeletons. Therefore, it is possible that a client may use a down-level stub to access a more recent skeleton, thereby breaking release-to-release binary compatibility. Java 2 has introduced a new product versioning API that can be used to specify how the packages of a system should evolve so that the goal of an open, scalable distributed system can be achieved.

10.5.1 Package versioning

A Java package is made up of class files plus optional resource files, with information to identify the contents of the package. The Java Product Versioning Specification defines the following attributes for a package as shown in table 10.1. The value of each attribute is a string.

Table 10.1 The Java Product Versioning Specification package attributes

Attribute	Description
Package-Title	Title of the package.
Package-Version	Package version number.
Package-Vendor	Company or organization.
Specification-Title	Title of the specification.
Specification-Version	Specification version number.
Specification-Vendor	Company or organization.

These attributes are stored in the JAR manifest format and are retrieved by programs using the `java.lang.Package` API, which is briefly described below.

The java.lang.Package class   The `java.lang.Package` class provides an object that can be used to locate and access information about a package. Package objects are created by class loaders and should be created before the first class in the package is defined. The attributes of each package, which are defined above, are stored in the JAR manifest and are retrieved by the classloader. The `Package` class has the definition shown in example 10.1.

Example 10.1: Package.java

```
package java.lang;
public class Package {
    public String getName();
    public String getSpecificationTitle();
    public String getSpecificationVersion();
    public String getSpecificationVendor();
    public String getImplementationTitle();
    public String getImplementationVersion();
    public String getImplementationVendor();
    public String isCompatibleWith(String desired);
```

```
public static Package getPackage(String classname);
public static Package[] getAllPackage();
public boolean equals(Object obj);
public int hashCode();
public String toString();
}
```

The getName() method returns the name of the package. The getSpecificationTitle() method returns the title of the specification of the package, and so on, for the rest of the get methods. The isCompatibleWith() method returns true if the package's specification version number is compatible with the desired version number. The getPackage() method locates the package for the class by name. And the getAllPackages() method returns an array of all the packages known to the current classloader. The equals() method returns true if the package has the same name and classloader as the object passed to it.

Additions to the java.lang.Class class   A new method to get the java.lang.Class class is available. The new method has the following definition:

```
package java.lang;
public class Class {
    . . . .
    public Package getPackage();
    . . . .
}
```

Additions to the java.lang.ClassLoader class   The ClassLoader class has been extended to keep track of the mapping from classes to packages. This also allows classloaders to define the Package instances for the classes they load. The java.lang.ClassLoader class has two new methods with the following definition:

```
package lang.lang;
public class ClassLoader {
    . . . .
    public static ClassLoader currentClassLoader();
    protected Package(String pkgname, String spectitle, String specversion,
String specvendor, String compatible, String implversion, String implven-
dor);
    . . . .
}
```

The currentClassLoader method is used to find the current ClassLoader. If this method is called from a classloader-loaded class, it will return the equivalent of this.getClass().getClassLoader(). Its behavior is identical to the current SecurityManager.currentClassLoader method.

The definePackage method is used by subclasses to define the packages of the classes it is loading. The classloader should supply the versioning attributes from the manifest, if they are available.

The JAR manifest format   The current manifest format has been extended to allow the specification of the attributes for package versioning information. A manifest entry should be created for each package; the name of the entry should be the directory within the archive that contains the package's class and resource files. For example:

```
Manifest-version: 1.0
Name: java/util/
Specification-Title: "Java Management Classes"
Specification-Version: "1.2"
Specification-Vendor: "Sun Microsystems Inc."
Package-Title: "java.mgmt"
Package-Version: "build44"
Package-Vendor: "Sun Microsystems Inc."
```

To insert these attributes in the manifest, you can create a prototype manifest and use the −m switch of the JAR tool to merge them into the manifest when it is built.

10.5.2   Product versioning and users

So far we have seen what is available and you should have an idea of how to use the Java Product Versioning API. But one question remains—how does this help users of our applications? It is up to the application developer to expose the available information to the user on demand or when errors occur. The following pieces of information can be reported:

- Which packages are loaded?
- What are the package versions?
- What version of the Java Runtime is active?
- What version of the JVM is active?

This information can be obtained using the methods in the Package class and the System.getProperties method of the java.lang class.

10.6   SUMMARY

- With the RMI enhancements in Java 2, it is now possible to establish secure communications between RMI clients and servers using SSL sockets. A number of SSL implementations can be used with Java. In this chapter we made use of the javax.net.ssl package, which is distributed with a number of JavaSoft products, including Java WebServer, Hot-Java, and the JavaServer Toolkit.
- A distributed system must be highly available. Therefore, object implementations must be active at all times. However, if objects remain active continuously, they would be taking up too many system resources. One of the enhanced RMI features in Java 2 is object activation, a mechanism for providing persistent references to objects and allowing them to begin executing on an as-needed basis.
- Prior to Java 2, there was no version control between RMI stubs and skeletons. It was possible for a client to use a down-level stub to access a more recent skeleton, thereby breaking release-to-release binary compatibility. Java 2 has introduced a new product-versioning API that can be used to specify how the packages of a system should evolve. Users should no longer complain, "If I upgrade, something will break."

CORBA

CHAPTER 11

Overview of CORBA

In previous chapters we have seen how Java objects can be distributed and accessed using Java's RMI. Now we'll shift our attention to an alternative approach for distributing and accessing objects. This approach is based on OMG's CORBA, which is an industry standard for creating and using distributed objects.

This chapter presents an overview of CORBA, its architecture, and applications. We'll discuss the components of CORBA, its services and facilities, and the new features that are being added to CORBA that will be part of CORBA 3.0.

11.1   *INTRODUCTION TO CORBA*

CORBA, which stands for Common Object Request Broker Architecture, is an industry standard developed by the OMG (a consortium of more than 700 companies) to aid in distributed objects programming. CORBA is just a *specification* for creating and using distributed objects; CORBA is *not* a programming language.

The CORBA architecture is based on the object model. This model is derived from the abstract core object model defined by the OMG in the *Object Management Architecture Guide,* which can be found at http://www.omg.org. The model is abstract in the sense that it is not directly realized by any particular technology; this allows applications to be built in a standard manner using basic building blocks such as objects. Therefore, a CORBA-based system is a collection of objects that isolates the requestors of services (clients) from the providers of services (servers) by a well-defined encapsulating interface. It is important to note that CORBA objects differ from typical programming objects in three ways:

- CORBA objects can run on any platform.
- CORBA objects can be located anywhere on the network.
- CORBA objects can be written in any language that has IDL mapping.

11.2 CORBA ARCHITECTURE

The OMG's Object Management Architecture (OMA) tries to define the various high-level facilities that are necessary for distributed object-oriented computing. The core of the OMA is the Object Request Broker (ORB), a mechanism that provides object location tranparency, communication, and activation. Based on the OMA, the CORBA specification which provides a description of the interfaces and facilities that must be provided by compliant ORBs was released.

CORBA is composed of five major components: ORB, IDL, dynamic invocation interface (DII), interface repositories (IR), and object adapters (OA). These are discussed in the following sections.

11.2.1 The object request broker

The CORBA specification must have software to implement it. The software that implements the CORBA specification is called the ORB. The ORB, which is the heart of CORBA, is responsible for all the mechanisms required to perform these tasks:

- Find the object implementation for the request.

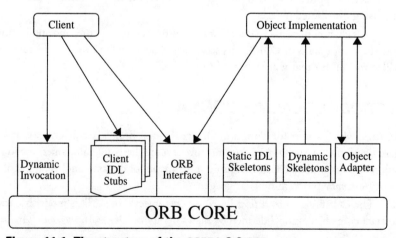

Figure 11.1 The structure of the CORBA 2.0 ORB

- Prepare the object implementation to receive the request.
- Communicate the data making up the request.

A number of implementations exist in the market today, including ORBIX from IONA Technologies (http://www.iona.ie), VisiBroker from Inprise (http://www.inprise.com), and JavaIDL from JavaSoft (http://java.sun.com/products/jdk.idl). Throughout this part of the book, we will use the VisiBroker ORB for Java, version 3.1. Figure 11.1 shows how the five major components of CORBA fit together.

Figure 11.2 shows a request being sent by a client to an object implementation. The client is the entity that wishes to perform an operation on the object, and the object implementation is the actual code and data that implements the object. Note that in this figure, the client, ORB, and object implementation are all on a single machine (meaning they're not separated by a network).

There are two important things to note about the CORBA architecture and its computing model:

- Both the client and the object implementation are isolated from the ORB by an IDL interface.

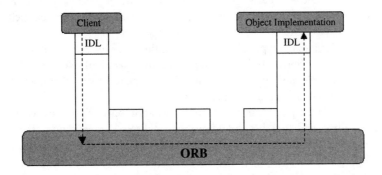

Figure 11.2 A request from a client to an object implementation

- All requests are managed by the ORB. This means that every invocation (whether it is local or remote) of a CORBA object is passed to an ORB. In the case of a remote invocation, however, the invocation passed from the ORB of the client to the ORB of the object implementation as shown in figure 11.3.

11.2.2   Different vendors and different   ORBs

Since there is more than one CORBA implementation, and these implementations are from different vendors, a good question at this point would be whether objects implemented in different ORBs from different vendors would be able to communicate with each other. The answer is this: all CORBA 2.0 (and above) compliant ORBs are able to interoperate via the Internet Inter-ORB Protocol, or IIOP for short. This was not true for CORBA 1.0 products, however. The whole purpose of IIOP is to ensure that your client will be able to communicate with a server written for a different ORB from a different vendor.

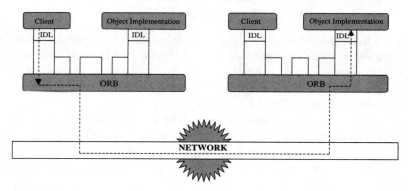

Figure 11.3 A request from a client to an object implementation within a network

11.2.3   Interface definition language

As with RMI, CORBA objects are to be specified with interfaces, which are the contract between the client and server. In CORBA's case, however, interfaces are specified in the special definition language IDL.

The IDL defines the types of objects by defining their interfaces. An interface consists of a set of named operations and the parameters to those operations. Note that IDL is used to describe interfaces only, not implementations. Despite the fact that IDL syntax is similar to C++ and Java, IDL is not a programming language.

Through IDL, a particular object implementation tells its potential clients what operations are available and how they should be invoked. From IDL definitions, the CORBA objects are mapped into different programming languages. Some of the programming languages with IDL mapping include C, C++, Java, Smalltalk, Lisp, and Python. Thus, once you define an interface to objects in IDL, you are free to implement the object using any suitable programming language that has IDL mapping. And, consequently, if you want to use that object, you can use any programming language to make remote requests to the object.

In chapter 13, I'll give you detailed coverage of IDL, and in chapter 14, I'll give you an overview of the IDL-to-Java mapping.

11.2.4   Dynamic invocation interface

Invoking operations can be done through either static or dynamic interfaces. Static invocation interfaces are determined at compile time, and they are presented to the client using stubs. The DII, on the other hand, allows client applications to use server objects without knowing the type of those objects at compile time. It allows a client to obtain an instance of a CORBA object and make invocations on that object by dynamically constructing requests. DII uses the interface repository to validate and retrieve the signature of the operation on which a request is made. CORBA supports both the dynamic and the static invocation interfaces.

11.2.5 Dynamic skeleton interface

Analogous to the DII is the server-side dynamic skeleton interface (DSI), which allows servers to be written without having skeletons, or compile-time knowledge, for the objects being implemented.

Unlike DII, which was part of the initial CORBA specification, DSI was introduced in CORBA 2.0. Its main purpose is to support the implementation of gateways between ORBs which utilize different communication protocols. However, DSI has many other applications beside interoperability. These applications include interactive software tools based on interpreters and distributed debuggers.

11.2.6 Interface Repository

The IR provides another way to specify the interfaces to objects. Interfaces can be added to the interface repository service. Using the IR, a client should be able to locate an object that is unknown at compile time, find information about its interface, then build a request to be forwarded through the ORB.

11.2.7 Object adapters

An object adapter is the primary way that an object implementation accesses services provided by the ORB. Such services include object reference generation and interpretation, method invocation, security of interactions, and object and implementation activation and deactivation.

11.3 CLIENT AND OBJECT IMPLEMENTATIONS

A distributed application consists of objects running within clients and servers. Servers provide objects to be used by clients as well as other servers. A client of an object has access to the object reference, which is the information needed to specify an object within an ORB; with that access, it can invoke operations on the object. A client knows the object through an interface, therefore the client knows nothing about how the object is implemented. A client generally sees objects and ORB interfaces through a language mapping.

11.4 OBJECT SERVICES

The OMA, which is shown in figure 11.4, is the next higher level that builds upon the CORBA architecture. The goal of the OMA is to allow applications to provide their basic functionality through a standard interface.

As you can see from figure 11.4, the OMA consists of two main components: *CORBAservices* and *CORBAfacilities*. CORBAservices provides basic services that almost every object needs; this includes naming service and event service. The CORBAfacilities provides higher-level functionality at the application level. As demonstrated in figure 11.4, CORBAfacilities are further divided into horizontal CORBAfacilities and vertical CORBAfacilities. Horizontal CORBAfacilities include user interface, information management, systems management, and task Management. Vertical (or Domain) CORBAfacilities are domain-based and provide functionality for a specific domain such as telecommunications, electronic commerce, or health care.

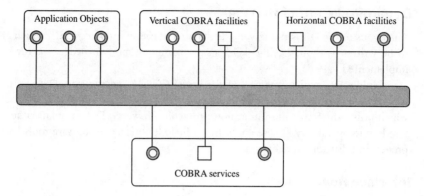

Figure 11.4 Object Management Architecture (OMA)

Object services are interfaces which are widely available and are most commonly used to support building well-formed applications in a distributed object environment built on a CORBA-compliant ORB. OMG object services have the following features:

- Objects may use few or many object services.
- The operations provided by object services are specified in IDL.

There have been a number of Request For Proposals (RFPs) issued for a set of specifications known as Common Object Services Specification, Volumes 1 and 2 (COSS 1 and COSS 2). They both include services for object naming, object events, object lifecycle, persistent object, object relationships, object externalization, object transactions, object concurrency, and object security. All of these services are now known as CORBA Services. Here is a description of some of these services.

- *Object naming service*   This service supports a name-to-object association called a name binding, which is always defined relative to a naming context. Different names can be bound to an object in the same or different context at the same time. This service supports a number of operations, including bind, unbind, and lookup.
- *Event service*   This service supports notification of events to interested objects. It provides asynchronous communications between cooperating, remote objects.
- *Persistent object service*   This service provides common interfaces for the mechanisms used for retaining and managing the persistent state of objects in a data-store independent manner. Of course, the object has the responsibility of managing its state, but it can use or delegate to this service for the actual work.
- *Concurrency control service*   This service defines how an object mediates simultaneous access by one or more clients, so that the objects it accesses remain consistent and coherent.

11.5 NEW FEATURES IN CORBA 3.0

Since its inception in 1991, CORBA has had to evolve to remain viable as a basis for distributed applications. As part of this continuing evolution, several significant new features are being added to CORBA that will be part of CORBA 3.0. The new features include Portable object adapter (POA), CORBA messaging, and objects by value. A brief overview of these new CORBA features is provided here.

11.5.1 Portable object adapter

Object adapters mediate between CORBA objects and programming language implementations (servants). Object adapters provide a number of services, including the creation of CORBA objects and their references, dispatching requests to the appropriate servant that provides an implementation for the target object, and activation and deactivation of CORBA objects.

In CORBA 2.0, the only standard object adapter defined by the OMG is called the basic object adapter (BOA), which only provides basic services to allow a variety of CORBA objects to be created. ORB vendors and developers, however, discovered that the BOA is ambiguous and missing some features. This led vendors to develop their own proprietary extensions, which resulted in poor portability between different ORB implementations.

The new standard object adapter, the POA, provides new features that allow applications and their servants to be portable between different ORBs supplied by different vendors. This new adapter provides a great deal of flexibility for server implementations. As I mentioned earlier, the POA mediates between the ORB and the server application. Figure 11.5 shows a request from a client to a server.

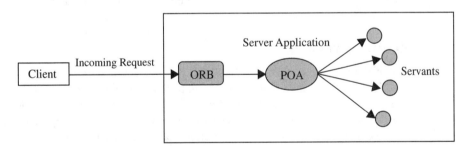

Figure 11.5 Request dispatching based on POA

The client invokes the request using a reference that refers to the target object. The request is then received by the ORB, which will dispatch the request to the POA that hosts the target object. The POA will then dispatch the request to the servant, which subsequently carries the request and sends the results back to the POA, to the ORB, and finally to the client. Note that an application may have multiple POAs, and in order for the ORB to dispatch the request to the right POA, it uses an *object key*, which is an identifier that is part of the request that is kept in the object reference. A part of the object key called the object ID is used by the POA to determine an association between the target object and a servant.

To summarize, the POA deals mainly with three entities: the *object reference*, the *object ID* (both of which are used for identification), and the *servant*, which actually implements CORBA objects.

11.5.2 CORBA messaging

CORBA 2.0 provides three different techniques for operation invocations:

- *Synchronous* The client invokes an operation, then pauses, waiting for a response.
- *Deferred synchronous* The client invokes an operation then continues processing. It can go back later to either poll or block waiting for a response.
- *One-way* The client invokes an operation, and the ORB provides a guarantee that the request will be delivered. In one-way operation invocations, there is no response.

Synchronous invocation techniques tend to tightly couple clients and servers. This has led many people to criticize CORBA as being unable to cope with large distributed systems. For this reason, a new specification (the CORBA messaging specification, which can be found at http://www.omg.org), has been adopted by the OMG. This new specification preserves the invocation techniques in CORBA 2.0 and adds two new asynchronous request techniques:

- *Callback* The client supplies an additional object reference with each request invocation. When the response arrives, the ORB uses that object reference to deliver the response back to the client.
- *Polling* The client invokes an operation that immediately returns a valuetype that can be used to either poll or wait for the response.

The callback and polling techniques are available for clients using statically typed stubs generated from IDL interfaces. These new techniques represent a significant advantage for most programming languages because static invocations provide a more natural programming model than the DII.

11.5.3 Objects by value

One of the ongoing criticisms of CORBA 2.0 is the lack of support for passing objects by value. This has been addressed by adding support for passing objects by value (see the document *Objects By Value*, which can be found at http://www.omg.org). This has led to the addition of a new construct to the OMG IDL called the valuetype. A valuetype supports both data members and operations, much the same as a Java class definition.

When a valuetype is passed as an argument to a remote operation, it will be created as a copy in the receiving address space. The identity of the valuetype copy is separate from the original, so operations on one have no effect on the other. It is important to note that operations invoked on valuetypes are local to the process in which the valuetype exists. This means that valuetype invocations never involve the transmission of requests and replies over the network.

11.6 SUMMARY

- CORBA stands for Common Object Request Broker Architecture. CORBA is an industry-standard developed by the OMG, a consortium of more than 700 companies.

CORBA is not a programming language; it's a specification for creating and using distributed objects.

- CORBA objects are different from typical programming objects in three ways: CORBA objects can run on any platform, they can be located anywhere on the network, and they can be written in any language that supports IDL mapping.
- CORBA is composed of five major components: ORB, IDL, DII, IR), andOA.
- The ORB is responsible for finding the object implementation for a request, preparing the object implementation to receive the request, and communicating the data making up the request.
- The OMA is the next higher level that builds upon the CORBA architecture. OMA consists of two main components: CORBAservices and CORBAfacilities. The OMA allows applications to provide their basic functionality through a standard interface.
- CORBA 3.0 will have several major new features, including POA, CORBA messaging, and objects by value. POA provides new features that allow applications and their servants to be portable between different ORBs supplied by different vendors. CORBA messaging adds two new asynchronous request techniques: *polling* and *callback*. These new techniques represent a significant advantage for most programming languages because static invocations provide a more natural programming model than the DII. Using objects by value, it is now possible to pass objects by value with CORBA.

C H A P T E R   1 2

Getting started with CORBA

12.1 CORBA implementations
12.2 Anatomy of a CORBA-based
application

12.3 CORBA vs. RMI
12.4 Summary

CORBA is merely a specification that does nothing if there is no software that implements it. There are a number of Java-based CORBA implementations; these are known as ORBs. Developing distributed applications in CORBA is similar to that of RMI in the sense that an interface must be defined first. However, unlike RMI, where interfaces are defined in Java, CORBA interfaces are defined in IDL.

This chapter shows you the anatomy of a CORBA-based application by walking you through the development and running of an example application. We'll also discuss the major differences between CORBA and RMI.

12.1 CORBA IMPLEMENTATIONS

The CORBA specification wouldn't be useful if there wasn't software to implement it. As you've already learned, the software that implements the CORBA specification is called an ORB. A number of ORBs exist today. Here are some of the most popular implementations that have Java support:

- VisiBroker from Inprise Corporation (http://www.inprise.com).

- OrbixWeb from IONA Technologies (http://www.iona.ie).
- JavaIDL from JavaSoft (http://www.java.sun.com/products/jdk/idl).

Other implementations of CORBA include PowerBroker from Expersoft (http://www.expersoft.com), DAIS from ICL (http://www.icl.co.uk), ObjectBroker from BEA Systems, (http:www.beasys.com) and ComponentBroker from IBM (http://www.software.ibm.com/ad/cb).

The CORBA programming examples in this book use the VisiBroker ORB for Java, version 3.1. To give you a brief history of the product, VisiBroker started as PostModern's Black Widow ORB. It was the first Java implementation of CORBA. In 1996, PostModern was acquired by Visigenic, a vendor for database middleware. Visigenic changed the name Black Widow to VisiBroker for Java. In 1997, Visigenic was acquired by Borland. In 1998, Borland changed its name to Inprise Corporation, but the ORB it acquired from Visigenic is still known as VisiBroker.

12.2 ANATOMY OF A CORBA-BASED APPLICATION

There are a number of steps for developing a CORBA-based application. Figure 12.1 illustrates the CORBA application development paradigm.

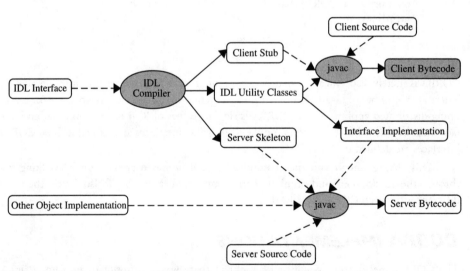

Figure 12.1 The CORBA application development paradigm

This section will outline the steps for developing a CORBA-based application using the VisiBroker ORB for Java. The following list is an overview of the steps.

1 Define interfaces using IDL.
2 Implement the CORBA classes.

3 Develop the server program.

4 Develop the client program(s).

5 Start the Smart Agent, the server, and the client(s).

I will explain each step separately by walking you through the development of the arithmetic server that we developed using sockets and RMI in chapters 3 and 8, respectively. The first step in developing the arithmetic server is to define an interface in IDL.

12.2.1 Defining an IDL interface

When defining an interface, keep in mind what types of operations the server will support. In the case of the arithmetic server, the operations that will be performed are of a mathematical nature—adding arrays, subtracting arrays, and so on. However, for the sake of simplicity, we will only consider the sum_arrays operation. As an exercise, you can modify the code and add more operations on your own.

Example 12.1 shows the IDL interface for the Add object. Note that the sum_arrays operation has three parameters. The first two are the input of the two arrays to be added, and the third parameter is the output holder (the sum of the two arrays). The first two parameters are declared in, and the third parameter is declared out. IDL defines three parameter-passing modes: in, out, and inout. As the names suggest, the in parameter is used for input, the out parameter is used for output, and the inout parameter is used for both input and output.

Example 12.1: Arith.idl

```
// Arithmetic IDL interface.
module Arith {
   interface Add {
      const unsigned short SIZE = 10;
      typedef long array[SIZE];
      void sum_arrays(in array a, in array b, out array c);
   };
};
```

Once we finish defining the IDL interface, we are ready to compile it. VisiBroker comes with an IDL compiler, idl2java, which is used to map IDL definitions into Java declarations and statements. We run the idl2java compiler from the command line and, as an argument, we feed it the idl module we want to compile, as follows:

```
% idl2java Arith.idl
Creating: Arith
Creating: Arith/AddPackage
Creating: Arith/AddPackage/SIZE.java
Creating: Arith/AddPackage/arrayHolder.java
Creating: Arith/AddPackage/arrayHelper.java
Creating: Arith/Add.java
Creating: Arith/AddHolder.java
Creating: Arith/AddHelper.java
Creating: Arith/_st_Add.java
Creating: Arith/_sk_Add.java
Creating: Arith/_AddImplBase.java
```

```
Creating: Arith/AddOperations.java
Creating: Arith/_tie_Add.java
Creating: Arith/_example_Add.java
%
```

As you can see, the idl2java compiler has generated a number of files; they are all stored in a subdirectory named Arith, which is the module name specified in the IDL file. As you will see in chapter 14, IDL modules are mapped to Java packages.

For this simple example, the generated files which are important to us are shown in table 12.1.

Table 12.1 Generated file list

Filename	Description
Add.java	The Arith interface declaration.
AddOperations.java	Declares the sum_arrays method.
_st_Add.java	Stub code for the Arith object on the client side.
_sk_Add.java	Stub code for the Arith object implementation on the server side.
_example_Add.java	Code you can fill in to implement the Arith object on the server side.

The Add.java file contains the Java code that was generated from the Arith.idl interface definition. The generated code in Add.java (without the comments) from the Arith.idl interface is shown in example 12.2. This segment of code will help implement the sum_arrays method.

Example 12.2: Add.java

```java
/**
 * Generated by the idl2java compiler.
 */
public interface Add extends org.omg.CORBA.Object {
    final public static short SIZE = (short) 10;
    public void sum_arrays(
        int a[],
        int b[],
        Arith.AddPackage.arrayHolder c
    );
}
```

At this point, we can implement the sum_arrays method.

12.2.2 Implementing the CORBA classes

Implementing the sum_arrays method is easy. As shown in the previous section, the idl2java compiler has generated a file named _example_Add.java. This file actually contains some constructors as well as the definition of the sum_arrays method. I copied the file into AddImpl.java and implemented the sum_arrays method as shown in example 12.3.

Example 12.3: AddImpl.java

```
/**
 * @(#)AddImpl.java
 */
public class AddImpl extends Arith._AddImplBase {
    /** Construct a persistently named object. */
    public AddImpl(java.lang.String name) {
        super(name);
    }
    /** Construct a transient object. */
    public AddImpl() {
        super();
    }
    public void sum_arrays(
        int[] a,
        int[] b,
        Arith.AddPackage.arrayHolder c
    ) {
        c.value = new int[10];
        for (int i < 0; i < Arith.AddPackage.SIZE.value; i++) {
            c.value[i] = a[i] + b[i];
        }
    }
}
```

Now we can compile it:

```
% javac AddImpl.java
```

We are now ready to develop our arithmetic server program.

12.2.3 Developing the server program

Example 12.4 shows an implementation of the Server class for the server side of our arithmetic server. The Server class does the following:

- Initializes the ORB.
- Initializes the BOA.
- Creates an AddImpl object.
- Activates the newly created object.
- Prints out a status message.
- Waits for incoming client requests.

As you can see from example 12.4, the Server class is small and fairly easy to follow and understand.

Example 12.4: Server.java

```java
import org.omg.CORBA.*;
/**
 * @(#)Server.java
 */
public class Server {
    public static void main(String argv[]) {
        try {
            // Initialize the ORB.
            ORB orb = ORB.init();
            // Initialize the BOA.
            BOA boa = orb.BOA_init();
            // Create the AddImpl object.
            AddImpl arr = new AddImpl("Arithmetic Server");
            // Export the newly created object.
            boa.obj_is_ready(arr);
            System.out.println(arr + " is ready. ");
            // Wait for incoming requests.
            boa.impl_is_ready();
        } catch (SystemException se) {
            se.printStackTrace();
        }
    }
}
```

Once we finish implementing the server program, we can compile it:

% javac Server.java

The next step is to implement a client program that uses one or more of the services offered by the server. In our application, adding arrays is the only service the server program offers.

12.2.4 Developing the client program

Most of the files needed to implement the client program are contained in the Arith package generated by the idl2java compiler. The Client class shown in example 12.5 performs the following actions:

- Initializes the ORB.
- Binds to an Add object.
- Requests the Add to sum two arrays with the specified input values.

- Gets the sum of the two arrays using the object reference returned by the sum_arrays method.
- Prints out the sum of the two arrays.

Example 12.5: Client.java

```java
import org.omg.CORBA.*;
/**
 * @(#)Client.java
 */
public class Client {
    public static void main(String argv[]) {
        int a[] = {1, 2, 3, 4, 5, 6, 7, 8, 9, 10};
        int b[] = {1, 2, 3, 4, 5, 6, 7, 8, 9, 10};
        Arith.AddPackage.arrayHolder result = new Arith.AddPackage.array-
Holder();
        try {
          // Initialize the ORB.
          ORB orb = ORB.init();
          // Locate an Add object.
          Arith.Add add = Arith.AddHelper.bind(orb,"ArithmeticServer");
          add.sum_arrays(a, b, result);
          System.out.print("The sum is: ");
          for (int i = 0; i < Arith.AddPackage.SIZE.value; i++) {
             System.out.print(result.value[i]+"    ");
          }
          System.out.println();
        } catch (SystemException se) {
           se.printStackTrace();
        }
    }
}
```

We'll now move on to the final step in the development lifecycle of a CORBA-based application: starting the smart agent, the server, and the client.

12.2.5   Starting the smart agent, the server, and the client

The VisiBroker smart agent, osagent, provides a fault-tolerant object location service and run-time licensing of VisiBroker applications. We start the smart agent as a background process on a Unix-based system with this command:

% osagent &

If you are running Windows NT, you can start the smart agent as an NT service through the Services Control Panel, or you can use this command:

prompt> osagent -c (or osagent -C)

The -c or -C option allows the osagent to run in console mode.

Once the osagent is running, we can start the server program. We will do this using the vbj command, which invokes the JVM and offers other special services such as setting paths.

```
% vbj Server
```

```
AddImpl[Server,oid=PersistentID[repID=IDL:Arith/Add:1.0,objectName=Arith-
metic Server]]is ready.
```

Finally, we can run the client program:

```
% vbj Client
The sum is: 2    4    6    8    10    12    14    16    18    20
```

In running the application in this chapter, we assumed that both the client and server are running on the same host. It is more common however, for the client and server to run on different hosts. One way to do this is by having an osagent run on each host. However, VisiBroker makes this unnecessary by providing the OSAGENT_ADDR property. To start a client or a server on a host that is not running the osagent, use the OSAGENT_ADDR property to specify the host that is running an osagent. For example, if there is an osagent running on the host "veda," the following command can used to start a client residing on a different host:

```
% java -DOSAGENT_ADDR=veda Client
```

12.3 CORBA VS. RMI

The arithmetic server developed in this chapter was also implemented using sockets (in chapter 3), and RMI (in chapter 8). In chapter 8, I briefly compared RMI with sockets. In this section, I will briefly compare CORBA with RMI.

Looking at the arithmetic server, the amount of code we had to write for each was almost the same. However, in CORBA's case, the code is more complex and the programmer has to be familiar with IDL for describing interfaces as well as with the IDL-to-Java mapping. You can see how RMI is a simpler system for developing distributed applications. In general, however, CORBA differs from RMI in the following areas:

- CORBA interfaces are defined in IDL, while RMI interfaces are defined in Java.
- CORBA was designed with language independence in mind, where objects run in a heterogeneous environment. On the other hand, RMI was designed for a single language where objects run in a homogenous language environment.
- CORBA objects are not garbage collected. They are language independent, and they therefore have to be consistent with languages that do not support garbage collection. Once it is created, a CORBA object exists until you get rid of it, and deciding when to get rid of objects can be a hard decision when designing CORBA-based applications. RMI objects, on the other hand, are garbage-collected automatically.
- RMI does not support out and inout parameters (CORBA does) since local objects are passed by copy and remote objects are passed by reference to a stub.

12.4 SUMMARY

- The software that implements the CORBA specification is called an ORB. Some of the most widely used ORBs are ORBIX from IONA Technologies, VisiBroker from Inprise Corporation, and JavaIDL from JavaSoft.

- Developing a CORBA-based application is similar to that of RMI in that the first step is to define an interface. However, unlike RMI, where an interface is defined in Java, CORBA interfaces are defined in IDL. Following the interface definition, we implement the interface, develop the server and client programs, start VisiBroker's Smart Agent, and finally start the server and client programs.
- There are a number of differences between RMI and CORBA:
    1 CORBA is a language-independent distributed environment. RMI is designed for a single language environment—Java.
    2 RMI objects are garbage-collected, but CORBA objects are not.
    3 Unlike CORBA, RMI does not support out and inout parameters since local objects are passed by copy and remote objects are passed by reference to a stub.

CORBA IDL: The interface definition language

A CORBA interface provides a description of the functionality provided by an object. An interface specifies all the information that a programmer needs to develop a client that uses that interface, such as all the attributes and methods supported by an object, including parameters.

IDL is a language for describing the interfaces of objects in a CORBA application. In this chapter, we'll cover IDL in detail, showing how it can be used to define even very complex interfaces.

13.1   IDL DEFINITIONS

An IDL definition fully specifies each operation's parameters and their types. A definition can be comprised of one or more types, as you will see later on in this chapter; these types include constant definitions, exception definitions, and module definitions. An IDL definition may also contain preprocessor directives (see section 13.11 for more information on preprocessing).

13.1.1 Comments

Two forms of comments are defined in the IDL specifications. The two examples in this section show how they can be used in an IDL definition file. The first type of comment starts with two forward slashes and ends at the end of the line:

```
// This is a comment
```

The other type of comment starts with the characters /* and ends with the characters */. It may contain any number of lines in between. This type of comment does not nest.

```
/*
 * This is another comment
 */
```

13.1.2 Identifiers

An identifier in an IDL specification consists of alphabetic characters (a to z , A to Z) and numeric characters (0 to 9). It may also contain the underscore character. An identifier must begin with an alphabetic character. There is no restriction on its length.

While identifiers are case sensitive, it is important to note that two identifiers that differ only in case cannot appear in the same scope; if they do, they will clash.

13.1.3 Literal values

A value such as the number 8 is known as a literal value. Such integer values can be specified in decimal, octal, or hexadecimal notation. An integer value can be specified in octal by having the prefix 0, and in hexadecimal by having either the prefix 0x or 0X.

Certain nonprintable characters can be represented by the escape sequences shown in table 13.1.

Table 13.1   Nonprinting and hard-to-print characters

Name of Character	DL notation
new line	\n
carriage return	\r
horizontal tab	\t
vertical tab	\v
backspace	\b
form feed	\f
backslash	\\
question mark	\?

(continued)

Table 13.2   Nonprinting and hard-to-print characters   (continued)

Name of Character	DL notation
single quote	\'
double quote	\"
octal number	\ooo
Hexadecimal number	\xhh

13.2   *IDL INTERFACES*

Interface definitions are central to IDL. An interface consists of a header and a body, and it gives a description of the functionality an object will provide. An interface also provides all the information needed to develop clients that use the classes that implement the interface. In addition, an interface typically specifies the attributes and methods of an object and it specifies the parameters of each method. An interface may inherit from another interface. In short, defining CORBA interfaces is conceptually similar to defining abstract interfaces in Java.

Consider an application that will perform arithmetic operations on arrays of integers. A user of a mathematical object may wish to add, subtract, or multiply arrays of integers. The arithmetic object can be made to hold the result of the arithmetic operation. The interface's header is introduced by the keyword `interface` and is followed by the name of the interface. Here is a sample interface:

```
interface Add {
    // Size of array
    const unsigned short SIZE = 10;
    /* A simple name for an array of longs */
    typedef long arr[SIZE];
    void add_arrays(in arr a, in arr b, out arr c);
};
```

The interface above provides one method, `add_arrays`, which has three parameters of type `arr` and is a `typedef`. An interface, however, may contain the following types of declarations:

- Attribute declarations
- Type declarations
- Method declarations
- Constant declarations
- Exception declarations

It is important to note that multiple interfaces can be defined in a single file. The next section shows a better way to group interfaces using modules.

13.3   *MODULE DECLARATION*

A module provides a way to group interfaces and other IDL-type definitions into logical units. A module also allows you to choose sensible names for interfaces so they won't clash with other names in the global name space. Therefore, we could define interfaces related to an arithmetic application with a module named `Arith` as follows:

```
module Arith {
    interface Add {
        .  .  .  .
    };

    interface Subtract {
        .  .  .  .
    };

    interface Multiply {
        .  .  .  .
    };
};
```

13.4 ATTRIBUTE DECLARATION

An interface can have attributes as well as operations. An attribute definition is equivalent to declaring a pair of *accessor* functions: one to set the value of the attribute and one to retrieve it. For example, in the following `BankAccount` interface, we have two attributes: `balance`, which is of type `float`, to represent the balance of the account, and `customer`, which is of type `string`, to represent the owner of the account.

```
// IDL
interface BankAccount {
    attribute float balance;
    readonly attribute string customer;
};
```

The optional `readonly` keyword indicates that there is only a function to retrieve the value. It does not mean that the value of the attribute cannot be changed.

13.5 TYPE DECLARATION

IDL, which is a C-like language that associates an identifier with a type, provides constructs for naming data types. It provides basic types such as `integer`, `char`, `float`, `boolean`, `octet`, and `any`. IDL also provides constructed types such as structures, discriminated unions, and enumerations. In the following sections, I will describe the *basic* and *constructed* type specifiers.

13.5.1 Basic types

As I mentioned earlier, the basic types supported in IDL include floating point type, integer type, char type, boolean type, octet type, and any type. The following sections contain brief descriptions of each one.

The floating-point type IDL supports two floating-point types: float and double. The float type represents IEEE single-precision floating-point numbers, and the double type represents IEEE double-precision numbers.

The integer type IDL defines two integer data types: long and short. They can be either signed or unsigned (only the unsigned types need to be specified). The long type represents the range -2^{31} to 2^{31}-1, while the unsigned long represents the range 0 to 2^{32}-1. The short type represents the range: -2^{15} to 2^{15}-1, while the unsigned short type represents the range: 0 to 2^{16}-1. There is no int type in IDL.

The char type IDL supports a char data type that is an 8-bit character.

The boolean type IDL defines a boolean data type that is used to denote a data item that can only have one of two values, true or false.

The octet type The octet type is an 8-bit quantity that is guaranteed not to undergo any conversion during transmission.

The any type The any type allows you to specify values that can express an arbitrary IDL type such as integer, float, or char. For example:

```
// IDL interface
 interface Hello {
    void sayHello(in any str);
};
```

13.5.2 Constructed types

IDL provides three constructed data types: *struct, union,* and *enum;* they are described below.

Structures A structure type is introduced by the struct keyword, followed by an identifier and a member list. For example, the following code creates the struct employeeData, which has three members: name, age, and salary.

```
// IDL
    struct employeeData {
    string name;
    short age;
    double salary;
};
```

Discriminated unions IDL defines the union type for which the amount of storage required is the amount necessary to store its largest element. A tag field is used to specify which member of a union instance currently has a value assigned to it.

```
// IDL
union myType switch (long) {
    case 1: long la;
    case 2: . . . .
    default: string name;
};
```

In this example, myType is now a new legal type. Notice that union must be discriminated, which means the header must specify a tag field that determines which union member is assigned a value. In the example above, the tag is called myType and is of type long.

Enumerations   An enumerated type consists of an ordered list of identifiers. For example:

```
// IDL
enum workdays { mon, tue, wed, thu, fri };
```

is an enumeration that defines a new legal type: workdays.

13.5.3   Template types

IDL provides two template types: *sequence* and *string*.

Sequences   A sequence is a one-dimensional array with two characteristics: a maximum size that is fixed at compile-time, and a length that is determined at run-time. There are two types of sequences: *bounded sequences* and *unbounded sequences*. For example, the following code segment:

```
// IDL
sequence<long, 15> arr;
```

defines a bounded sequence of size 15, so the sequence arr can be of any length up to the maximum bound (15). On the other hand, this code segment defines an unbounded sequence:

```
// IDL
sequence<long arr>;
```

Strings   IDL defines the type string that is similar to a sequence of char. A string can either be bounded or unbounded depending on the way it is declared. The following example demonstrates this.

```
// IDL
string str;        // unbounded string
string name<20>;   // bounded string
```

13.6   ARRAYS

IDL provides multidimensional, fixed-size arrays. The array size in each dimension is fixed at compiletime. Therefore, the size of each dimension must be specified as follows:

```
// IDL
short a[15];        // 1-D array
short table[5][7];  // 2-D array
```

When an array is passed as a parameter in an operation invocation, all elements of the array are transmitted.

13.6.1 Arrays vs. sequences

An array is different from a sequence in the sense that an array is always fixed, whereas a sequence can be of variable size (it may shrink and grow up to the bound in the case of a bounded sequence).

13.7 TYPEDEF DECLARATION

As with struct, union, and enum, a typedef can be used to associate a simple or a more meaningful name with a data type. For example,

```
typedef short size
```

defines size as a synonym for short. Thus, the declaration

```
size m;
```

is equivalent to

```
short m;
```

Similarily, the declaration

```
const unsigned short SIZE = 10;
typedef long array[SIZE];
```

allows a subsequent definition as

```
array a;
```

13.8 CONSTANT DECLARATION

IDL constants can be defined in an interface or a module. For example, the size of an array can be defined as follows:

```
module Arith {
  interface Add {
    const unsigned short SIZE = 15;
    // Rest of definition
  };
};
```

13.9 EXCEPTION DECLARATION

An exception declaration permits the declaration of a data structure which may be used to indicate that an exceptional condition has occurred during the performance of a request. An exception can be specified as follows:

```
// IDL
exception TooMany {
```

```
    string why;
};
```

An exception is declared by the keyword exception followed by the exception type identifier and the members of the exception within braces. A developer can access the values of the members when an exception is raised.

13.10 OPERATIONS DECLARATION

An operation is a function that can be applied to an object, and its declaration is similar to C function declarations. For example, the following interface declares one operation:

```
// IDL
interface BankAccount {
    void deposit(in float amt, out float balance);
};
```

The operation is named deposit() and its return type is specified as void, meaning that the operation does not return a result. The return type of an operation can be any valid type that can be defined in IDL. Also, an operation may specify one or more parameters in its parameter list. For example, the deposit operation above specifies two parameters separated by a comma.

13.10.1 Parameter declaration

A parameter declaration must specify the direction in which the parameter is to be passed. There are three possible directions:

- *in*   The parameter is passed from client to server as input.
- *out*   The parameter is passed from server to client as output.
- *inout*   The parameter is passed in both directions.

13.10.2 Nonblocking operations

The caller of an operation is normally blocked while the operation is being processed. However, if the operation is defined as oneway then the caller is not blocked. A oneway operation must specify a void return type and it cannot have out or inout parameters; it also cannot include a raises expression. The following code segment shows an example:

```
// IDL
interface SnailMail {
    oneway void send(in string letter);
};
```

13.10.3 Raises expressions

An operation may include a raises expression that specifies which exceptions may be raised as a result of an invocation of the operation. The saveFile operation below shows an example of a raises expression:

```
// IDL
interface File {
```

```
    exception Reject {
      string why;
    };
    exception alreadyExists{};
    someInterface saveFile(in string name)
      raises (Reject, alreadyExists);
};
```

The saveFile operation may raise exceptions of type Reject and alreadyExists. An operation may raise any number of exceptions which are listed between the parentheses and separated by commas. However, standard system exceptions that are defined by CORBA cannot be listed in a raises expression. Therefore, even if an operation does not include a raises expression, an invocation of that operation may raise a standard system exception.

13.11 PREPROCESSING

An IDL file may contain preprocessor directives that will be processed before the IDL compiler is invoked. IDL preprocessing is based on ANSI C++ preprocessing. Thus, preprocessor directives allow macro substitution, conditional compilation, and source file inclusion.

A preprocessor directive is specified by placing a # as the first non-white-space character on a line. It may be continued on the next line by placing a backslash (\) character right before the new line at the end of the line to be continued.

13.12 KEYWORDS

The following identifiers are reserved for use as keywords in IDL.

any	default	inout	out	switch
attribute	double	interface	raises	TRUE
boolean	enum	long	readonly	typedef
case	exception	module	sequence	unsigned
char	FALSE	Object	short	union
const	float	octet	string	void
context	in	oneway	struct	

13.13 SUMMARY

- In the CORBA world, the IDL is used to describe the interfaces of objects. IDL itself is part of the OMG CORBA specification.

- An IDL definition consists of one or more text files, which can contain both IDL directives and preprocessor directives. IDL preprocessing is based on the ANSI C++ preprocessing, allowing macro substitution, conditional compilation, and source file inclusion. All pre-processor directives start with a # as the first non-white-space character on the line.

IDL-to-Java mapping

CORBA applications can be developed in any programming language that supports IDL mapping—Java, C, C++, and Lisp are just a few. Once we define an interface to some objects in IDL, we are free to implement the objects using any suitable programming language that supports IDL mapping. To develop a CORBA application in a specific programming language, we need to know how IDL is mapped to that language.

In this chapter, I'll present an overview of the IDL-to-Java mapping 1.0, as defined by the joint submission of different companies to the OMG, and as implemented by VisiBroker's idl2java compiler. Each section will have an example which shows the IDL code first, then the corresponding Java code.

14.1   NAMES

IDL names and identifiers are mapped to the same names and identifiers in Java without any changes. If there is a name collision in the mapped Java code, the name collision is resolved by prepending an underscore (_) to the mapped name in Java.

A single IDL construct may be mapped to several Java constructs. The additional names are constructed by appending a descriptive suffix. For example, the IDL interface foo is mapped to the Java interface foo, and two additional Java classes are created: fooHelper and fooHolder.

14.2 MODULES

An IDL module is mapped to a Java package with the same name. For all IDL types within the module that are mapped to Java classes or Java interfaces, the corresponding Java class or interface is declared inside the Java package that is generated. For example:

```
// IDL
module Example { . . . . };
```

is mapped to:

```
// Generated Java
package Example;
    . . . .
```

14.3 HOLDER CLASSES

Support for out and inout parameter passing modes requires the use of additional *holder* classes.

For the basic IDL types, the holder class name is the Java name (with its initial letter capitalized) to which the type is mapped, with an appended "Holder"—for example, ByteHolder.

Each holder class has a constructor from an instance, a default constructor, and a public instance member (value, which is the typed value). The default constructor sets the value field to the default value for the type as defined by the Java language: false for Boolean, 0 for numeric and char types, and null for strings and object references.

The holder classes for some of the basic data types are defined below. These holder classes are defined in the org.omg.CORBA package. For more information on holder and helper classes, please refer to http://www.omg.org/library/schedule/Technology_Adoptions.html.

```java
// Java
package org.omg.CORBA;

final public class ShortHolder {
   public short value;
   public ShortHolder() {}
   public ShortHolder(short initial) {
      value = initial;
   }
}

final public class IntHolder {
   public int value;
   public IntHolder() {}
   public IntHolder(int initial) {
```

```
        value = initial;
    }
}

final public class LongHolder {
    public long value;
    public LongHolder() {}
    public LongHolder(long initial) {
        value = initial;
    }
}

final public class ByteHolder {
    public byte value;
    public ByteHolder() {}
    public ByteHolder(byte initial) {
        value = initial;
    }
}

final public class FloatHolder {
    public float value;
    public FloatHolder() {}
    public FloatHolder(float initial) {
        value = initial;
    }
}

final public class CharHolder {
    public char value;
    public CharHolder() {}
    public charHolder(char initial) {
        value = initial;
    }
}
```

The following example shows the holder class for a mapping of a user-defined type <foo>:

```
// Java
final public class <foo>Holder implements org.omg.CORBA.portable.Streamable
{
    public <foo> value;
    public <foo>Holder() {}
    public <foo>Holder(<foo> initial) {}
    public void _read(org.omg.CORBA.portable.InputStream i) { . . . . }
    public void _write(org.omg.CORBA.portable.OutputStream o) { . . . . }
    public org.omg.CORBA.TypeCode _type() { . . . . }
}
```

Note that the holder class for the user-defined type (<foo>) above implements the org.omg.CORBA.portable.Streamable interface. This is needed in order to support portable stubs and skeletons.

14.4 CONSTANT VALUES

Constants are mapped differently, depending upon where they appear—one within an interface will appear different from one outside an interface.

14.4.1 Constants within an interface

Constants declared within an IDL interface are mapped to public static final fields in the Java interface corresponding to the IDL interface.

```
// IDL
module Example {
    interface Foo {
        const long aLong = -321;
    };
};
```

```
// Generated Java
package Example;
public interface Foo {
    public static final int aLong = (int) (-321L);
}
```

14.4.2 Constants not within an interface

Constants not declared within an IDL interface are mapped to a public interface with the same name as the constant. This new interface contains a public static final field named value, which holds the constant's value.

```
// IDL
module Example {
    const long aLongOne = -6789;
};
```

```
// Generated Java
package Example;
public interface aLongOne {
    public static final int value = (int)(-6789L);
}
```

14.5 BASIC TYPES

As we discussed in section 13.5.1, IDL provides basic types, such as integer, char, float, boolean, octal, and any. In this section, I will explain how these basic IDL types are mapped into Java.

14.5.1 Boolean

The IDL boolean constants TRUE and FALSE are mapped to the corresponding Java constants true and false.

```
// IDL
module Example {
   const boolean married = FALSE;
};
```

```
// Generated Java
package Example;
final public class married {
   final public static boolean value = false;
}
```

14.5.2 Char

The IDL char is mapped to a Java char.

```
// IDL
module Example {
   const char aChar = 'K';
};
```

```
// Generated Java
package Example {
final public class aChar {
   final public static char value = (char) 'K';
}
```

The IDL wchar maps to the Java primitive type char.

14.5.3 Octet

An IDL octet, an 8-bit quantity, is mapped to the Java type byte.

```
// IDL
interface anOctet {
   void foo(in octet x);
};
```

```
// Generated Java
public interface anOctet extends CORBA.Object {
   public void foo(byte x) throws CORBA.SystemException;
}
```

14.5.4 String

The IDL string, both bounded and unbounded, is mapped to java.lang.String.

```
// IDL
module Example {
   const string aString = "Distributed Programming";
```

```
    };

    // Generated Java
    package Example;
    final public class aString {
        final public static String value = "Distributed Programming";
    }
```

14.5.5   Integer

IDL supports four integer data types: short, long, unsigned short, and unsigned long.
Java has only three integer data types: short, int, and long. The following examples show
what each IDL integer type is mapped to in Java.

```
    // IDL
    module Example {
        const short aShort = -3;
        const unsigned short unsignedShort = 1998;
        const long aLong = -6753;
        const unsigned long unsignedLong = 874321;
    };

    // Generated Java for Example/aShort.java
    package Example;
    final public class aShort {
        final public static short value = (short) (-3L);
    }

    // Generated Java for Example/unsignedShort.java
    package Example;
    final public class unsignedShort {
        final public static short value = (short) 1998;
    }

    // Generated Java for Example/aLong.java
    package Example;
    final public class aLong {
        final public static int value = (int) -6753;
    }

    // Generated Java for Example/unsignedLong.java
    package Example;
    final public class unsignedLong {
        final public static int value = (int) 874321;
    }
```

14.5.6   Floating point

The IDL floating point types float and double map to a Java class containing the corresponding data type.

```
// IDL
module Example {
   const float aFloat = 2.01;
   const double aDouble = 3.827612321;
};


// Generated Java for Example/aFloat.java
package Example;
final public class aFloat {
   final public static float value = (float) 2.01;
}


// Generated Java for Example/aDouble.java
package Example;
final public class aDouble {
   final public static double value = (double) 3.827612321;
}
```

14.6 CONSTRUCTED TYPES

IDL supports the following constructed types: enum, struct, union, and array. The following sections describe how these constructed IDL types are mapped into Java.

14.6.1 Enum

The IDL enum type is mapped to a Java final class with the same name as the enum type,
which declares a value method, two static data members per label, an integer conversion
method, and a private constructor.

One of the members is a public static final that has the same name as the IDL
enum label. The other has an underscore (_) prepended to it and is intended to be used in
switch statements.

```
// IDL
module Example {
   enum Weekend { Sat, Sun };
};


// Generated Java
package Example;
public final class Weekend {
   public static final  int _Sat = 0;
   public static final Weekend Sat = new Weekend(_Sat);

   public static final int _Sun = 1;
   public static final Weekend Sun = new Weekend(_Sun);

   public int value() { . . . . }
   public static Weekend from_int(int value) { . . . . };
```

```
    // Constructor
    private Weekend(int) { . . . . }
}
```

14.6.2   Structure

The IDL type struct is mapped to a Java class that provides instance variables for the fields and a constructor for all values. A null constructor is also provided so that the fields can be filled in later.

The holder class for the struct is also generated. Its name is the struct's mapped Java classname with Holder appended to it, as shown in the following example.

```
// IDL
struct structType {
    long field1;
    string field2;
};
```

```
// Generated Java
final public class structType {
    // Instance variables
    public int field1;
    public String field2;
    // Constructors
    public structType() {}
    public structType(int field1, String field2) { . . . .}
}
```

```
final public class structTypeHolder implements org.omg.CORBA.porta-
ble.Streamable {
    public structType value;
    public structTypeHolder() {}
    public structTypeHolder(structType initial) { . . . . }
    public void _read(org.omg.CORBA.portable.InputStream i) { . . . . }
    public void _write(org.omg.CORBA.portable.OutputStream o) { . . . . }
    public org.omg.CORBA.TypeCpde _type() { . . . . }
}
```

14.6.3   Union

An IDL union is mapped to a final Java class with the same name as the IDL union that provides the following: a default constructor, an accessor method for the union's discriminator, a method for setting each of the union's branches, and a method for retrieving each of the union's branches.

The holder class for the union is also generated. Its name is the union's mapped Java classname with Holder appended to it.

```
// IDL
module Example {
    union unionType switch (EnumType) {
        case first: long win;
```

IDL-TO-JAVA MAPPING

```
            case second: short place;
            case third:
            case fourth: octen show;
            default: boolean other;
    };

    // Generated Java
    final public class unionType {
        // Constructor
        public unionType() { . . . . }

        // Discriminated accessor
        public<switch-type>discriminator() { . . . . }

        // Win
        public int win() { . . . . }
        public void win(int value) { . . . . }

        // Place
        public short place() { . . . . }
        public void place(short value) { . . . . }

        // Show
        public byte show() { . . . . }
        public void show(byte value) { . . . . }
        public void show(int discriminator, byte value) { . . . . }

        // Other
        public boolean other() { . . . . }
        public void other(boolean value) { . . . . }
    }

    final public class unionTypeHolder implements org.omg.CORBA.porta-
    ble.Streamable {
        public unionType value;
        public unionTypeHolder() { }
        public unionTypeHolder(unionType initial) { . . . . }
        public void _read(org.omg.CORBA.portable.InputStream i) { . . . . }
        public void _write(org.omg.CORBA.portable.OutputStream o) { . . . . }
        public org.omg.CORBA.TypeCode _type() { . . . . }
    }
```

14.6.4 Sequence

An IDL sequence is mapped to a Java array with the same name. Anywhere the sequence type is needed, an array of the mapped type of elements is used.

The holder class for the sequence is also generated. Its name is the sequence's mapped Java classname with `Holder` appended to it.

```
// IDL
typedef sequence< long > UnboundedData;
typedef sequence< long, 42 > BoundedData;
```

```
// Generated Java
final public class UnboundedDataHolder implements org.omg.CORBA.porta-
ble.Streamable {
    public int[] value;
    public UnboundedDataHolder() { };
    public UnboundedDataHolder(int[] initial) { . . . . }
    public void _read(org.omg.CORBA.portable.InputStream i) { . . . . }
    public void _write(org.omg.CORBA.portable.OutputStream o) { . . . . }
    public org.omg.CORBA.TypeCode _type() { . . . . }
}

final public class BoundedDataHolder implements org.omg.CORBA.porta-
ble.Streamable {
    public int[] value;
    public BoundedDataHolder() { };
    public BoundedDataHolder(int[] initial) { . . . . };
    public void _read(org.omg.CORBA.portable.InputStream i) { . . . . }
    public void _write(org.omg.CORBA.portable.OutputStream o) { . . . . }
    public org.omg.CORBA.TypeCode _type() { .... }
}
```

14.6.5 Array

An IDL array is mapped to a Java array. Actually, it is mapped the same way as an IDL bounded sequence. Anywhere the array type is needed, an array of the mapped type of element is used.

The holder class for the array is also generated for other constructed data types. Its name is the array's mapped Java classname with `Holder` appended to it.

```
// IDL
const long ArrayBound = 16;
typedef long larray[ArrayBound];

// Generated Java
final public class larrayHolder implements org.omg.CORBA.portable.Stream-
able {
    public int[] value;
    public larrayHolder() { };
    public larrayHolder(int[] initial) { . . . . };
    public void _read(org.omg.CORBA.portable.InputStream i) { . . . . }
    public void _write(org.omg.CORBA.portable.OutputStream o) { . . . . }
    public org.omg.CORBA.TypeCode _type() { . . . . }
}
```

14.7 EXCEPTIONS

An exception in IDL is mapped in the same way that an IDL struct is mapped. A Java class is generated that provides instance variables for each of the fields of the exception.

Exceptions can be one of two types: user-defined exceptions and CORBA system exceptions.

14.7.1 User-defined exceptions

User-defined exceptions are mapped to final Java classes that extend org.omg.CORBA.User-Exception (the user-defined exceptions indirectly inherit from java.lang.Exception); otherwise, they are mapped just like the IDL struct type.

```
// IDL
module Example {
    exception ex1 { string reason; };
};

// Generated Java
package Example;
final public class ex1 extends org.omg.CORBA.UserException {
   public String reason;
   public ex1() { . . . . }
   public ex1(String str) { . . . . }
}

final public class ex1Holder implements org.omg.CORBA.portable.Streamable {
   public ex1 value;
   public ex1Holder() { }
   public ex1Holder(ex1 initial) { . . . . }
   public void _read(org.omg.CORBA.portable.InputStream i) { . . . . }
   public void _write(org.omg.CORBA.portable.OutputStream o) { . . . . }
   public org.omg.CORBA.TypeCode _type() { . . . . }
}
```

14.7.2 System exceptions

Standard IDL system exceptions are mapped to final Java classes that extend org.omg.CORBA.SystemException. The Java class name for each standard IDL exception is the same as its IDL name, and it is declared to be in the package. For a list of all the system exceptions, please refer to http://www.omg.org/library/schedule/Technology_Adoptions.html.

14.8 INTERFACES

An IDL interface is mapped to a public Java interface with the same name, and an additional helper Java class with the suffix Helper is appended to the interface name. The Java interface extends the org.omg.CORBA.Object interface, and it contains the mapped operations' signatures. The helper class holds a static narrow method that allows an org.omg.CORBA.Object to be narrowed to the object reference of a more specific type.

Attributes are mapped to a pair of Java accessor and modifier methods; they will have the same name as the IDL attributes.

The holder class for the interface is also generated. Its name is the interface's mapped Java class name with Holder appended to it.

```
// IDL
module Example {
```

```
        interface Foo {
            long method(in long arg) raises (e);
            attribute long assignable;
            readonly attribute long nonassignable;
        }
    }


// Generated Java
package Example;

public interface Foo extends org.omg.CORBA.Object {
    int method(int arg) throws Example.e;
    int assignable();
    void assignable(int I);
    int nonassignable();
}

public class FooHelper {
    // . . . . some standard helper methods . . . .
    public static Foo narrow(org.omg.CORBA.Object obj) { . . . . }
}
final public class FooHolder implements org.omg.CORBA.portable.Streamable {
    public Foo value;
    public FooHolder() { }
    public FooHolder(Foo initial) { . . . . }
    public void _read(org.omg.CORBA.portable.InputStream i) { . . . . }
    public void _write(org.omg.CORBA.portable.OutputStream o) { . . . . }
    public org.omg.CORBA.TypeCode _type() { . . . . }
}
```

14.8.1 Parameter-passing modes

As we discussed in chapter 13, there are three parameter-passing modes: in, out, and inout. IDL in parameters, which implement call-by-value semantics, are mapped to normal Java actual parameters. The results of IDL operations are returned as the result of the corresponding Java method.

IDL out and inout parameters cannot be mapped directly into the Java parameter-passing mechanism. The mapping defines additional holder classes for all the IDL basic and user-defined types that are used to implement these parameter modes in Java. The client supplies an instance of the appropriate holder Java class that is passed (by value) for each IDL out or inout parameter. Here is an example:

```
// IDL
module Example {
    interface Modes {
        long operation(in long inArg, out long outArg, inout long inoutArg);
    };
};


// Generated Java
```

```
package Example;
public interface Modes {
    int operation(int inArg, IntHolder outArg, IntHolder inoutArg);
}
```

Here are some examples showing how these modes might typically be used:
```
// Developer Java code
// Select a target object.
Example.Modes target = . . . .;
// Get the in actual value.
int inArg = 26;
// Prepare to receive out.
IntHolder outHolder = new IntHolder();
// Set up the in side of the inout.
IntHolder inoutHolder = new IntHolder(115);
// Make the invocation.
int result = target.operation(intArg, outHolder, inoutHolder);
// Use the value of the outHolder.
. . . . outHolder.value . . . .;
// Use the value of the inoutHolder.
. . . . inoutHolder.value . . . .;
```

14.9 TYPEDEF MAPPING

Since Java does not have a typedef construct, the mapping depends whether the typedef is
for simple or complex IDL types.

14.9.1 Simple IDL types

Typedef declarations for simple types are mapped to the original wherever the typedef type
appears. IDL types covered by this rule are covered in section 14.5. However, note that helper
classes are generated for all typedefs.

14.9.2 Complex IDL types

Typedefs for nonarrays and sequences are unwound to their original type until a simple IDL
type or a user-defined type is encountered. Helper classes are generated for sequence and array
typedefs only.

```
// IDL
struct EmpName {
    string firstName;
    string lastName;
};
typedef EmpName EmpRec;

// Generated Java
// Regular struct mapping for EmpName.
// Regular helper class mapping for EmpRec.
final public class EmpName {
    . . . .
```

```
}

public class EmpRecHelper {
    . . . .
}
```

14.10 SUMMARY

- IDL names and identifiers are mapped to Java names and identifiers with no change. However, if there is a name collision in the mapped Java code, it is resolved by prepending an underscore to the mapped name.
- A single IDL construct may be mapped to several Java constructs. The additional names are constructed by appending a descriptive suffix. The IDL interface foo, for example, is mapped to the Java interface foo, plus two additional Java classes: fooHelper and foo-Holder.
- We have described the IDL-to-Java mapping 1.0, as defined by the joint submission of different companies to the OMG, and as implemented by VisiBroker's idl2java compiler. As the IDL-to-Java mapping is constantly changing, you are advised to refer to the latest documentation on the topic by referring to IDL/Java Language Mapping at http://www.omg.org/techprocess/meetings/schedule and The Common Object Request Broker: Architecture and Specification, Revision 2.0. at http://www.omg.org/corba/corbai-iop.html.

C H A P T E R   1 5

Naming and binding

When creating a CORBA object, a server must specify an object name if that object is to be made available to clients through the VisiBroker's Smart Agent (osagent). If an object name is not specified in the bind() method, then the osagent will return any suitable object with the specified interface. A client, on the other hand, must first obtain an object reference using the bind() method before invoking methods on an interface.

In this chapter, I'll demonstrate the bind() method and show you how to uniquely identify objects by developing a simple banking application, which I'll modify throughout this chapter and the next few chapters.

15.1   A BANKING APPLICATION

The arithmetic server we developed in chapter 12 is a simple CORBA application with just one interface. In this chapter, we will develop a more sophisticated CORBA application (a banking application) with two interfaces using some advanced IDL constructs such as readonly. The banking application will use a server to administer and manage bank account objects.

Following the steps for developing a CORBA-based application, which we discussed in chapter 12, the first step is to define an IDL interface that shows the functionality required for the application.

15.1.1 Defining interfaces in IDL

We will need two interfaces for the banking application: an account interface and a manager interface, grouped together in a module. Example 15.1 shows our interfaces as a module.

Example 15.1: Bank.idl

```
// Bank Example
module Bank {
   interface Account {
      readonly attribute float balance;

      void Deposit(in float f);
      void Withdraw(in float f);
   };

   interface Manager {
      Account createAccount(in string customerName);
      Void deleteAccount(in Account acct);
   };
};
```

Compiling Bank.idl with the idl2java compiler generates a number of files, as explained in chapter 12.

15.1.2 Implementing the CORBA classes

Now we can implement the operations defined in the interfaces above. The idl2java compiler has generated two template files we can use to implement the operations: _example_ Account.java and _example_Manager.java. I renamed them AccountImpl.java and Manager-Impl.java respectively.

We'll start by implementing the operations defined in the Account interface. This is shown in example 15.2. I have deleted all the HTML tags generated by the idl2java compiler so the code will be easier to read.

Example 15.2: AccountImpl.java

```
//package Bank;
/**
 * @(#)AccountImpl.java
 * Most of this code was generated by the idl2java compiler.
 * I only had to provide the implementation for the methods.
 */
public class AccountImpl extends Bank._AccountImplBase {
   private float bal;

   /** Construct a persistently named object. */
   public AccountImpl(java.lang.String name) {
     super(name);
   }
   /** Construct a transient object. */
```

```
    public AccountImpl() {
      super();
    }

    public AccountImpl(float balance) {
      bal = balance;
    }

    public void Deposit(
      float f
    ) {
      // IMPLEMENT: Operation
      bal += f;
    }

    public void Withdraw(
      float f
    ) {
      // IMPLEMENT: Operation
      bal -= f;

    }

    public float balance() {
      // IMPLEMENT: Reader for attribute
      return bal;
    }
}
```

Now we can implement the operations defined in the Manager interface. Example 15.3 shows our implementation. I have deleted all the HTML tags that were generated by the idl2java compiler to make the code more compact and easier to read.

Example 15.3: ManagerImpl.java

```
import java.util.*;
/**
 * @(#)ManagerImpl.java
 * Part of this code was generated by the idl2java compiler
 */
public class ManagerImpl extends Bank._ManagerImplBase {
  private Dictionary _accounts = new Hashtable();
  private Random rand = new Random();

  /** Construct a persistently named object. */
  public ManagerImpl(java.lang.String name) {
    super(name);
  }
  /** Construct a transient object. */
  public ManagerImpl() {
    super();
  }
```

```java
public Bank.Account createAccount(
    java.lang.String customerName
) {
    // IMPLEMENT: Operation
    Bank.Account acct = (Bank.Account) _accounts.get(customerName);
    if (acct == null) {
        float bal = Math.abs(rand.nextInt()) % 100000 / 100f;
        acct = new AccountImpl(bal);
        _boa().obj_is_ready(acct);
        System.out.println("Account created.");
        _accounts.put(customerName, acct);
    }
    return acct;
}
public void deleteAccount(
    Bank.Account acct
) {
    // IMPLEMENT: Operation
    Bank.Account account = (Bank.Account) _accounts.get(acct);
    if (account == null) {
        System.out.println("No such account exists");
    } else {
        _accounts.remove(account);
        System.out.println("deleted");
    }

}
}
```

15.1.3   Developing the server

Now we are ready to develop our server program, which is very similar to the server in chapter 12 except that this server creates an object of type `Manager`. Example 15.4 shows our server.

Example 15.4: Server.java

```java
import org.omg.CORBA.*;
/**
 * @(#)Server.java
 */
public class Server {
    public static void main(String argv[]) {
        try {
            ORB orb = ORB.init();
            BOA boa = orb.BOA_init();
            Bank.Manager  manager = new ManagerImpl("Bank");
            boa.obj_is_ready(manager);
            System.out.println("Manager is ready");
            boa.impl_is_ready();
        } catch(SystemException e) {
            e.printStackTrace();
        }
```

```
        }
    }
```

15.1.4 Developing the client

Finally, we can develop our client. The client binds to the server and invokes some operations. The client, which is shown in example 15.5, performs the following operations:

- Creates an account.
- Deposits some money.
- Prints out the balance.
- Withdraws some money.
- Shows the new balance.

Example 15.5: Client.java

```java
import org.omg.CORBA.*;
/**
 * @(#)Client.java
 */
public class Client {
    public static void main(String argv[]) {
        String name = "Qusay H. Mahmoud";
        float bal = 0.0;
        try {
            ORB orb = ORB.init();
            Bank.Manager manager = Bank.ManagerHelper.bind(orb,"Bank");
            Bank.Account account = manager.createAccount(name);
            account.Deposit((float)128.4);
            bal = (float) account.balance();
            System.out.println("Balance = "+bal);
            account.Withdraw((float)400.0);
            bal = (float) account.balance();
            System.out.println("Balance = "+bal);
        } catch (SystemException e) {
            e.printStackTrace();
        }
    }
}
```

15.1.5 Running the application

Now we can run our application by first running the osagent, then running the server and the client.

```
% osagent &

% vbj Server
Manager is ready

% vbj Client
```

```
Balance = 733.77
Balance = 633.77
```

If you look at the Client.java code and wonder how we got such a balance, take another look at the ManagerImpl.java code and notice that when we create a new account, we give it an initial random balance.

15.2 NAMING OBJECTS

The name of an object represents its unique object reference. The object's interface name and its object name are unique within the object's server. Therefore, when creating an object, a server must specify an object name if that object is to be made available to clients through the osagent.

When the server calls the BOA.obj_is_ready() method, the object's interface will only be registered with the osagent if the object is named. If an object is given a name at creation time, it will return a persistent object reference.

Having names for objects helps in distinguishing between multiple instances of an interface. Thus, the use of an object name by your client application is required if it plans to bind to more than one instance of an object at a time. However, if an object name is not specified in the bind() call, then the osagent will return any suitable object with the specified interface.

As you saw in the bank application earlier in this chapter, the Server class instantiated a Manager object using the ManagerImpl constructor that accepts an object name. Example 15.6 shows the server code for creating a ManagerImpl object called NovaBank.

Example 15.6: NovaServer.java

```java
import org.omg.CORBA.*;
/**
 * @(#)NovaServer.java
 */
public class NovaServer {
   public static void main(String argv[]) {
     try {
       ORB orb = ORB.init();
       BOA boa = orb.BOA_init();
       Bank.Manager  manager = new ManagerImpl("NovaBank");
       boa.obj_is_ready(manager);
       System.out.println("Manager is ready");
       boa.impl_is_ready();
     } catch(SystemException e) {
       e.printStackTrace();
     }
   }
}
```

15.3 BINDING TO OBJECTS

Your client application must first obtain an object reference using the bind method before it can invoke methods on an interface. The following code segment from the bank client shows how the client would connect to the manager at NovaBank.

```
public class Client {
   public static void main(String argv[]) {
      String name = "Qusay H. Mahmoud";
      float bal = 0.0;
      try {
        ORB orb = ORB.init();
        Bank.Manager manager = Bank.ManagerHelper.bind(orb,"NovaBank");
        Bank.Account account = manager.createAccount(name);
        account.Deposit((float)128.4);
        // . . . . more code . . . .
      } catch {}
   }
}
```

As you can see from the example above, the bind method requires that an ORB object be supplied as the first parameter. The bind method has two forms; the first is where the only parameter to bind is the ORB object. This form of bind will connect your client to a suitable implementation of the object being referenced. The second form, like the one used in the first example in this section, has a string argument in addition to the ORB object. If the string represents a URL, however, the ORB uses the URL Naming Service to bind to an object.

15.3.1 The binding functionality

Invoking the bind method from the client causes the ORB to perform several functions on behalf of your client application.

- The ORB communicates with the osagent to locate an object server that is offering the requested interface.
- When an object implementation is located, the ORB attempts to establish a connection between the object implementation that was located and your client application.
- If the connection is successfully established, the ORB will create a proxy object, if necessary, and return a reference to that object.

15.3.2 Specifying bind options

The behavior of the bind process can be controlled by specifying options to the bind method. The following code, for example, shows the bind method generated by the idl2java compiler for the ManagerHelper class, which allows you to specify bind options.

```
abstract public class ManagerHelper {
   . . . .
   public static Bank.Manager bind(org.omg.CORBA.ORB orb, java.lang.String
name, java.lang.String host, org.omg.CORBA.BindOptions options) {
      . . . .
```

```
                   . . . .
        }
                   . . . . .
                   . . . . .
}
```

The BindOptions class allows you to control various aspects of the connection between the client and the server. The class has two Boolean values: defer_bind and enable_rebind.

If defer_bind is set to true, a connection will not be established with the object implementation when bind is invoked; rather, it will be established when your client invokes a method on the object. If defer_bind is set to false, the connection will be established when bind is invoked. This is the default behavior.

The enable_rebind field can be used for fault tolerance. For example, if the connection between the client and object implementation fails for some reason (such as a network error), then VisiBroker will automatically attempt to rebind to the server or a replica of that server. To prevent the rebinding process, set enable_rebind to false; otherwise, it will automatically be set to true, which is the default behavior.

15.3.3   Local vs. remote object location

If a client requests an object that resides on a remote host, a TCP/IP connection will be established between the client and the object server. The ORB will instantiate a stub for your client to use. When a method is invoked on the proxy object, it will be marshaled and sent to the server, and the server will, in return, unmarshal the request, invoke the requested method, and send the results back to the client. On the other hand, if the client requests an object that resides in the same address space, then once your client invokes a bind method, the ORB returns a pointer to the object implementation. All methods invoked on the client's object will then get directly called as regular Java methods on the object implementation.

15.3.4   Operations on object references

When a client invokes the bind method, an object reference will be returned to the client. Your client can use this object reference to invoke methods on the object that have been defined in the object's interface. There are also a number of methods which an ORB object inherits from the org.omg.CORBA.Object class that you can use. Some of these methods are listed below.

- *_is_a*   Determines if an object implements a specified interface.
- *_is_bound*   Returns true if a connection is currently active for this object.
- *_is_local*   Returns true if the object is implemented in the same address space.
- *_is_remote*   Returns true if the object's implementation does not reside in the local address space.
- *_object_name*   Returns this object's name.

15.3.5 Narrowing object references

Narrowing is the process of converting an object reference's type from a general supertype to a more specific subtype. Narrowing can be accomplished with VisiBroker using the object's narrow method, as shown below:

```
abstract public class ManagerHelp {
    . . . .
    public static Bank.Manager narrow(org.omg.CORBA.Object object) {
        . . . .
    }
}
```

If the narrow method determines that it is not possible to narrow an object to the requested type, it will return null.

15.4 SUMMARY

- The name of an object represents its unique object reference. If an object is to be made available to clients through the VisiBroker's Smart Agent (osagent), then a server must specify an object name when creating that object. If an object name is not specified in the bind() method, then the osagent will return any suitable object with the specified interface.
- A client must first obtain an object reference using the bind() method before invoking methods on an interface. The client's call to bind() causes the ORB to perform several functions on behalf of the client: the ORB communicates with the osagent to locate an object server offering the requested interface; the ORB attempts to establish a connection between the object implementation and the client; and, finally, if the connection is successfully established, the ORB creates a proxy object if necessary, and returns a reference to that object.
- You can control the behavior of the binding process by specifying options to the bind() method. The BindOptions class has two Boolean values: defer_bind and enable_bind. Depending on the value (true or false) they are set to, defer_bind and enable_bind can be used to determine when a connection should be established. They can also be used for fault tolerance.
- The process of converting an object reference's type from a general supertype to a more specific subtype is called narrowing. In VisiBroker, you accomplish this by calling the object's narrow() method.

C H A P T E R 1 6

Registering and activating objects

A CORBA object is created when its implementation class is instantiated by a server. The server uses the BOA to activate its objects so clients can use them. The BOA provides several functions to client applications and the object implementations they use.

In this chapter, we'll discuss the functionality provided by the BOA for client applications and object implementations, along with an overview of the several adapter types supported by VisiBroker. You'll learn about the various activation modes, the Implementation Repository, and how VisiBroker's implementation (object activation daemon) of the Implementation Repository activates objects.

16.1   THE BASIC OBJECT ADAPTER

VisiBroker's BOA provides several functions to client applications and the object implementations they use, including providing several activation modes, registering object implementations with VisiBroker's Smart Agent, and storing information about object implementations residing on a server within the Implementation Repository.

VisiBroker for Java supports several adapter types. Object adapters are initialized with `BOA_init()` and they may be one of the following types:

- *TPool*   Thread pooling.
- *TSession*   Thread per session.
- *SSLTPool*   SSL with thread pooling.
- *SSLTSession*   SSL with thread per session.

There are two versions of `BOA_init()`:

- If you call the `BOA_init()` with no arguments, you get the default thread policy, which is thread pooling. This call will return an instance of `TPool`.
- You can pass arguments to `BOA_init()` to get the adapter type and its properties. Pass `null` if you do not want to set any properties.

16.2   OBJECT ACTIVATION MODES

VisiBroker provides a number of activation modes for launching servers. These activation modes apply only to objects with a global scope. The three supported modes are:

- *Shared server mode*   In this mode, an object with the same implementation in the server can be accessed by multiple clients. Only one implementation will be activated by the object activation daemon (OAD) at a time.
- *Unshared server mode*   In this mode, servers are accessed by one client only. If multiple clients wish to bind to the same object implementation, a separate server is activated for each client application.
- *Server-per-method mode*   This activation mode requires a server process to be started for each method that is invoked. After the method has been completed, the server will exit. Any subsequent method invocation on the same object will require a new server process to be started.

16.3   OBJECT REFERENCES

An ORB object is created when its implementation class is instantiated by an object implementation or a server. An object implementation uses the BOA to activate its ORB objects so that clients can use them. There are two types of object references: *transient* and *persistent*.

16.3.1   Transient object references

Transient object references are those objects that are only available during the lifetime of the server that creates them. A transient object reference can be created simply by not specifying an object name when instantiating the object, as shown in the following code segment:

```
public class Server {
   public static void main(String argv[]) {
      try {
         ORB orb = ORB.init();
         BOA boa = orb.BOA_init();
         Bank.Manager manager = new ManagerImpl();
         boa.obj_is_ready();       // Export the object.
```

```
        boa.impl_is_ready();     // Wait for incoming requests.
      } catch (SystemException e) {
        e.printStackTrace();
      }
    }
  }
```

16.3.2 Persistent object references

Persistent object references differ from transient object references in the sense that persistent object references remain valid beyond the lifetime of the server that created them.

A persistent object reference can be created when instantiating an object and specifying an object name. This type of object reference is registered with VisiBroker's directory service. Therefore, it can be allocated by the osagent and used by client applications. The following example shows how to create a persistent object reference.

```
public class Server {
  public static void main(String argv[]) {
    try {
      ORB orb = ORB.init();
      BOA boa = orb.BOA_init();
      Bank.Manager manager = new ManagerImpl("Bank Manager");
      boa.obj_is_ready(manager);   // Export the object.
      boa.impl_is_ready();         // Wait for incoming requests.
    } catch (SystemException e) {
      e.printStackTrace();
    }
  }
}
```

Your client applications can check whether an object reference is persistent or transient using the Object._is_persistent method. This method returns true if the reference is persistent and false if it is transient. This method is useful because some methods (such as object_to_string) will fail if an object is transient.

16.4 REGISTERING AN OBJECT

Once a server has instantiated the ORB objects that it offers, the BOA must be notified of the object initialization. The BOA is also notified when the server is ready to receive requests from clients. We have seen examples of this already, such as when we used the obj_is_ready method to notify the BOA that an ORB object was ready to receive requests from clients. Bear in mind that if your server offers more than one object, it must invoke the obj_is_ready method for each object, with the object reference as an argument. If the object reference is persistent, it will be registered with VisiBroker's directory service, and if it is transient, no such registration takes place.

Once an object has been instantiated and all the required obj_is_ready methods have been invoked, the server must invoke the impl_is_ready method to wait for client requests.

If obj_is_ready has not been invoked on an object and a client attempts to bind to it, the exception NO_IMPLEMENT will be raised.

If an object is registered by calling the obj_is_ready method, then that object can be deactivated by calling deactivate_obj, which will allow the Java garbage collection to reclaim the object. Once this method is invoked, the object implementation will not be available to service clients.

16.5 *THE IMPLEMENTATION REPOSITORY*

The Implementation Repository provides a run-time database of information about the classes a server provides, the objects that are instantiated, and their identifiers. The details of the Implementation Repository are not part of the CORBA standard.

VisiBroker ORB provides an implementation for CORBA's Implementation Repository. The implementation is known as the OAD. The OAD however, is also used to automatically activate an implementation when a client requests a bind to an object; figure 16.1 shows a client requesting a bind to an object. The object is started manually, without the use of the OAD.

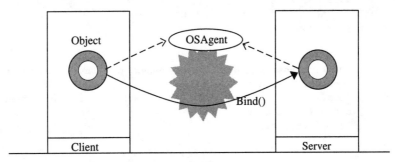

Figure 16.1 An object started manually

Figure 16.2 shows a client requesting a bind to an object and the object being started through the OAD.

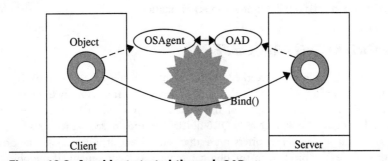

Figure 16.2 An object started through OAD

Registering object implementations can either be done using a command-line utility (oadutil) or using the ORB interface to the OAD. For example, to register an object implementation from the command line, the oadutil command can be used with the required parameters (the interface name, object name, and path name). If an activation policy is not specified, shared server is the default. If you do not specify a host, then the OAD will only look for the object locally. As an example, the following command registers the server from the Bank example:

```
% oadutil reg -i Bank:Manager -o BankManager -java Server -p Shared
```

The oadutil has options not only for registering object implementation, but also for unregistering and listing object implementations. Please refer to the VisiBroker Reference Manual, available at http://www.inprise.com, for the options.

Note that all implementation repository data are stored in a file named impl_rep; its path is dependent on where VisiBroker was installed. For example, if VisiBroker was installed on /opt/vbroker/, the path to the file would be /opt/vbroker/adm/impl_dir/impl_rep/.

The OAD is a separate process that only needs to be run on hosts where objects are to be activated on demand.

16.6 SUMMARY

- The BOA provides several functions to client applications and the object implementations they use, including registering object implementations with VisiBroker's Smart Agent, storing information about object implementations residing on a server within the Implementation Repository, and providing several activation modes. The three supported activation modes are shared server mode, unshared server mode, and server-per-method mode.

- Two versions of the BOA_init() are available. You can pass arguments to BOA_init() to get the adapter type and its properties; otherwise, you get the default thread policy (thread pooling).

- There are two types of object references: transient and persistent. Transient objects are only available during the lifetime of the server that created them. Persistent objects remain valid beyond the lifetime of the server that created them.

- Once a server instantiates the ORB objects that it offers, the BOA must be notified of this initialization. The obj_is_ready() method notifies the BOA that an ORB object is ready to receive requests from clients.

- The implementation repository provides a run-time database of information about the classes a server provides. VisiBroker's implementation of the Implementation Repository is known as the OAD. OAD also automatically activates an implementation when a client requests a bind to an object.

CHAPTER 17

Inheritance and the tie mechanism

An IDL interface can extend the functionality of one or more existing interfaces via the inheritance mechanism. Despite the fact that a Java class may implement multiple interfaces, Java does not support multiple inheritance of classes. So how can we inherit from a server skeleton and another class?

This chapter presents an overview of interface inheritance, and it discusses an alternative approach—the tie mechanism—for inheriting from a skeleton and another class. I'll compare both approaches to help you determine when to use what.

17.1   INTERFACE INHERITANCE

IDL allows a new interface to extend the functionality of an existing interface via the inheritance mechanism. The existing interface is known as the *base* interface, and the new interface is known as the *derived* interface. A derived interface may declare new elements such as constants, types, attributes, operations, and exceptions. Unless they are redefined in the derived interface, the elements of a base interface can be referred to as if they were elements of the derived interface. To refer to a base element explicitly, the name resolution operator (: :) can be used.

An interface may be derived from any number of base interfaces. In other words, IDL supports multiple inheritance in which a new interface may have two or more immediate base interfaces.

17.1.1 Example

Suppose we want to extend the bank example discussed in chapter 15 to handle checking accounts. The new module of interfaces would then be as follows:

```
module Bank {
    interface Account {
       readonly attribute float balance;
       void Deposit(in float f);
       void Withdraw(in float f);
    };

    // Extending Account.
    interface checkingAccount : Account {
        readonly attribute float overLimit;
    };

    interface Manager {
        Account createAccount(in string customerName);
        void deleteAccount(in Account acct);
        checkingAccount createCheckingAcct(in string customerName, in float
limit);
    };
};
```

Notice how the new interface checkingAccount extends, or inherits from, the Account interface. Also, note the new operation, createCheckingAcct, that we added to the Manager interface.

17.2 THE TIE MECHANISM

All the CORBA-based server programs we have developed so far extend a CORBA skeleton; however, there are times when inheriting a skeleton is not appropriate. For example, Java does not support multiple inheritance, so we cannot inherit from a skeleton and another class. In such cases, the *tie mechanism*, which offers an alternative approach to inheritance, can be used.

One thing to be aware of, however, is that inheritance is easier to use since implementation objects look like normal object references. Also, if object implementations are in the same process as the client using them, then method invocations would be cheaper—they involve fewer overheads since no delegation is required. The tie mechanism provides a delegator implementation class that inherits from CORBA.Object. This delegator simply delegates every invocation to the real implementation class, which can be implemented separately and can inherit from whichever class it needs to.

17.2.1 Example

This section contains a version of the bank example using the tie mechanism. As you will see, you only need to make minor modifications in order to use the tie mechanism instead of inheritance.

As you learned in chapter 12 when we discussed the idl2java compiler, a number of files are automatically generated when you run the idl2java compiler on an IDL file. One important file to note is _tie_interfaceName, where *interfaceName* is the name of the interface. So for this example, we would have two tie files: _tie_Account and _tie_Manager. These two files are actually delegator implementations for the interfaces Account and Manager. Now the AccountImpl and ManagerImpl classes no longer need to inherit from the skeleton classes _sk_Account and _sk_Manager. Both classes are now free to inherit from another class.

The next three sections show the various modifications needed for the implementation classes.

17.2.2 Changes to the Server class

The Server class needs to be modified to accommodate the extra step needed for creating an instance of _tie_Manager. Therefore, the Server class will perform four major tasks:

- Create a manager.
- Create a _tie_Manager and initialize it with the manager.
- Export the _tie_Manager object.
- Wait for requests from clients.

Example 17.1 shows the modifications to the Server class.

Example 17.1: Server.java

```
/**
 * @(#)Server.java
 */
public class Server {
   public static void main(String argv[]) {
      try {
         CORBA.ORB orb = CORBA.ORB.init();
         CORBA.BOA boa = orb.BOA_init();
         Manager manager = new Manager();
         Bank.Manager manager2 = new Bank._tie_Manager(manager, "Bank");
         // Export the object reference.
         boa.obj_is_ready(manager);
         System.out.println("The Acct Manager is ready.");
         // Wait for requests.
         boa.impl_is_ready();
      } catch (SystemException e) {
         e.printStackTrace();
      }
   }
}
```

17.2.3 Changes to the AccountImpl class

With the availability of the tie mechanism, classes no longer need to inherit from skeletons. The only change that needs to be made to the Account class is that it should no longer extend the skeleton _sk_Account.

17.2.4 Changes to the ManagerImpl class

A few changes need to be made to the ManagerImpl class.

- The Manager class should no longer extend the skeleton _sk_Manager.
- When a new account is created, a _tie_Account is also created and initialized.
- The _tie_Account is exported.

Example 17.2 shows the modifications to the ManagerImpl class. These modifications are to be made to the createAccount method in example 15.3.

Example 17.2: ManagerImpl.java

```
/**
 * @(#)ManagerImpl.java
 */
class Manager implements Bank.ManagerOperations {
    // . . . .
    // Everything else is the same as in example 15.3.
    // . . . .

    // When an account is created we do this:
    Account acct = new Account(name);
    // Create the tie object for the account.
    acct = new Bank._tie_Account(acct);
    // Everything else is the same as in example 15.3.

    // Export the object reference.
    CORBA.ORB.init().BOA_init().obj_is_ready(acct);
    // Everything else is the same as in example 15.3.
}
```

17.3 SUMMARY

- IDL supports single and multiple inheritance. A new interface is allowed to extend the functionality of one or more existing interfaces via the inheritance mechanism.
- Throughout our study of CORBA so far, we have been extending a CORBA skeleton. There are times, however, when extending the functionality of a skeleton is not a valid solution. For example, Java does not support multiple inheritance (even though a class may implement multiple interfaces). Therefore, in Java we cannot inherit from a skeleton and another class. In this situation, the tie mechanism offers an alternative.

- The tie mechanism provides a delegator implementation class that inherits from a CORBA.object. The delegator simply delegates every invocation to the real implementation class. The real implementation class can then inherit from whichever class it needs.
- Inheritance is easier to use than a tie, since implementation objects look like normal object references. Use inheritance if you want to inherit from a CORBA skeleton only, and use the tie mechanism if you want to inherit from a CORBA skeleton and another class.

C H A P T E R   1 8

The Dynamic Invocation/ Skeleton Interface

The IDL interfaces used by a client are determined when the client is compiled. The programmer is therefore limited to using servers that contain objects that implement those interfaces. But what if an application such as a distributed debugger requires the use of interfaces that are not defined at the time the application was developed?

The solution is provided by CORBA's DII and DSI. DII allows an application to invoke operations from any interface. DSI provides a way to deliver requests from an ORB to an object implementation without any compile-time knowledge of the type of the object it is implementing. Clients use the IR to learn about unknown object interfaces and they use DII to invoke methods on the object.

In this chapter, I'll discuss DII, DSI, and the IR in detail, and I'll show you how to combine these mechanisms to develop sophisticated CORBA applications.

18.1 THE DYNAMIC INVOCATION INTERFACE

The IDL interfaces a client can use are determined when the client program is compiled. Therefore, the client's programmer is limited to using servers that contain objects that implement those interfaces. However, some applications and tools (such as distributed debuggers) require the use of interfaces which were not defined at the time the application was developed. CORBA supports a DII that allows an application to invoke operations from any interface, even if that interface was unknown at the time the application was compiled. Figure 18.1 shows a client invoking a request using the DII.

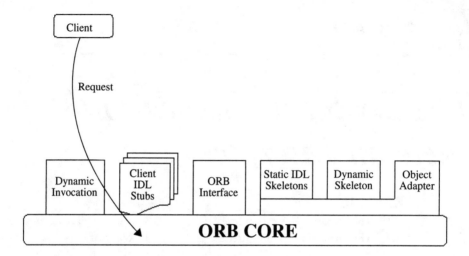

Figure 18.1 A client invoking a request using DII

It is important to note that client applications that use DII are not as efficient as applications that use static operation requests; however, the use of DII offers two main advantages:

- Client applications may issue requests for any operation, even if that operation was unknown at the time the application was compiled.
- Client applications do not need to be recompiled in order to access newly activated object implementations.

18.1.1 Using DII

In order for a client to use DII, the client's programmer must follow these steps:

1 Obtain an object reference for the target object he wants to use.
2 Create a Request object.
3 Initialize the request parameters and the result to be returned.
4 Invoke the request.
5 Get the results.

The idl2java compiler has a flag (-portable). If this flag is switched on, the compiler will generate stub code using DII.

The code that follows illustrates some of the steps defined above:

```
// Obtain an object reference.
CORBA.Object object;
object = orb.string_to_object(ior);

// Create a request object.
CORBA.Request request = object._request("create");

// Initialize parameters.
request.arguments().add_value("name", new
CORBA.Any().from_string(acctName), CORBA.ARG_IN.value);
request.result().value().from_Object(null);

// Invoke the request.
request.invoke();

// Retrieve the result.
float balance = request.result().value().to_float();
```

Let's now take a closer look at what is actually happening in this code. The code is performing the following tasks:

1 Using the CORBA.Object.string_to_object method to obtain a reference to an object. The ior stands for Internet object reference, and it is created by calling the method string_to_object on the server object. So ior in this example is really a string that is given by the user.

2 Creating a request whose operation is named "create".

3 Using the CORBA.Request.add_value method to set the input argument.

4 Setting the type of the return value. Since the purpose of DII is to be able to invoke operations without compile-time information, we do not know the actual type of the argument. Therefore, we use the type CORBA.Object.

5 Invoking the DII request.

6 Retrieving the resulting object from the request.

18.1.2   Request parameters

Before you can send a request, you must first define the type and usage of each parameter. The type of the parameter defines how that parameter will be marshaled and unmarshaled. The use of the parameter is defined as one of the following:

- in   Used for input.
- out   Used for output.
- inout   Used for both input and output.

The parameters must be initialized before a request is sent; if its not, marshaling errors will occur.

18.2 THE DYNAMIC SKELETON INTERFACE

The DSI is a way to deliver requests from an ORB to an object implementation without any compile-time knowledge of the type of the object it is implementing. Figure 18.2 shows an object implementation receiving a request through DSI.

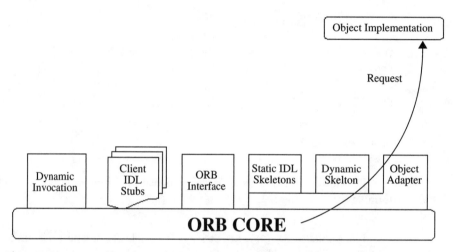

Figure 18.2 An object implementation receiving a request through DSI

DSI is analogous to DII in the sense that DII is for the client side and DSI is for the server side. Both DII and DSI have many applications beyond interoperability solutions. These uses may include interactive software development tools based on interpreters, and distributed debuggers.

18.2.1 Using DSI

In order to use DSI for your server object implementation, you must follow these steps:

1 Design your object implementation so that it extends the abstract class `org.omg.CORBA.DynamicImplementation` instead of extending a skeleton object.

2 Declare and implement the `invoke` method that the ORB will use to dispatch client requests to your object.

3 Register your object implementation with the BOA using the `boa.obj_is_ready` method.

The following code segment shows the declaration of the `Account` object to be implemented with DSI:

```
class AccountImpl extends org.omg.CORBA.DynamicImplementation {
    AccountImpl(float balance) {
```

```
    Super(name, "IDL:Bank:Account:1.0");
  }
  void invoke(org.omg.CORBA.ServerRequest request) {

     . . . .

  }

   . . . .

}
```

The `invoke` method is included in the `AccountImpl` class because the class is extending the `DynamicImplementation` class. The ORB will use the `invoke` method to pass client operation requests to the object in the form of `ServerRequest` objects.

In the example above, we are calling the `DynamicImplementation` class's constructor, which allows us to create a server object by specifying a string that represents the repository identifier of that object being implemented. Notice that we are specifying the correct repository identifier (`IDL:Bank/Account:1.0`). If we have an interface named `Hello:SayHi`, the corresponding repository identifier would be `IDL:Hello/SayHi:1.0`.

18.3   *THE INTERFACE REPOSITORY*

The IR is like a database that contains data that describes CORBA interfaces or types. The information contained in an IR is equivalent to that in an IDL file except that information in the IR is represented in such a way that makes it easier for clients to use. Figure 18.3 shows the structure of the interface and implementation repositories.

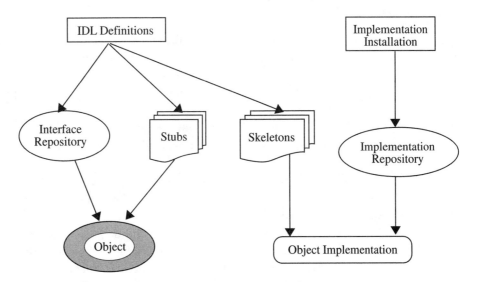

Figure 18.3 Interface and implementation repositories

Clients use the IR to learn about unknown object interfaces, and they use DII to invoke methods on that object. However, this does not mean that IR and DII are tied together in any way.

Using VisiBroker, an IR can be created using the irep server program, and you can update or populate an IR using the idl2ir utility. Note that interface repositories are like normal objects, so there is no limit on the number of IRs you can create. However, you should follow some kind of convention on the number of IRs you want to deploy for your site—for example, create one central IR for all production objects, then developers can create their own IRs for testing.

18.3.1 Creating an IR

The irep program can be used to create and view interface repositories. Here is the syntax to use irep:

```
% irep [-console] IRname [file.idl]
```

where `-console` directs the program to present a command line interface instead of a GUI interface. `IRname` specifies the instance name of the IR, so clients can bind to it using this name. And `file.idl` specifies the IDL file whose contents will be loaded into the created IR. If no files are specified, irep creates an empty IR.

The following command shows how an interface repository named MyIR can be created from a file called MyInterface.idl.

```
% irep MyIR MyInterface.idl
```

18.4 SUMMARY

- The IDL interfaces used by a client are determined when the client is compiled. The programmer is therefore limited to using servers containing objects that implement those interfaces. But some applications—for example, distributed debuggers—may require the use of interfaces that are not defined at the time the application was developed.
- CORBA's DII allows an application to invoke operations from any interface, even if an interface was unknown at the time the application was compiled. DII is for the client side.
- The DSI differs from DII in that it is for the server side. DSI provides a way to deliver requests from an ORB to an object implementation without any compile-time knowledge of the type of the object it is implementing.
- The interface repository is a database that contains data about CORBA interfaces and types. Information contained in the IR is equivalent to that in an IDL file except that the data in the IR is represented in such a way that makes it easier for clients to use. Clients use the IR to learn about unknown object interfaces, and DII to invoke methods on the object. However, IR and DII are not tied together in any way.

C H A P T E R   1 9

Caffeine

Unlike RMI interfaces, CORBA interfaces are defined in IDL. This means that to develop a CORBA-based application, we not only need to know IDL syntax, we must also know how IDL is mapped to Java.

Caffeine is a set of features that has been added to VisiBroker for developing distributed applications. The main idea of Caffeine is that we can use Java instead of IDL to define CORBA interfaces. Caffeine's java2iiop compiler then generates IIOP-compliant stubs and skeletons. Caffeine also has other advantages, as you will see throughout the chapter.

In this chapter, I'll give you an overview of Caffeine and show it can be used to develop distributed applications that are IIOP-compliant.

19.1   OVERVIEW OF CAFFEINE

Inprise Corporation has added a set of features to VisiBroker for Java that is collectively known as Caffeine. In some ways, Caffeine is similar to RMI in the sense that interfaces are defined in Java rather than in IDL (such as with CORBA). Here are the features that constitute Caffeine:

- The java2iiop compiler, which allows you to stay in a Java environment. The java2iiop compiler generates IIOP-compliant stubs and skeletons from your Java interfaces. As you learned in chapter 11, objects in CORBA are passed by reference. One advantage of using the java2iiop compiler is that through the use of complex data structures, it becomes possible to pass objects by value.
- The java2idl compiler turns your Java interfaces into IDL interfaces, which then allows you to generate stubs and skeletons for the language of your choice.
- Web Naming allows URL-based naming, in which URLs can be associated with objects—you can obtain an object reference by specifying a URL.

19.2   USING THE JAVA2IIOP COMPILER

As I mentioned above, the java2iiop compiler allows you to define interfaces in Java (rather than IDL) which can be used in CORBA. Note that the java2iiop compiler reads bytecodes, not Java source code. This means it reads .class files, not .java files. The java2iiop compiler generates the IIOP-compliant stubs and skeletons needed for marshaling and communication in CORBA.

The java2iiop compiler generates the same files (including helper and holder classes) as if the interface was written in IDL. It understands all data types, and each one is mapped to its corresponding type in IDL.

When you're using the java2iiop compiler, such as with RMI (where an interface must extend the Remote interface), interfaces must be defined as remote interfaces by having them extending the org.omg.CORBA.Object interface. The following code segment illustrates this:

```
// myInterface.java
public interface myInterface extends org.omg.CORBA.Object {
    int sayHi();
}
```

Once you have an interface, you must compile it with javac to generate bytecodes; then we can run the java2iiop compiler on it, as follows:

```
% javac myInterface.java

% java2iiop myInterface
```

19.3   ANATOMY OF A CAFFEINE-BASED APPLICATION

To develop an application using Caffeine, follow these steps.

1 Define a remote interface (as shown above) in Java and compile its bytecodes with java2iiop.

2 Use the skeleton class to create an implementation of the server object.

3 Compile the server class using javac.

4 Write the client code.

5 Compile the client code using javac.

6 Start the server object.

7 Start the client.

To demonstrate how to use Caffeine, I will walk you through these seven steps as we program the arithmetic server we developed in previous chapters using sockets, RMI, and CORBA. Remember, the arithmetic server takes two arrays of integers from a client, adds them item by item, and then returns the sum, as an array, to the client.

Using Caffeine, the first step is to define an interface for the arithmetic server.

19.3.1 Defining an interface

The interface should contain enough information about the signature of the methods so the client will have an idea of how to invoke them. The arithmetic interface in this example is simple; it will provide just one method that takes two arrays of integers as an argument and returns the sum as an array of integers. Example 19.1 shows the Arith interface.

Example 19.1: Arith.java

```
/**
 * @(#)Arith.java
 */
public interface Arith extends org.omg.CORBA.Object {
    int[] add(int a[], int b[]);
}
```

Notice how the interface is extending the CORBA Object interface. In RMI, we had to extend the Remote interface.

Now we can compile the interface using the javac compiler to generate bytecodes. Once we have the bytecodes, we can run the java2iiop compiler on them. Remember that the java2iiop compiler takes bytecodes as input.

```
% javac Arith.java


% java2iiop Arith
Creating: ArithPackage
Creating: ArithPackage/sequence_of_longHolder.java
Creating: ArithPackage/sequence_of_longHelper.java
Creating: ArithHolder.java
Creating: ArithHelper.java
Creating: _st_Arith.java
Creating: _ArithImplBase.java
Creating: ArithOperations.java
Creating: _tie_Arith.java
Creating: _example_Arith.java
```

The generated files are the same files that would have been generated by the idl2java compiler, which we discussed in chapter 12.

19.3.2 Writing a server object

The second step in developing an application using Caffeine is to write a server object. This server object will have to extend the skeleton class `ArithImplBase`. The code for the server object is shown in example 19.2:

Example 19.2: ArithServer.java

```
/**
 * @(#)ArithServer.java
 */
public class ArithServer extends _ArithImplBase {
    ArithServer(String name) {
        super(name);
    }

    public int[] add(int a[], int b[]) {
        int sum[] = new int[10];
        for(int i=0; i<a.length; i++) {
            sum[i] = a[i] + b[i];
        }
        return sum;
    }

    public static void main(String argv[]) {
        org.omg.CORBA.ORB orb = org.omg.CORBA.ORB.init(argv, null);
        org.omg.CORBA.BOA boa = orb.BOA_init();
        Arith math = new ArithServer("Math Server");
        boa.obj_is_ready(math);
        System.out.println(math +" is ready.");
        boa.impl_is_ready();
    }
}
```

The server object implementation looks as simple as it is. In the object implementation, we implement the add method that was defined in the `Arith` interface. In the main body of the server, we initialize the ORB and the BOA, create an instance of the `ArithServer`, and have this server object ready to listen for client requests.

19.3.3 Compiling the server

This step is simple. We just have to compile the server using the javac compiler.

% javac ArithServer.java

19.3.4 Writing the client code

It is now time to write the client code. This code, which is shown in example 19.3, is also simple. We have two arrays, we initialize the ORB, we bind it, and we invoke the add method from the object server.

Example 19.3: ArithClient.java

```
/**
 * @(#)ArithClient.java
 */
public class ArithClient {
    public static void main(String argv[]) {
        org.omg.CORBA.ORB orb = org.omg.CORBA.ORB.init(argv, null);
        Arith m = ArithHelper.bind(orb);
        int a[] = {2, 2, 2, 2, 2, 2, 2, 2, 2, 2};
        int b[] = {2, 2, 2, 2, 2, 2, 2, 2, 2, 2};
        int result[] = new int[10];
        result = m.add(a, b);
        for(int i=0; i<a.length; i++) {
            System.out.print(result[i] +"    ");
        }
        System.out.println("");
    }
}
```

19.3.5 Compiling the client code

Next, we compile the client code using the javac compiler.

```
% javac ArithClient.java
```

At this point, we are ready to run the application. To do so, the Smart Agent (osagent) must be already running. Then we can run the server and the client.

19.3.6 Running the server

The VisiBroker's Smart Agent, osagent, has to be running, so first we'll start the osagent:

```
% osagent &
```

Now we can run the server using the vbj command. Note that vbj is a script that comes with VisiBroker for Java.

```
% vbj ArithServer
```

19.3.7 Running the client

Finally, we can run the client using the vbj command, which produces the following output:

```
% vbj ArithClient

4    4    4    4    4    4    4    4    4    4
```

19.4 DATA TYPE MAPPING

The marshaling of the Java primitive data types, which represent an operation request that can be transmitted to the object server, is handled by the entities or client stubs generated by java2iiop. Marshaling a Java primitive type in this case means that the data type must be converted into an IIOP-compliant format. Table 19.1 shows how the Java primitive data types are mapped to IDL/IIOP types.

Table 19.1 Mapping Java types to IDL/IIOP

Java Type	IDL/IIOP Types
boolean	boolean
byte	octet
char	char
double	double
float	float
int	long
long	long long
package	module
short	short
String	string
org.omg.CORBA.	Anyany
org.omg.CORBA.Object	Object
org.omg.CORBA.Principal	Principal
org.omg.CORBA.TypeCode	TypeCode

Mapping complex data types is done differently, however. In the rest of this section we'll discuss the mapping of some of the complex data types.

Let's start with Java interfaces which are represented in IDL as CORBA interfaces. They must inherit from the `org.omg.CORBA.Object` interface. Interfaces that do not extend the `org.omg.CORBA.Object` interface are mapped to an extensible struct, as shown below, by the java2iiop compiler. One important thing to note about the java2iiop compiler is that it doesn't support overloaded methods on Caffeine interfaces.

Arrays are another complex data type. They are mapped to CORBA unbounded sequences by the java2iiop compiler.

Java classes in which you define arbitrary data types are mapped to IDL structs, provided that a class satisfies all of the following requirements:

- The class is `final`.
- The class is `public`.
- The class does not use implementation inheritance.
- The data members of the class are `public`.

For example, the following class fits these requirements, so therefore it is mapped to an IDL struct.

```
final public class Employee {
  public int id;
  public String name;
  public double salary;
}
```

If a class doesn't satisfy these requirements, it is mapped to an extensible struct, which is an upwardly compatible extension of CORBA structs. When extensible structs are used, objects are passed by value. However, the use of extensible structs is a VisiBroker extension to the OMG IDL—they use Java Object Serialization to compress a Java object's state into a serial stream of octets that can be passed as part of the request. It is important to understand, however, that extensible structs behave like any other CORBA data type with an additional advantage—you can pass arbitrary Java serializable objects where objects are passed by value.

19.5 SUMMARY

- Caffeine is a set of features that were introduced by Inprise Corporation in its VisiBroker for Java. There are advantages to using Caffeine:
  You can define interfaces in Java rather than IDL.
  You can pass objects by value rather than by reference.
- Caffeine generates IIOP-compliant skeletons.
- The anatomy of a Caffeine-based application is similar to that of an RMI-based application. In both, an interface must first be defined in Java. The main difference is that Caffeine uses the java2iiop compiler to generate IIOP-compliant stubs and skeletons.

PART IV

Mobile agents and Voyager

C H A P T E R   2 0

Overview of mobile software agents

Mobile software agents are programming entities that can freely roam the network on behalf of the user in an autonomous fashion. Java is particularly well suited to programming agents because of its platform independence; you can write and debug an agent on one machine, and it can run on all computers on the network that have a Java Virtual Machine.

In this chapter, I'll present an overview of mobile software agents, including the applications of mobile software agents, the problems they solve, and the problems they raise, together with some of the mobile agent implementations that are available in the market today.

20.1   INTRODUCTION TO SOFTWARE AGENTS

We all know what software is. But before we try to define what a software agent is, let us first try to understand the meaning and characteristics of an agent. We are all, in one sense or another, familiar with the concept of an agent. Most of us have probably dealt with travel agents and we know the role they play. The main role of a travel agent, for example, is that he or she *acts on behalf of others*. This characteristic can be considered the first fundamental property of an agent. The travel agent also exhibits another fundamental agent characteristic—he or she enjoys a variable degree of *autonomy*. Yet another important characteristic of an agent is the degree of proactivity and reactivity in its behavior. For example, once an agent receives the details of its tasks, it proactively tries to attain the goals defined by the assigned tasks, and it reacts to changes in the available data by modifying its plans. Agents also exhibit other attributes, including learning, cooperation, and mobility. Therefore, an agent can be defined, along with its characteristics, as an entity that:

- Acts on behalf of others in an autonomous fashion.
- Performs its actions in some level of proactivity and reactivity.
- Exhibits some levels of the key attributes of learning, cooperation, and mobility.

(This definition is borrowed from *Software Agents: A Review*, Shawn Green, Leon Hurst, Brenda Nangle, Padraig Cunningham, Fergal Somers, and Richard Evans)

The characteristics above are equally true for software agents. But what exactly is a software agent and how does it differ from a software object? A software agent is a software component that conforms to the characteristics of agents and also performs such tasks as inhibiting computers and networks assisting users with computer-based tasks. It is the programmer's responsibility to determine what an agent can do, and to determine what information is required from the user or software for the agent to perform its actions in a reactive manner. The agent's behavior can be set by another software package, which you can think of as a sort of super agent that creates a new agent when a task requires extra help.

20.2 MOBILE SOFTWARE AGENTS

A software agent must be a *mobile* software agent if it is to migrate from host to host to work in a heterogeneous network environment. This means you need to consider the software environments in which mobile agents exist. A mobile agent environment is a software system distributed over a network of heterogeneous computers; its primary task is to provide an environment in which mobile agents can execute. The agent not only transports itself, but it transports its state as well. When it reaches the new host, the agent should be able to perform appropriately in the new environment.

20.3 A NEW PARADIGM FOR DISTRIBUTED COMPUTING

The central principle of today's distributed programming is RPC, which we discussed in chapter 1. As I pointed out in section 1.4.2, the RPC approach has its own limitations. Most notably, all interactions between the client and the server must go through the network.

Another approach that is forming a new paradigm for distributed computing is one that employs mobile agents. Initially, this approach, known as remote programming.

The remote programming approach views computer-to-computer communication as one computer not only calling procedures in another, but also supplying the procedures to be performed. Each message that goes through the network includes a procedure that the receiving computer is to perform and the data for the procedure's arguments. The procedure and its state are called a mobile agent, since they represent the sending computer even while they are in the receiving computer. This approach is attractive since the reliability of the network is not crucial for the following reasons:

- Mobile agents do not consume much network bandwidth. They only consume bandwidth when they move.
- Mobile agents continue to execute after they move, even if they lose network connectivity with their creators.

Therefore, if a client requires extensive communication with a particular server somewhere on the network, then it is a good idea to implement such a system using mobile agents—an agent can move closer to the remote server (thereby reducing the network traffic), perform all tasks, and come back. During that period the client machine does not have to be switched on. The client machine will have to be turned on only when it is time to welcome back the agent. Figure 20.1 demonstrates the idea of this paradigm.

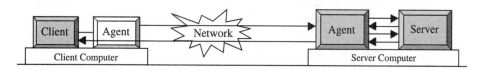

Figure 20.1 The mobile agents computing paradigm

At this point, you might be thinking, "This is exactly what process migration is all about—this has been done since the '60s." If you think so, you are absolutely right. However, mobile agents are different now, since they exhibit the characteristics of a software agent as described earlier in section 20.2.

20.4 MOBILE AGENT APPLICATIONS

Before we go any further with mobile agents, it is important to understand what this technology can do for both software developers and end users.

With the explosive growth of the Internet and the world wide web, and as we come close to the end of the 20th century, we are seeing as many untrained computer users as we have microprocessors. This gap is becoming more apparent as the computing age moves on. For example, current computer interfaces do nothing unless you give them commands from the keyboard, mouse, or touch screen. The computer is merely a passive entity that waits to execute your commands. It does not provide us with any help whenever we want to perform complex tasks. We are also carrying out more and more actions that take a long time to process, such as searching the web for information. Why doesn't the computer perform such tasks for us and present us with the results? Researchers in the area of agent technology have high hopes for software agents, which may know users' interests and can act autonomously on their behalf.

An attractive area in which to use mobile agents is in processing data over unreliable networks. In such environments, the low-reliability network can be used to transfer agents, rather than a chunk of data, from place to place. In this paradigm, the agent can travel to the nodes on the network, process the information on those nodes (without the risk of network disconnection), then return home. Another interesting area that is attracting attention is electronic commerce. For example, instead of spending a considerable amount of time going through on-line bookstores to find the best deal on a book, firing up an agent to do this would save us a considerable amount of time. The agent would be programmed to visit a number of bookstores and find the best deals on books we're looking for.

Yet another interesting application area for mobile agents is in network management. In today's heterogeneous network environments, network operators are required to have extensive knowledge of the diverse networks in order to manage them. Such management requires them to collect a large amount of data from nodes on the network. Mobile agents represent an ideal tool for collecting the data and analyzing it.

Mobile agents seem to be useful for many different applications. You may say, however, that virtually any task that can be performed with mobile agents can also be performed with other technologies such as remote method invocation. Despite the fact that there are not many distributed computing problems that cannot be solved without mobile agents, mobile agents can make certain applications easier to develop and may improve reliability and efficiency. Table 20.1 contains some of the claimed advantages of mobile agents over conventional approaches; this table is based on *Software Agents: A Review*.

Table 20.1 Possible advantages of mobile software agent

Possible advantage	Justification
Efficiency	Mobile agents consume fewer network resources since they move the computation to the data rather than the data to the computation.
Less bandwidth	Most communication protocols involve several interactions, which cause a lot of network traffic. Mobile agents consume bandwidth only when they move.
Robustness and fault tolerance	The ability of mobile agents to react dynamically to adverse situations makes it easier to build fault-tolerant behavior in complex distributed systems.
Support for heterogeneous environments	Mobile agent systems are computer and network independent. Therefore, a Java mobile agent can target any system that has a Java Virtual Machine.
Support for electronic commerce	Mobile agents are being used to build electronic markets since they embody the intentions, desires, and resources of the participants in the market.
Easier development paradigm	Constructing distributed systems can be made easier with mobile agents. Mobile agents are inherently distributed in nature. Therefore, they are a natural view of a distributed system.

20.5 SECURITY IN MOBILE AGENTS

Although mobile agents represent a useful new paradigm for distributed computing, they have seldom been used in practice. There are a number of related technical and social challenges to implementing mobile agents. Technical challenges include, among others, difficulties with portability and security. The security issues can also be considered as a social challenge—convincing people to use mobile software agents to buy items over the Internet is not always easy. The security challenge, however, is a complicated one.

Mobile agents raise issues similar to Java applets. There are several security issues to be considered in mobile agent-based computing. Some people think of mobile agents as viruses since they may exhibit similar behavior. Mobile agent security can be split into two areas, according to *Software Agents: A Review*:

- Protecting host nodes from destructive mobile agents.
- Protecting mobile agents from malicious hosts.

A mobile agent is an open system, so the host nodes are subject to a variety of attacks. These attacks can be in one of the following forms:

- *Leakage* Acquisition of data by an unauthorized party.
- *Tampering* Altering of data by an unauthorized party.
- *Resource stealing* Use of facilities by an unauthorized party.

The standard approach to these problems is to use authentication and digital signatures and to reject all unknown mobile agents from entry into a host. However, this does not really seem like a good solution.

The other area of security deals with the issue of protecting mobile agents from hosts which may want to scan the agent for information, alter the agent's state, or even kill the agent. The crucial issue here is that the agent will have to expose its data and information to the host in order to run on it. It seems it is computationally impossible to protect a mobile agent from a malicious host. Some researchers are tackling the problem from a sociological point of view by means of enforcing good host behavior.

20.6 MOBILE AGENT IMPLEMENTATIONS

Mobile agents can be written in any language (Perl, Python, and Tcl, for example), and they may be executed in either machine or interpreted language. However, in order to support heterogeneity, it is best to write agents in an interpreted, platform-independent language. Java represents an ideal host language for developing mobile agents because Java bytecodes will run on any platform that has a Java interpreter.

Mobile agent technology has been under serious development for a number of years. However, it was only in late 1996 that useful mobile agent systems appeared. Most of today's Java-based mobile agent systems are built as class libraries on top of Java. In this section, I'll provide an overview of the most widely available mobile agent systems.

20.6.1 General Magic's Odyssey

The Odyssey product inherits many features from a previous General Magic product: Telescript. Telescript is a C++-based language and environment for creating mobile agents. It was the most widely talked-about agent system before Java came on the scene. The three principal concepts implemented in Telescript are *agents*, *place*, and *go*. These three terms together form the best behavior to describe mobile agents: *agents go places*.

With Java promising platform independence, General Magic started making changes to its system, which is now implemented in Java. The agent system is now known as Odyssey. It is more or less a generic system that implements the basic functionality needed for creating mobile agents. It also supports Java RMI, Microsoft Distributed Component Object Model (DCOM), and CORBA IIOP. For more information on Odyssey, see http://www.generalmagic.com/technology/techwhitepaper.html.

As a sidenote, General Magic first coined the term *mobile agents*; it received a patent for it in 1997.

20.6.2 IBM Japan's Aglets

The Aglet Workbench from IBM Japan was one of the early Java-based development tools for mobile agents. The name *aglet* was derived from *agent* and *applet*. The aglet model is a simple framework in which the programmer overrides predefined methods to add desired functionality. Conceptually, an aglet is a mobile Java object (since it supports the ideas of autonomous execution) that travels from one Aglet-enabled host to another. However, only the state is maintained as an aglet travels from host to host. For more information on the Aglet Workbench, see http://www.trl.ibm.co.jp/aglets.

It is worth noting that Danny Lang, who was the head of the Aglet's project, is now working on Odyssey for General Magic.

20.6.3 ObjectSpace's Voyager ORB

Voyager is a Java agent-enhanced object request broker. Voyager seems to have a tighter integration with Java than any other mobile agent system does. The nice thing about Voyager is that it can be used for creating both mobile agents and conventional distributed systems. For more information on Voyager, see http://www.objectspace.com.

I believe that Voyager is the most widely used mobile agent system. Table 20.2 presents a feature summary of the mobile agent systems discussed above.

Table 20.2 A summary of mobile agent system feature

Mobile agent system	Portability	Mobility	Security
Aglets	Java	Aglet Transfer Protocol	Sandbox model
Odyssey	Java	Java RMI, CORBA IIOP, DCOM	Sandbox model
Voyager	Java	Java Object Serialization, Reflection	Sandbox model, secure channels

20.7 SUMMARY

- Mobile software agents are programming entities that can freely roam the network on behalf of the user in an autonomous fashion. They represent a new paradigm for distributed computing. This paradigm is attractive since the reliability of the network is not crucial. Mobile agents are attractive for processing data over unreliable networks and for electronic commerce.

- Despite the fact that most distributed computing problems can be solved without mobile agents, mobile agents nevertheless make certain applications easier to develop and may improve reliability and efficiency. Construction of distributed systems can be easier with mobile agents, since they are inherently distributed in nature.

- Mobile agents can be written in any language, but in order to support heterogeneity it is best to write them in an interpreted, platform-independent language. Java represents the ideal host language for writing mobile agents. A number of mobile agent systems are built as class libraries on top of Java, including General Magic's Odyssey, IBM's Aglets, and ObjectSpace's Voyager.

Getting started with Voyager

Voyager is a Java distributed-computing platform that can be used to produce high-impact distributed systems quickly. Like RMI, Voyager allows you to use regular message syntax to construct remote objects and send them messages. More importantly, Voyager allows you to move messages between programs.

Voyager offers many benefits, including ease of use, compatibility, performance, and flexibility. For example, you can create a Voyager server from the command line by running the voyager server program. The created server accepts objects and messages from other Voyager programs.

This chapter provides an overview of Voyager ORB 3.0 and its major features. I'll show you how to use Voyager for developing distributed and mobile agent applications.

21.1   OVERVIEW

Voyager is a Java product from ObjectSpace Inc. that can be used to develop high-impact distributed applications quickly and easily. Voyager is described as a 100% Java distributed computing platform that helps you produce high-impact distributed systems quickly. (For more information on Voyager, see http://www.objectspace.com.)

As with RMI, Voyager allows you to use regular message syntax to construct remote objects and send them messages. It also allows you to move messages between programs. In this chapter, I'll present an overview of Voyager, discuss its features, and show you how it can be used to build distributed applications. Proclaimed as a high-performance state-of-the-art ORB, Voyager offers many benefits, including:

- *Productivity* You can remote-enable any Java class without modifying its code in any way.
- *Compatibility* It has full native CORBA support for IDL and IIOP. Therefore, Java objects will be CORBA-enabled at run time without modification.
- *Performance* It makes efficient use of bandwidth, which makes its ORB one of the world's fastest for enterprise solutions.
- *Flexibility* Voyager's multilayered, scalable architecture makes it ideal for enterprise applications and embedded solutions.

The Voyager system has a number of great innovative features that are invaluable for constructing distributed applications. Some of Voyager's features are:

- *Remote-enabling a class* A Java class does not have to be modified in any way to remote-enable it. Java classes are remote-enabled at run time and no additional files are created.
- *Exception handling* If a remote exception is thrown, it is caught at the remote site and rethrown locally.
- *Distributed garbage collection* The distributed garbage collector reclaims objects when there are no more local or remote references to them.
- *Dynamic aggregation* This is an innovative feature in Voyager that allows you to add secondary objects (also called *facets*) to a primary object at run time.
- *CORBA* There is a full native support for IDL, IIOP, IDL to Java, and Java to IDL translation. No stub generators or helper classes are required.
- *Mobility* You can move any serializable object between programs at run time.
- *Autonomous mobile agents* You can create mobile autonomous mobile agents that move themselves between programs and continue to run upon arrival.
- *Activation* Voyager's activation framework allows objects to be persisted to any kind of database and automatically reactivated in case that program is restarted.
- *Security* An enhanced security manager is included. Hocks are also provided for installing custom sockets such as SSL.

The communication facility provided in Voyager is very flexible—it provides asynchronous, synchronous, and future remote method calls, which are delivered by lightweight agents called messengers. Method calls across address spaces have the same semantics as local calls. They are also polymorphic in the sense that they allow access to local as well as remote objects through virtual object proxies using the same syntax.

21.2   WORKING WITH VOYAGER

So far, I have presented the main concepts of Voyager and its features. In this section, I will explain some technical aspects of Voyager. I'll also show you how to start and stop a Voyager program, how to create a remote object, and how to send messages.

21.2.1 Starting and stopping a Voyager program

A Voyager server can be created from the command line using the `voyager` server program. The created server will accept objects and messages from other Voyager programs. To start a Voyager program that accepts connections on port 8080, for example, type:

% voyager 8080

If everything goes as it should, you will see this message:

```
voyager orb 3.0, copyright 1997-1998 objectspace
```

To terminate the created server from the command line, use CNTL-C.

To see usage information, type `voyager` at the command line with no arguments. (Voyager expects an argument list.) Table 21.1 shows the valid arguments and a description of each one.

Table 21.1 Voyager command-line argument list

Argument	Meaning
url	Typically, a port on which to start the server.
-b <classname>	Load and start this application.
-c <url>	Enable network class loading from the specified URL.
-l <string>	Log level: *silent, exceptions, verbose.*
-i <interpreter>	Use this interpreter instead of Java (for example: Voyager -i jview).
-q	Quiet mode. Do not display the copyright on startup.
-r	Enable resource, or class file serving.
-s	Install the Voyager security manager.
-t <int>	The maximum thread pool size.
-x	Pass the remaining parameters to the Java interpreter.

A more practical way to start and stop a Voyager program is by invoking methods from within your programs. To start a Voyager program and be able to use any Voyager features, your program must invoke one of the following variations of `Voyager.startup()`:

- *Voyager.startup()*   Starts Voyager as a client that does not initially accept incoming messages.
- *Voyager.startup(String url)*:   Starts a Voyager server that accepts incoming messages on the specified URL. If the URL is `null`, it will accept connections on a random port number.

NOTE   Another form is `Voyager.startup(Object obj, String url)`, which must be used by Voyager applets and servlets. But since they are not discussed in this chapter, we will not discuss them in this book.

Here are a few ways to start a Voyager program:

```
Voyager.startup();      // Start up as a client.
Voyager.startup("8080");            // Start up as a server on port 8080.
Voyager.startup("//ultra:1500");    // Start up as a server on the machine
name "ultra" on port 1500.
```

To shut down a Voyager program, call `Voyager.shutdown()`, which kills Voyager's non-daemon threads and terminates the main program.

21.2.2 Logging information to the console

Voyager allows you to log information to the console. This information may include stack traces of remote exception. There are three levels of logging: *silent*, *exception*, or *verbose*.

Setting the logging level can be done from either the command line or within your programs. To set the logging level from the command line, use the `voyager -1` option with the arguments `silent`, `exceptions`, `verbose`. To set the logging level from within your programs, use `Console.setLogLevel` to select a logging level:

- *Console.SILENT* Displays no output to the console.
- *Console.EXCEPTIONS* Displays stack traces of remote and unhandled exceptions.
- *Console.VERBOSE* Displays stack traces of remote and unhandled exceptions, as well as internal debug information.

21.2.3 Remote interfaces

The version of Voyager we are using here (Voyager ORB 3.0) follows a similar approach to RMI in defining the methods of a remote class as an interface. An interface in Java consists of a series of declarations that are subject to these two restrictions:

- Method declarations must not include implementation code.
- Variable declarations can only have constant initializers.

For example, consider the following valid Java code:

```
interface Hello {
   void sayHi();
}
```

The interface `Hello` has the method `sayHi()` declared in it.

Voyager interfaces start with an "I" so the above interface would be `Ihello`, for example. I recommend you follow this rule when programming with Voyager; however, your own code does not have to follow this rule if you choose otherwise.

There's one important thing you should know about Java interfaces. Look at the interface below:

```
interface IHello {
  sayHi();
}
```

If a class `HelloThere` implements the interface `IHello`, then it is legal to write:

```
IHello hello = new HelloThere();
```

Java interfaces certainly simplify distributed computing, and Voyager (just like RMI) takes great advantage of interfaces to simplify the lives of distributed application programmers. In Voyager, a remote object is represented by a proxy that implements the same interfaces as its remote counterpart. Therefore, a variable whose type is an interface may refer to a remote object via a proxy, as you will see later in the examples.

21.2.4 Creating remote objects

To create an object at a specified location, use the Factory.create() method. It returns a proxy to the newly created object and creates the proxy class dynamically if it does not already exist. The create() method has a number of variations which depend on whether you want to create the object locally or on a remote machine. For example, to create an instance of a class named Hello in the local program, you would write something like this:

```
IHello obj = (IHello) Factory.create("Hello");
```

On the other hand, to create an instance of a class named Hello in the program running on port 9000 of the machine ultra (as illustrated in figure 21.1), you would write something like this:

```
IHello obj = (IHello) Factory.create("Hello", "//ultra:9000");
```

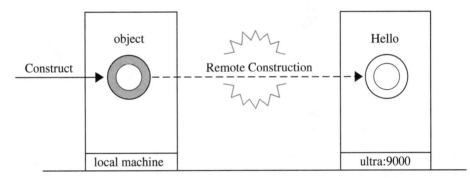

Figure 21.1 The remote construction of an object

Another variation of create() depends on whether the constructor of the class you are creating an instance of takes any arguments. For example, let's say the Hello class has a constructor that takes two arguments, a message of type String, and an int that represents the number of times the message to be shown. Creating an instance of Hello and its constructor would be done as follows:

```
Object args[] = new Object[] {"Hi there", new Integer(4)};

IHello obj = (IHello) Factory.create("Hello", args, "//ultra:9000");
```

It is very important to note that the primitive arguments are wrapped in an Object.

21.2.5 Anatomy of a Voyager-based application

Developing a distributed application with Voyager involves five steps. The steps may vary depending on the approach used to develop the application. In general, however, these are the steps to follow:

1 Define a remote interface.
2 Implement the remote interface.
3 Develop a client that uses the remote interface.
4 Start the Voyager server.
5 Run the client.

Let's examine each step through the development of a simple distributed application. The featured application is the same arithmetic server we developed using sockets in chapter 3, using RMI in chapter 8, and using CORBA in chapter 12. Again, given two arrays of integers and an operation to perform (such as add), the arithmetic server will perform the requested operation on the two arrays and return the resulting array back to the client as shown in figure 21.2.

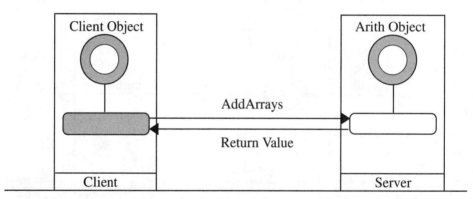

Figure 21.2 The arithmetic client/server application

In this example, we will only implement the add operation. As an exercise, you may want to modify the application by adding more related arithmetic methods.

The first step is to define a remote interface.

Defining a remote interface   Our interface will have only one method; it will take two arrays of integers as arguments and return an array of integers. The arithmetic interface, IArith, is shown in example 21.1.

Example 21.1: IArith.java

```
/**
 * @(#)IArith.java
 */
public interface IArith {
```

```
   int[] addArrays(int a[], int b[]) {
}
```

Implementing the remote interface   The second step in the development cycle of a distributed application using Voyager is to implement the remote interface we defined above. This is done by writing a class that implements the IArith interface. Our implementation is shown in example 21.2.

Example 21.2: Arith.java

```
import java.io.*;
/**
 * @(#)Arith.java
 */
public class Arith implements IArith, Serializable {
   public Arith() {   // Constructor
     System.out.println("construct arith object");
   }
   public int[] addArrays(int a[], int b[]) {
     int len = a.length;
     int c = new int[len];
     for(int i=0; i<len; i++) {
       c[i] = a[i] + b[i];
     }
     return c;
   }
}
```

The most important thing to note about the Arith class is that besides implementing the IArith interface, we are also implementing the Serializable interface. We are doing this because Voyager, just like RMI, makes extensive use of object serialization for marshaling, unmarshaling, and object mobility.

Developing a client   We are now ready to develop a client that can remotely invoke a method. In this case, we want to invoke the addArrays method defined in the IArith interface. We want to create a remote object in our client and send it a message. But first we must start Voyager from within our program as a client. A sample client implementation is shown in example 21.3.

Example 21.3: ArithClient.java

```
import com.objectspace.voyager.*;
/**
 * @(#)ArithClient.java
 */
public class ArithClient {
   public static void main(String argv[]) {
       int a[] = {4, 4, 4, 4, 4, 4, 4, 4, 4, 4};
       int b[] = {4, 4, 4, 4, 4, 4, 4, 4, 4, 4};
       int result[] = new int[10];
       // Start Voyager as a client.
```

```
Voyager.startup();
// Create a remote arithmetic object.
IArith arithObj = (IArith) Factory.create("Arith", "//local-
host:8000");
// Send the message to the remote object.
result = arithObj.addArrays(a, b);
for (int i=0; i<result.length; i++) {
    System.out.println(result[i]);
}
Voyager.shutdown();
    }
}
```

The client code is simple. Notice how we are starting Voyager as a client. Also notice how we are creating a remote object using `Factory.create()` and sending a message to that object.

Starting Voyager   We are now ready to test our arithmetic application. To do that, we first need to start a voyager server. The following command starts Voyager on port 8000.

% voyager 8000

Running the client   It's time to run our client. Once we run the client, the message contained in the `Arith`'s constructor will be displayed in the window where Voyager was started. To start the client, we simply write:

% java ArithClient

This will start the client, and if everything goes well, you will see the sum of the arrays.

21.2.6   Naming services and proxies

In the example above, we used simple Voyager features to write the arithmetic server distributed application. Real applications, however, use more advanced Voyager features such as proxies and the naming service for binding names to objects and finding objects by name. In this section we will revise the arithmetic server application to demonstrate how to send a remote message to a proxy that was obtained using the `lookup` method of naming services. But first, let me present a brief overview of Voyager's naming services and proxies and how to use them.

Working with naming services and proxies   A naming service allows names to be associated with an object for later lookup; Voyager's naming service can be used to bind names to objects for later lookup. To bind a name to an object in Voyager, invoke `Namespace.bind (String name, Object obj)`. This method associates the specified name with the object, or it will throw an exception if the name already has an association. For example, the following code segment creates an `Arith` object on the host //ultra2:9000, then binds it to the name add for later lookup:

```
IMath m = (IMath) Factory.create("Arith", "//ultra2:9000");
Namespace.bind("//ultra2:9000/add", m);
```

Alternatively, the two lines above can be combined:

```
IMath m = (Imath) Factory.create("Arith", "//ultra2:9000/add");
```

Now we need to obtain a proxy to a named object by invoking `Namespace.lookup(String name)`. This method returns a proxy to the object associated with the specified name, or `null` if no such object is found. For example, to obtain a proxy to the object that was created and named add above, we need to write:

```
IMath m = (IMath) Namespace.lookup("//ultra2:900/add");
```

The `Namespace.lookup()` method is just one way of getting a proxy to an object. This proxy can also be obtained using the following methods:

```
Factory.create(String classname, String url); // Returns a proxy to a newly
created object.
Proxy.of(Object obj); // Returns a proxy to the specified object.
```

The arithmetic server revisited   We will now revise our arithmetic server code to use Voyager's naming service and proxies. The `IArith` interface and the `Arith` class will remain the same. We will modify the `ArithClient` code and we'll also add a new class for starting up Voyager and binding the `Arith` object to a name. Figure 21.3 illustrates the interaction between the arithmetic client and the server objects via a proxy.

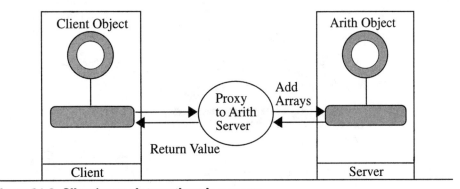

Figure 21.3 Client/server interaction via a proxy

Let's start by adding a new class. In this class we will start Voyager, export the new `Arith` object, and bind it to name. The new class, `Arith2`, is shown in example 21.4.

Example 21.4: Arith2.java

```
import java.io.*;
import com.objectspace.voyager.*;
/**
 * @(#)Arith2.java
 */
public class Arith2 {
   public static void main(String argv[]) throws Exception {
      Voyager.startup();
```

```
IArith m = (IArith) Proxy.export(new Arith(), "9000");
Namespace.bind("9000/add", m);
    }
}
```

The most important thing to note about the `Arith2` class is that we are exporting the `Arith` object explicitly—in order for an object to receive remote messages, that object must be explicitly exported to exactly one local URL. Of course, this is done automatically for us when a proxy to the object is passed to a remote program for the first time. In this case, however, we are explicitly exporting an object on a specific port. One of the following methods can be used to explicitly export an object:

```
export(Object obj, String url);  // Exports the obj to the specific URL.
export(Object obj);              // Exports the obj to the default URL.
```

To unexport an object, invoke `unexport(Object obj)`.

Another important thing to note about the `Arith2` class is that we are starting the Voyager server explicitly. This is how you actually should start Voyager from your own sophisticated applications.

Now, we turn to modifying the `ArithClient` class. In the new class, `ArithClient2`, we want to `lookup` an object. This means we need to change only one line in the old `Arith-Client` class. The line:

```
IArith arithObj = (IArith) Factory.create("Arith", "//localhost:8000");
```

should be replaced with:

```
IArith arithObj = (IArith) Namespace.lookup("//localhost:9000/add");
```

The new class, `ArithClient2`, is shown in example 21.5.

Example 21.5: ArithClient2.java

```
import com.objectspace.voyager.*;
/**
 * @(#)ArithClient2.java
 */
public class ArithClient2 {
    public static void main(String argv[]) throws Exception {
        int a[] = {4, 4, 4, 4, 4, 4, 4, 4, 4, 4};
        int b[] = {4, 4, 4, 4, 4, 4, 4, 4, 4, 4};
        int result[] = new int[10];
        Voyager.startup();
        IArith arithObj = (IArith) Namespace.lookup("//localhost:9000/add");
        result = arithObj.addArrays(a, b);
        for (int i=0; i<result.length; i++) {
            System.out.println(result[i]);
        }
        Voyager.shutdown();
    }
}
```

21.3 SUMMARY

- Voyager is a 100 percent Java-distributed computing platform that helps you produce high-impact distributed systems quickly. Like RMI, Voyager allows you to use regular message syntax to construct remote objects and send them messages. It also allows you to move messages between programs.
- You can create a Voyager server from the command line by running the voyager utility. The created server accepts objects and messages from other Voyager programs.
- As with RMI, building a distributed application using Voyager involves a number of steps:

  Defining a remote interface that acts as the contract between the client and the server.

  Implementing the remote interface.

  Developing a client.

  Starting a Voyager server.

  Running the client.

CHAPTER 22

Programming mobile agents

Voyager has introduced a number of innovative features that are important for developing distributed applications. Suppose you are building a system that requires adding behavior to third-party components whose source is not available. How is it possible to extend the behavior of an object at run time? Voyager enables you to attach secondary objects, known as *facets*, to a primary object at run time. Together, the primary object and its facets are known as an *aggregate*.

A mobile agent can be made up of one or more mobile objects. The first step in creating a mobile agent is making your objects mobile. Mobility refers to the ability to move your objects around the network, is a useful ability. For example, you can move objects that exchange large numbers of messages closer to each other to reduce network traffic and increase throughput.

In this chapter, we'll discuss dynamic aggregation and I'll show examples of how to create, add, and access facets. Then we'll discuss mobility as it enables agents to move. Finally, I'll show, through examples, how to develop mobile agents easily using Voyager.

22.1 DYNAMIC AGGREGATION

Dynamic aggregation is an innovative feature that has been added to Voyager. The beauty of this feature is that it allows you to attach secondary objects (known as *facets*) to a primary object at run time. The primary object and its facets form an *aggregate*, which is acted upon as a single unit. Figure 22.1 illustrates this idea.

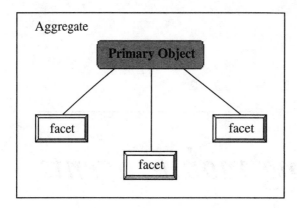

Figure 22.1 An aggregate: a primary object with three facets

To understand the usefulness of this feature, consider the following scenarios:

- You are building a new system and you would like to add behavior to some third-party components whose source is not available to you.
- A particular object is used by many subsystems, and each requires a customized version of the object.

You may think that these problems can be solved with some object-oriented (OO) features such as inheritance and polymorphism. Actually, these OO features will not help you much, especially if you want to extend the behavior of an object at run time. Dynamic aggregation is an innovative feature that complements inheritance and polymorphism. It is very useful in modeling OO systems in a more flexible, dynamic way. Using this innovative feature of Voyager, you can dynamically add a visit facet to a patient's history record, for example.

Having said that, there are a few rules that we have to follow when working with facets.

- Facets cannot be nested—a facet cannot have a facet.
- Facets cannot be removed. Once a facet is added, it stays for the life span of the aggregate.
- A primary object and its facets have the same life span. For example, they are garbage collected as a single unit when there are no references to either the primary object or its facets.

- A class does not have to be modified in order for its instances to play the role of the primary object and/or facet.

22.1.1 Working with facets

To work with facets, you need to be able to *add* one or more facets to a primary object and *access* a primary object's facets.

A primary object's facets are represented by an instance of Facets, which is initially set to null. To access an object's facets, use one of the following static methods:

- *get(Object obj)*   Returns the object's facets, which may be null.
- *of(Object obj)* Returns the object's facets. If it is null, it will be set to an initialized instance.

Other methods that are useful for manipulating an object's facets include:

- *get(String interfacename)*   Returns a proxy to a facet that implements the specified interface. A null will be returned if no match is found.
- *of(String interfacename)*   Returns a proxy to a facet that implements the specified interface. If no match is found, a proxy will be added automatically.
- *getPrimary()*   Returns a proxy to the primary object.
- *getFacets()*   Returns an array of proxies to the primary object's facets.

22.1.2 Facet creation and remote access

In this example, I will demonstrate facets by adding a payment facet to a customer object. Then we will access the facet remotely. Let's start by writing the Customer class; an instance of Customer will be our primary object in this example. First, let's write the Customer interface, ICustomer. It will have two methods: one for the customer's name and one for the location. The ICustomer interface is shown in example 22.1.

Example 22.1: ICustomer.java

```
/**
 * @(#)ICustomer.java
 */
public interface ICustomer {
   String getName();
   String getLocation();

}
```

Now we will implement the ICustomer interface. Our implementation is shown in example 22.2.

Example 22.2: Customer.java

```
/**
 * @(#)Customer.java
 */
public class Customer implements ICustomer {
   String name;
```

```
    String location;

    public Customer(String name, String location) {
        this.name = name;
        this.location = location;
    }

    public String toString() {
        return "Customer(" +name+","+location+")";
    }

    public String getName() {
        return name;
    }

    public String getLocation() {
        return location;
    }
}
```

We are now ready to develop the Payment class. Again, we start by writing the interface. Let's call it IPayment, and give it two methods: payBill() and getBalance(), as shown in example 22.3.

```
/**
 * @(#)IPayment.java
 */
public interface IPayment {
    void payBill(int amount);
    int getBalance();
}
```

An implementation to the IPayment interface is shown in example 22.4.

```
/**
 * @(#)Payment.java
 */
public class Payment implements IPayment {
    int balance;

    public String toString() {
        return "Payment("+balance+")";
    }

    public void payBill(int amount) {
        balance += amount;
    }
```

```
public int getBalance() {
    return balance;
  }
}
```

The Payment object is our secondary object, meaning it is the *facet* that we will be adding to the primary object, Customer. The addition of the Payment facet to the Customer object is accomplished using the AddFacet class shown in example 22.5.

Example 22.5: AddFacet.java

```
import com.objectspace.lib.facets.*;
import com.objectspace.voyager.*;
/**
 * @(#)AddFacet.java
 */
public class AddFacet {
    public static void main(String argv[]) {
        try {
          Voyager.startup("8000");
          ICustomer customer = new Customer("J. Giles", "Ottawa");
          // Return the customer's facet.
          IFacets facets = Facets.of(customer);
          // Return a proxy to the facet that implements the IPayment
             interface.
          IPayment payment = (IPayment) facets.of("IPayment");
          payment.payBill(2300);
          System.out.println("primary = "+facets.getPrimary());
          Object objs[] = facets.getFacets();
          for(int i=0; i<objs.length; i++) {
            System.out.println("facet["+i+"]="+objs[0]);
          }
          Namespace.bind("Giles", customer);
        } catch(Exception e) {
          System.err.println(e);
        }
    }
}
```

In example 22.5, we first start up a Voyager server, then we create a Customer object, which is the primary object. We then return the customer's facet and proxy to the facet that implements the IPayment interface. The IFacets.getFacets() method returns an array of proxies to the primary object's facets. In this example, only one proxy will be returned.

Now, in order to remotely access the Payment facet, we need another class. The AccessFacet class shown in example 22.6 does exactly that.

Example 22.6: AccessFacet.java

```
import com.objectspace.lib.facets.*;
import com.objectspace.voyager.*;
/**
 * @(#)AccessFacet.java
```

```
    */
public class AccessFacet {
    public static void main(String argv[]) {
        try {
            Voyager.startup();
            ICustomer customer = (ICustomer) Namespace.lookup("//local
                host:8000/Giles");
            IPayment payment = (IPayment) Facets.of(customer).of("IPayment");
            System.out.println("Payment ="+payment);
        } catch(Exception ex) {
            System.err.println(ex);
        }
        Voyager.shutdown();
    }
}
```

22.2 MOBILITY

Mobility refers to the idea that you can move your objects around the network. But why would you want to do that? As you saw in chapter 20, many applications could benefit from mobile agent technology. You might want to move your objects around the network for one of the following reasons:

- If you have objects around the network that exchange a large number of messages, they are going to increase network traffic and decrease throughput. Moving your objects closer to each other reduces network traffic and increases throughput. ObjectSpace claims that local messages are between 1000 and 100000 times faster than remote messages.
- In a mobile world, you may want to move objects into a mobile device (such as a Palmtop) so that objects will remain with the device after it has been disconnected from the network.

22.2.1 Moving objects around

Moving an object to a new location on the network is easy with Voyager. It involves two steps:

1 Using `Mobility.of()` to obtain the object's mobility facet.

2 Using one of the following methods defined in the `IMobility:` interface:

- *moveTo(String url* Moves to the program with the specified URL.
- *moveTo(Object obj)* Moves to the program that contains the object that is specified by a proxy. The `moveTo("ultra:8000")` operation. The `moveTo` operation is illustrated in figure 22.2.

When `moveTo()` is invoked, the relating object performs a number of tasks in the following order:

- Messages that the object is currently processing will complete, and new messages that arrive at the object will be suspended.

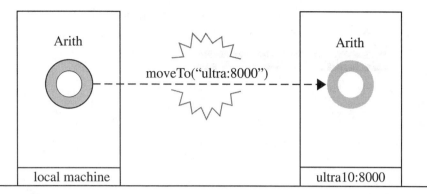

Figure 22.2 Illustrates the `moveTo()` **operation.**

- The object and all its nontransient parts are copied to the new location using Java object serialization. An exception is thrown if any part of the object is not serializable or if a network error occurs.
- The new addresses of the object (including all its nontransient parts) are cached at the old location.

NOTE   The new addresses cached at the old location are not treated as references by the garbage collector. A moved object is reclaimed when there are no more local or remote references to it.

- The old object is destroyed.
- Suspended messages sent to the old object are resumed.
- When a message sent via a proxy arrives at the old address of the object, an exception containing the new address of the object is thrown back to the proxy. The proxy traps this exception, rebinds to the new address, and resends the message to the new address.
- `moveTo()` returns after the object is successfully moved or when an exception is thrown. In the case of an exception, the object is restored to its original condition.

22.2.2   Mobility and messaging

In this section, I'll use a simple example to demonstrate mobility and messaging by developing a greetings program in which we construct an object, move it, and send it greetings messages. As usual, when working with Voyager, we start by creating an interface. Our interface (`IHello`) contains one method (`sayHi`) which is shown in example 22.7.

Example 22.7: IHello.java

```
/**
 * @(#)IHello.java
 */
public interface IHello {
   void sayHi(String msg);
}
```

Now we simply implement the IHello interface. The implementation is shown in example 22.8.

Example 22.8: Hello.java

```java
import java.io.*;
/**
 * @(#)Hello.java
 */
public class Hello implements IHello, Serializable {
    public void sayHi(String msg) {
        System.out.println(msg);
    }
}
```

The most important thing to note about the Hello class is that, in addition to implementing the IHello interface, it is implementing the Serializable interface. This is because objects are copied to new locations using Java object serialization. Therefore, every mobile object must implement the Serializable interface; otherwise, an exception will be thrown during mobility.

It is now time to write the class that will do the actual work of moving the object and sending it messages as illustrated in figure 22.3. The class implementation is shown in example 22.9.

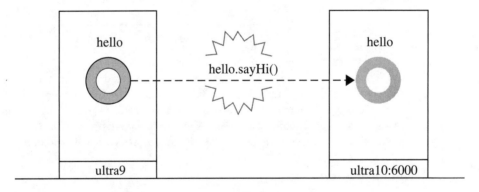

Figure 22.3 The `moveTo("ultra:8000");` **operation**

Example 22.9: Action.java

```java
import com.objectspace.voyager.*;
import com.objectspace.voyager.mobility.*;
/**
 * @(#)Action.java
 */

public class Action {
    public static void main(String argv[]) {
```

```
      boolean onHost = false;
      try {
        Voyager.startup("9000");
        IHello hello = (IHello) Factory.create("Hello");
        IMobility mob = Mobility.of(hello);
        if(!onHost) {
          mob.moveTo("//ultra10/6000");
          hello.sayHi("hi from my creator on ultra9");
        } else {
          mob.moveTo("//localhost:9000");
          hello.sayHi("hi to myself");
        }
      } catch(Exception e) {
          System.err.println(e);
      }
      Voyager.shutdown();
      }
}
```

In example 22.9, we start a Voyager server on port 9000 on the machine on which the Action class exists. We then move the object to the machine ultra10 on which a Voyager server is running on port 6000. Note that a Voyager server must be started on port 6000 on ultra10.

Be aware that the movement of the object is transparent to the client. Also, the client's reference to the moving object is valid whether the object is local, remote, or on the move.

To experiment with the code, change the machine name ultra10 to some other name that exists on your network, or to localhost if you do not have access to other machines. Then, compile the IHello.java, Hello.java, and Action.java classes. Start a Voyager server on port 6000 (either on a local or remote machine) and run the Action class. If everything goes well, you should see a greeting message on the window where you started a Voyager server on port 6000.

22.2.3 Getting notified

The Hello example demonstrates how to move an object to a new location and send it a message. Some objects, however, may want to be called back when they are about to move, or have just been moved. This callback capability is provided through the IMobile interface. In order for an object to receive callbacks during the move, it must implement the IMobile interface. An object is then qualified to receive the following sequence of callbacks:

- *preDeparture(String src, Sing dest)* This method is executed on the object at the original location.
- *preArrival()* This method is executed on the copy of the object at the destination.
- *postArrival()* This method is executed on the copy of the object at the destination.
- *postDeparture()* This method is executed on the stale object at the original location.

Let's now modify our Hello example above by qualifying it to get mobility callbacks using the IMobile interface. The IHello interface remains the same. The new Hello implementation (Hello2) of the IHello interface will have to implement the IMobile interface by providing implementations for the pre- and post-methods described in this section. The Hello2 class is shown in example 22.10. Our implementation is simple and it is only for demonstration purposes. Normally, you'd want to perform some actions in the callbacks. For example, in the postDeparture method, you might want to remove the stale object from persistence.

Example 22.10: Hello2.java

```java
import java.io.*;
import com.objectspace.voyager.mobility.*;
/**
 * @(#)Hello2.java
 */
public class Hello2 implements IHello, IMobile, Serializable {
    public void sayHi(String msg) {
        System.out.println(msg);
    }

    public void preDeparture(String src, String dest) {
        System.out.println("preDeparture()");
    }

    public void preArrival() {
        System.out.println("preArrival()");
    }

    public void postArrival() {
        System.out.println("postArrival");
    }

    public void postDeparture() {
        System.out.println("postDeparture");
    }
}
```

As for the Action class, only one change needs to be made. Replace the line

```java
IHello hello = (IHello)Factory.create("Hello");
```

with this one:

```java
IHello hello = (IHello)Factory.create("Hello2");
```

When I did this and ran the Hello2 example, I saw the messages preArrival() and postArrival() displayed at the remote host, and the messages preDeparture() and postDeparture() displayed on the local host.

22.3 MOBILE AGENTS

In chapter 20, I presented an overview of mobile agents and their advantages and areas of applications. Here I'll show you how mobile agents can be created and deployed using Voyager.

22.3.1 Working with mobile agents

A mobile agent is made up of one or more *mobile* objects. Therefore, the first step in building a mobile agent is to make an object become a mobile agent. To do that, use `Agent.of()` to obtain the object's facet. The second step is to use the following methods defined in the `IAgent` interface.

- `moveTo(String url, String callback, Object argv[])` Moves the program to the specified URL and restarts it by executing a callback that returns no value. The argument `argv`, which is an array of objects, is optional.

- `moveTo(Object obj, String callback, Object argv[])` Moves the agent to the program containing the specified object and restarts the program by executing a callback (that returns no value) with the proxy to the object as the first argument. Again, the argument `argv` is optional.

- `setAutonomous(boolean flag)` Allows you to set an agent to be autonomous. An autonomous agent is not reclaimed by the garbage collector even if there are no more references to it. An agent is initially autonomous by default. When an agent achieves its goals and wishes to be garbage collected, it will invoke `setAutonomous(false)`.

- `isAutonomous()` Returns `true` if the agent is autonomous; otherwise, it returns `false`.

- `getHome()` Returns the home of the agent, which is defined by a URL.

As a simple example, the following line of code makes an object become a mobile autonomous agent. The object then moves itself to the machine ultra10 (as shown in figure 22-4), which has a Voyager server running on port 6000, using `sayHi`:

```
Agent.of(this).moveTo("//ultra10:6000", "sayHi");
```

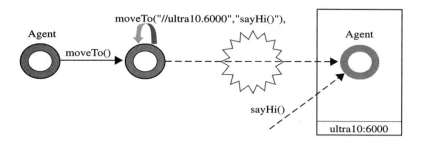

Figure 22.4 A mobile agent moving to machine ultra10

In this case, if the `moveTo()` call is successful, it will cause the thread of control to stop in the agent before it moves and resumes from the callback method in the agent after it has moved.

22.3.2 Developing mobile agents

Let's walk through a mobile agent example to demonstrate mobile agent development using Voyager. We will use our classic arithmetic server example. The server will run on a remote machine, and an array adder will move itself to the remote machine to perform its computations.

To start with, let's write our first interface and implementation for the arithmetic server. In this interface, we define the addArrays method as shown in example 22.11.

Example 22.11: IArith.java

```
/**
 * @(#)IArith.java
 */
public interface IArith {
    int[] addArrays(int a[], int b[]);
}
```

Next, we implement the IArith interface as shown in example 22.12.

Example 22.12: Arith.java

```
import java.io.*;
/**
 * @(#)Arith.java
 */
public class Arith implements IArith, Serializable {
    public Arith() {
        System.out.println("construct math object");
    }

    public int[] addArrays(int a[], int b[]) {
        int len = a.length;
        int c[] = new int[10];
        for(int i=0; i<len; i++) {
            c[i] = a[i] + b[i];
        }
        return c;
    }
}
```

Now we need a class that is capable of moving to a remote machine and using the computing facilities available there. First, however, let's write an interface for the class. This interface will have one method, add, that takes the IArith interface as an argument. The new interface, IAdder, is shown in example 22.13.

Example 22.13: IAdder.java

```
/**
 * @(#)IAdder.java
 */
public interface IAdder {
```

```
      void add(IArith arith);
}
```

Next, we implement the IAdder interface as shown in example 22.14.

Example 22.14: Adder.java

```
import java.io.*;
import com.objectspace.voyager.*;
import com.objectspace.voyager.agent.*;
/**
 * @(#)Adder.java
 */
public class Adder implements IAdder, Serializable {
    int a[] = {4, 4, 4, 4, 4, 4, 4, 4, 4, 4};
    int b[] = {4, 4, 4, 4, 4, 4, 4, 4, 4, 4};

    public Adder() {
        System.out.println("construct an array adder");
    }

    public void finalize() {
        System.out.println("finalize array adder");
    }

    public void add(IArith arith) {
        System.out.println("remote adder");
        addAt(arith);
        System.out.println("local adder");
        try {
          Agent.of(this).moveTo(arith, "atMachine");
        } catch(Exception e) {
          System.err.println(e);
        }
    }

    public void atMachine(IArith arith) {
        System.out.println("at remote machine, home = "+Agent.of(this).getH-
ome());
        addAt(arith);
        Agent.of(this).setAutonomous(false);
    }

    public void addAt(IArith arith) {
        int result[] new int[10]; // Hold the new result.
        System.out.println("start adding");
        result = arith.addArrays(a, b);
        // Print the result.
        for(int i=0; i<10; i++) {
            System.out.println(result[i]);
        }
        System.out.println("stop adding");
```

```
        }
    }
```

Note that the `Adder` class is also implementing the `Serializable` interface. Again, this is because Voyager uses object serialization to marshal objects. Most of the work of the `Adder` class is done by the `add` method, which will communicate with the remote arithmetic server and move to it to perform the `addArrays` locally. The `atMachine` method is used to perform operations locally once the `Adder` has moved itself to the arithmetic server running on a remote machine. The `setAutonomous(false)` method is invoked to allow the `Adder` object to be garbage collected once it has achieved its goal. Finally, the `addAt` method is used to do the actual work by calling the `addArrays` method once it has arrived at a destination.

Finally, we need to write an agent that will produce the objects on local and remote machines. Our agent is shown in example 22.15.

Example 22.15: MyAgent.java

```
import com.objectspace.voyager.*;
/**
 * @(#)MyAgent.java
 */
public class MyAgent {
    public static void main(String argv[]) {
        try {
            Voyager.startup();
            IArith arith = (IArith)Factory.create("Arith", "//ultra10:7000");
            IAdder add = (IAdder)Factory.create("Adder");
            add.add(arith);
        } catch(Exception e) {
            System.err.println(e);
        }
        Voyager.shutdown();
    }
}
```

`MyAgent` simply starts Voyager as a client, then creates an arithmetic server on a machine named ultra10, on which a Voyager server is running on port 7000. Then it calls the `add` method of the `Adder` class, which does most of the work.

To experiment with the code, change the machine name ultra10 to another name on your network. Start a Voyager server on port 7000 on that machine. Now, on a different machine, run `MyAgent`. When I ran it on my network, `MyAgent` added the two arrays by making a remote call to the arithmetic server. Then the agent co-located itself with its target on the remote machine to perform the array addition locally to the arithmetic server.

I have changed the code to add the arrays 100 times. It took 56 milliseconds using remote methods, and it went down to 6 milliseconds after the agent colocated closer to the arithmetic server. If you would like to measure how it performs on your network, replace the `addAt` method in the `Adder` class with the following `addAt` method:

```
public void addAt(IArith arith) {
    int result[] = new int[10];
    System.out.println("start adding");
```

```
      Stopwatch watch = new Stopwatch();
      watch.start();
      for(int i=0; i<100; i++) {
        result = arith.addArrays(a, b);
      }
      watch.stop();
      System.out.println("stop adding");
      System.out.println("time = "+watch.getTotalTime()+ " ms");
  }
```

The Stopwatch class is one of Voyager's timer services. You can use a Stopwatch object to clock time intervals and print measurement statistics. It's a very nice class, indeed. In order for the method above to compile, you need to add the following import statement to the Adder class:

```
import com.objectspace.lib.timer.*;
```

We will cover more of the Voyager's timer services in the next chapter.

22.4 SUMMARY

- Dynamic aggregation allows you to attach secondary objects, known as facets, to a primary object at run time. The primary object and its facets form an aggregate, which is acted upon as a single unit. Voyager provides a number of methods for creating, adding, and accessing facets.
- A mobile agent can be made up of one or more mobile objects. The first step in creating a mobile agent is making your objects mobile. Mobility refers to the ability to move your objects around the network. Voyager's moveTo() method moves a program to a specified location, making mobility simple.

CHAPTER 23

Advanced Voyager programming

Voyager provides a number of advanced features that are useful for developing secure and highly available distributed systems. It supports the standard Java security manager by providing a customized security manager. It also provides a number of other features, including a scalable architecture known as a *Space* for event replication, an activation framework that allows an object to survive program restarts, and timers to clock time intervals. This chapter presents an overview of these advanced features, along with hints on how to use them.

23.1   *SECURITY*

Voyager deals with security by including support for the standard Java security manager. While Java applets are automatically initialized with a restrictive security manager called AppletSecurityManager, Java applications have no security manager by default. This means that objects in a Java application are free to perform any operation. But as you saw in chapter 6, you can develop your own policy and implement a security manager. Voyager includes a security manager known as VoyagerSecurityManager, which you can install in your Voyager applications to restrict operations.

271

23.1.1   Installing a security manager

If you want, you can install the `VoyagerSecurityManager` in your Voyager applications. However, once you install a security manager, it will be active for the duration of the program and it cannot be uninstalled or replaced. If you are developing a mission-critical application, it is a good idea to install a security manager as objects attempt to execute operations that could compromise security. The Java run-time system checks with the program's security manager to see if such operations are allowed.

The `VoyagerSecurityManager` can be installed in two different ways:

- From the command line using the −s option, where s stands for security.
- From within a program by creating a new instance of the `VoyagerSecurityManager` and installing it like this: `System.setSecurityManager(new VoyagerSecurity-Manager())`.

It is important to note that the `VoyagerSecurityManager` distinguishes between objects residing in the program's CLASSPATH (known as native objects) and objects whose classes were dynamically loaded across the network (known as foreign objects). The `VoyagerSecurityManager` allows native objects to perform any operation, while the operations of foreign objects are restricted. For example, a native object is allowed to exit the program and a foreign object is not allowed to do so. Table 23.1 indicates some of the operations that the `VoyagerSecurityManager` allows an object to perform as a native object and as a foreign object.

Table 23.1 Object authority

Operation	Native objects	Foreign objects
Accept connections from any host	Allowed	Allowed
Connect to any host	Allowed	Allowed
Listen on any port	Allowed	Allowed
Manipulate threads	Allowed	Not allowed
Execute a process	Allowed	Not allowed
Exit the program	Allowed	Not allowed
Create windows	Allowed	Allowed
Create class loaders	Allowed	Not allowed
Delete files	Allowed	Not allowed
Access security APIs	Allowed	Not allowed
Link to dynamic libraries	Allowed	Not allowed
Access packages	Allowed	Allowed
Print	Allowed	Not allowed

23.2 ADVANCED MESSAGING

So far, the types of messages we have been using in Voyager are known as *synchronous* messages. Voyager messages are synchronous by default. This means that when a caller sends a message, the caller pauses until the message completes and the return value (if any) is received. Some applications, however, may need to use asynchronous messages where the caller does not block while the message completes.

Voyager provides you with the ability to send a synchronous message *dynamically* using the static Sync.invoke() method, which returns a Result object (such as a placeholder for return values or exceptions) when the message completes. You can then retrieve the return values or exceptions from the Result object. The Sync.invoke() method expects the following arguments: a target object, the name of the method you want to call, and the arguments to the dynamically invoked method in an array of Objects. For example, the following code segment uses Sync to dynamically invoke an add() message on an instance of a simple math object to add two numbers:

```
Result res = Sync.invoke(m, "addNums", new Object[]
                                    {new Integer(4), new Integer(7)});
int sum = res.readInt();
```

In this example, we are retrieving an integer value using the readInt() method. Equally likely, you can use readTTT() where TTT can be Boolean, Byte, Char, Short, Int, Long, Float, Double, or Object to retrieve return values of such types.

If you wish to query whether a Result object has received its return value, you can call isInvoke() which returns true if the Result has received its return value.

In addition to dynamically invoking synchronous messages, Voyager provides the following types of asynchronous messages:

- *One-way messages* A one-way message is a message that does not return a result. Sending a one-way message is fast, though, as the caller does not block while the message completes. As with Sync, to send a one-way message dynamically, call the static method OneWay.invoke().
- *Future messages* A future message immediately returns a Result object, which is really a placeholder for the return value. Again, the caller does not block while the message completes. Once the message is completed, the Result object is then used to retrieve return values. Again, to send a future message dynamically, call the static method Future. invoke().

23.3 PUBLISH/SUBSCRIBE

Imagine an Internet-based news service that wants to send news events to readers who are interested in a particular topic. One way to do this is to write a distributed system that uses a single repeater object to replicate an event to each object in the group, as shown in figure 23.1.

This approach works well if the number of objects is small. However, it does not scale well as the number of objects becomes larger. Voyager provides a scalable architecture, known as a *Space*, for event replication, as illustrated in figure 23.2.

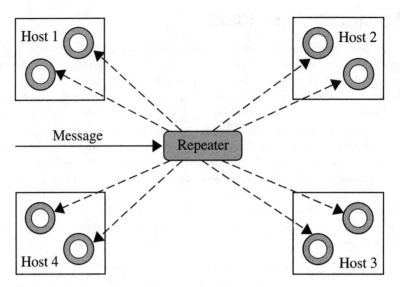

Figure 23.1 A repeater object replicating a message

A *Space* is one or more subspaces linked together and it can span multiple programs. A subspace is a local container of objects.

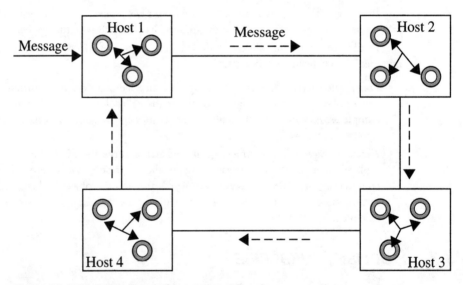

Figure 23.2 Voyager Space for event replication

23.4   ACTIVATION

If a message is sent to a remote object whose program has been terminated or restarted, an `ObjectNotFoundException` is thrown. Voyager's activation framework allows an object to survive program restarts, and the program will receive messages as if it had never shut down. This is accomplished by having an activation proxy that catches the `ObjectNotFoundException` and attempts to rebind to the object using activation information. This activation information is passed to the activation manager in the object's program, which in turn uses the activator class to locate the object's activator. If no instance of the activator class is found, Voyager automatically constructs one and registers it with the activation manager. Figure 23.3 shows a typical activation setup.

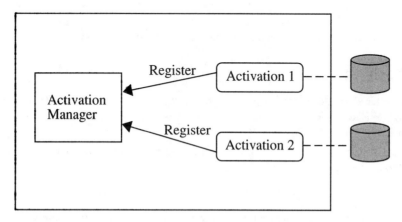

Figure 23.3 A typical activation setup

Once the object's activator is located, the activation manager sends it the message `activate(memento)`. The object will be then be loaded into memory and a proxy will be returned to the newly restored object. The rebind process is then completed and the original message is resent to the activated object. This whole process is transparent to the user.

23.4.1   Writing an activator

Each Voyager application contains a single activation manager that manages zero or more activators. An activator is associated with a database and can be registered using `Activation.register()` at startup. In order to enable your objects for activation, you must implement an activator by implementing the activation interface `IActivator`, which has two methods:

* `getMemento(Proxy proxy)`   Returns a memento string, which is a database key that can be used to reactivate the proxy's object using the `activate()` method.
* `activate(String memento)`   Loads the object associated with the memento and returns a proxy to the activated object.

Now, to enable an object for activation, pass the object or proxy to `Activation.enable()`, which in turn invokes `getMemento()` and `activate()`.

To implement the getMemento(Proxy proxy) method, do the following:

- Use Snapshot.of(proxy) to obtain a snapshot of the proxy's object.
- Use Snapshot.getObject() to obtain the object.
- Locate the object in the activator's database. If it is found, return a string memento that will allow activate() to retrieve the object from the database.
- If the object is not found in the database, an activator can either store the object or throw an ActivationException. In order to store the object, save the Snapshot object directly or save its parts individually.

Implementing the activate(String memento) can be done in one of these two ways:

- If a snapshot of the object was stored directly into the database, load the snapshot using the memento key. Otherwise, you can load each part separately using Snapshot. from() to recreate the original snapshot.
- Return the result of sending restore() to the snapshot.

23.5 TIMERS

Voyager provides timer services through the Stopwatch and Timer classes. Use the Stopwatch class to clock time intervals, and use the Timer class if you need an alarm clock for your objects.

To use any of Voyager's timer services, you must include the following line among your import statements:

```
import com.objectspace.voyager.lib.timer.*;
```

In the following example, we use a Stopwatch object to clock time intervals and print measurement statistics. The following code segment from example 22.15 in chapter 22 demonstrates how to use the Stopwatch class to print measurements.

```
public void addAt(IArith arith) {
   System.out.println("start adding");
   Stopwatch watch = new Stopwatch();
   watch.start();
   for(int i=0; i<100; i++) {
     arith.addArrays(a, b);
   }
   watch.stop();
   System.out.println("stop adding");
   System.out.println("time = "+watch.getTotalTime()+ " ms");
}
```

The Stopwatch class defines other useful methods, which include getDate(), which returns the current date; reset(), which resets the stopwatch by clearing lap times and setting the lap count to zero; lap(), which stops the stopwatch temporarily to record the lap time and immediately restarts it; and getLapCount(), which returns the current completed lap count. For more information on the Stopwatch and Timer classes, please refer to Voyager's documentation.

23.6 SUMMARY

- Voyager deals with security by including support for the standard Java security manager. Voyager includes a security manager known as `VoyagerSecurityManager`, which you can install in your Voyager applications to restrict operations.
- Voyager messages are synchronous by default. This means that when a caller sends a message, the caller pauses until the message is sent and the returned value, if any, is received.
- Voyager enables you to send synchronous messages dynamically using the static `Sync.invoke()` method, which returns a `Result` object when the message has completed. You can then query the `Result` object to retrieve the return value or exception.
- Voyager provides two other message types: one-way messages and future messages. A one-way message is a message that does not return a result. A future message immediately returns a `Result` object.
- Voyager provides a number of other advanced features, including a scalable architecture known as a Space for event replication, an activation framework that allows an object to survive program restarts, and timers to clock time intervals.

CHAPTER 24

Voyager and CORBA integration

Voyager has integrated native CORBA support, and it can communicate with other ORBs regardless of their implementation language. It has full native support for all IDL types and IIOP with bidirectional IDL/Java translation. This integration allows Voyager to be used as a CORBA client or server. The beauty of this system is that proxy classes are generated at run time, so no stub generators, IDL repository, or helper files are required.

In this chapter, I'll demonstrate the anatomy of Voyager CORBA applications and show you how to integrate Voyager with a third-party CORBA server (such as VisiBroker) by walking you through a variety of examples, including the development of a complete Voyager CORBA application.

24.1 PROGRAMMING WITH VOYAGER CORBA

Programming a Voyager CORBA application has been made easy, as the call to Voyager.startup() automatically CORBA-enables the program. This, however, depends on whether you have voyager.corba.*, voyager.corba.advanced.*, or both in your CLASSPATH. If you have voyager.corba.* in your CLASSPATH, then the class to Voyager.startup() will automatically CORBA-enable your program by adding IIOP capabilities to the underlying communication subsystems. However, that will only support a subset of CORBA, including object references, exceptions, and IOR import/export. If you want to get full CORBA support, you must have `voyager.corba.advanced.*` in your CLASSPATH.

Importing and exporting CORBA objects is done using interoperable object references (IORs). An IOR is a string that encodes the hostname, port number, type, and key of a single CORBA object.

24.1.1 Exporting and importing CORBA objects

The simplest way for a server to export an object to a client is to write the object's IOR to a file. This means that the server will have to obtain the object's IOR, which is done by passing the object to `Corba.asIOR()`. Once the IOR is written to a file, the client can read the file, retrieve the IOR, and bind to it. The client can then obtain a proxy to a CORBA object by passing its IOR to `Namespace.bind()`. Once this is accomplished, messages then can be sent to remote CORBA objects. These messages will be transmitted using IIOP. In the case of an exception during the remote method call, a run-time exception, `CorbaSystemException`, is thrown.

24.2 ANATOMY OF A VOYAGER CORBA APPLICATION

The development lifecycle of a Voyager CORBA application involves the following steps:

- Developing the required interfaces.
- Implementing the interfaces.
- Developing the server program.
- Developing the client program.
- Compiling all the above, then running the server and client programs.

Let's look at each of the above steps separately by developing our classic arithmetic server example.

24.2.1 Developing the interfaces

The first step in the development lifecycle of a Voyager CORBA program is to develop the interface. This will be easy, since we have developed the same interface more than once throughout this book. Again, the example we will be using is the arithmetic server, where the server is capable of adding arrays of integers. The interface will have one method that takes two arguments as arrays of integers and returns an array, which is the sum of the two supplied arrays. Example 24.1 shows our arithmetic interface.

Example 24.1: IArith.java

```
/**
 * @(#)IArith.java
 */
public interface IArith {
    int[] addArrays(int a[], int b[]);
}
```

24.2.2 Implementing the interfaces

The second step is to implement the IArith interface in example 24.1. Implementing this interface is a straightforward process—there is nothing special about its implementation. Our implementation is shown in example 24.2.

Example 24.2: Arith.java

```
/**
 * @(#)Arith.java
 */
public class Arith implements IArith {
   public int[] addArrays(int a[], int b[]) {
      int c[] = new int[10];
      for(int i=0; i<c.length; i++) {
        c[i] = a[i] + b[i];
      }
      return c;
   }
}
```

24.2.3 Developing the server program

The third step in developing our Voyager CORBA program is to develop the server program. Our server will create an Arith object, retrieve its IOR, and write this IOR to a file. The IOR, which is really a string, is retrieved by invoking the method Corba.asIOR(obj) where obj is the object we are retrieving the IOR for. Writing the IOR to a file is accomplished using the writeUTF() method. Example 24.3 shows our Server class.

Example 24.3: Server.java

```
import java.io.RandomAccessFile;
import com.objectspace.voyager.*;
import com.objectspace.voyager.corba.*;
/**
 * @(#)Server.java
 */
public class Server {
   static IArith arith;
   public static void main(String argv[]) {
      try {
        Voyager.startup("6000");
        arith = new Arith();
        String ior = Corba.asIOR(arith);
        System.out.println("Arith IOR =: "+ior);
        RandomAccessFile file = new RandomAccessFile("Arith.IOR", "rw");
        file.writeUTF(ior);
        file.close();
        System.out.println("CORBA server is ready to serve clients");
      } catch (Exception e) {
        System.err.println(e);
```

```
                }
            }
        }
```

24.2.4 Developing the client program

Now we have everything we need to develop our client program. Our client will simply retrieve the object's IOR (using the readUTF method) from the file Arith.IOR file, which was created by the server program. Then it will bind to the Arith object using a Namespace.lookup on the IOR, and send a message to the Arith object. Our client program is shown in example 24.4.

Example 24.4: Client.java

```java
import java.io.RandomAccessFile;
import com.objectspace.voyager.*;
import com.objectspace.voyager.corba.*;
/**
 * @(#)Client.java
 */
public class Client {
    public static void main(String argv[]) {
        int a[] = {4, 4, 4, 4, 4, 4, 4, 4, 4, 4};
        int b[] = {4, 4, 4, 4, 4, 4, 4, 4, 4, 4};
        int result[] = new int[10];
        try {
          Voyager.startup();
          RandomAccessFile file = new RandomAccessFile("Arith.IOR", "r");
          String ior = file.readUTF();
          file.close();
          System.out.println("Arith IOR =: "+ior);
          IArith arith = (IArith) Namespace.lookup(ior);
          result = arith.addArrays(a, b);
          System.out.print("Sum = ");
          for(int i=0; i<result.length; i++) {
            System.out.print(result[i]+"    ");
          }
          System.out.println();
        } catch(Exception e) {
          System.err.println(e);
        }
        Voyager.shutdown();
    }
}
```

24.2.5 Compiling and running the application

We are finally ready to compile and run the application. We'll start by running the server program, then we'll run the client program.

Let's start by compiling. Assuming that the files IArith.java, Arith.Java, Server.java, and Client.java are all in a directory by themselves, we can compile them all at once using this command:

```
% javac *.java
```

If everything goes well, we shouldn't see any error or warning messages.

We are now ready to run our application. To do that, we'll run the server program in one window as follows:

```
% java Server
Arith IOR
=IOR:000000000000000f49444c3a4941726974683a312e300000000000010000000000000
01c0001000000000008756c7472613131300017700000000000000400000000
      CORBA server is ready to serve clients
```

We'll run the client program in a different window on the same machine, as follows:

```
% java Client
Arith IOR =
IOR:000000000000000f49444c3a4941726974683a312e30000000000000010000000000000
1c0001000000000008756c7472613131300017700000000000000400000000
Sum = 8   8   8   8   8   8   8   8   8   8
```

As you can see, in both the server and the client programs we are displaying the IORs. On the client side, we have the result: an array of 8s, which is the sum of the two arrays.

24.3 *VOYAGER CORBA INTEGRATION*

So far in this chapter we have discussed how to write Voyager client/server applications in CORBA mode. There is not really much use for such applications. A more realistic and practical use would be to have either a Voyager client communicate with a third-party CORBA server, or a third-party CORBA client communicate with a Voyager server.

In order for a CORBA client to communicate with a Voyager server, IDL interfaces must be generated from the classes in your application. On the other hand, if you want a Voyager client to communicate with a CORBA server, some Java interfaces must be generated from the IDL interfaces. In either case, the *cgen* utility can be used to translate IDL to Java and vice versa. For example, to translate a Java file into IDL, run cgen on the .java or .class file. cgen searches the directories, .zip, and .jar files in the CLASSPATH for the specified files and it generates IDL interfaces. Table 24.1 shows the valid arguments to cgen and a description of each.

Table 24.1 Command-line cgen argument list

Argument	Meaning
-d <path>	Store packages relative to <path>.
-h	Disable holder/helper files generation.
-i <interpreter>	Use <interpreter> instead of Java.
-I <path>	Add to list of #include paths.
-f	Force the flat idl structure to the output.
-q	Quiet mode. Do not display copyright notice.
-v	Verbose mode. Display status while processing.
-x	Pass the list of the remaining command-line arguments to the Java interpreter.

24.3.1 Voyager client and CORBA server

In this section, I'll show you how to develop a Voyager client that is capable of communicating with a third-party CORBA server (such as VisiBroker). We'll write a Voyager arithmetic client to communicate with the CORBA-based arithmetic server we developed in chapter 12 using VisiBroker for Java. Doing this involves a number of steps.

Let's start by reviewing the IDL interface for our CORBA-based arithmetic server. The IDL interface is shown in example 24.5.

Example 24.5: Arith.idl

```
// Arith.idl
module Arith {
   interface Add {
      const unsigned short SIZE = 10;
      typedef long array[SIZE];
      void sum_arrays(in array a, in array b, out array c);
   };
};
```

Nothing is special about this IDL interface, but we will need it later on. The implementation of this IDL interface is shown in example 12.3 in chapter 12. Nothing is going to change for that example.

As I mentioned in section 24.1, Voyager imports and exports objects based on their IORs. This means that we have to modify our arithmetic server, example 12.4. Mainly, we need to find out the server object's IOR and write it in a file to be used by a Voyager client. The new arithmetic server is shown in example 24.6.

Example 24.6: VisiServer.java

```
import org.omg.CORBA.*;
import java.io.RandomAccessFile;
/**
 * @(#)VisiServer.java
 */
```

```
public class VisiServer {
    public static void main(String argv[]) {
        try {
            ORB orb = ORB.init();
            BOA boa = orb.BOA_init();
            // AddImpl is defined in chapter 12.
            AddImpl arr = new AddImpl("Arithmetic Server");
            boa.obj_is_ready(arr);
            String ior = orb.object_to_string(arr);
            System.out.println("Arith IOR = "+ior);
            RandomAccessFile file = new RandomAccessFile("arith.ior", "rw");
            file.writeUTF(ior);
            file.close();
            System.out.println(arr + " is ready");
            boa.impl_is_ready();
        } catch(SystemException se) {
            se.printStackTrace();
        } catch (Exception e) {
            e.printStackTrace();
        }
    }
}
```

The most important thing to notice in example 24.6 is that we are retrieving the IOR (which is a string that encodes the hostname, port, type, and key of a single CORBA object) of the object using the method orb.object_to_string(). We are also saving the IOR of the object in a file named arith.ior for later retrieval by the Voyager client.

At this point, we are ready to develop our Voyager arithmetic client. To start, we need to create a new directory to which we will copy the IDL interface (Arith.idl). We'll then generate Java interfaces from the Arith.idl file using the cgen utility as follows:

prompt> cgen -d ./ Arith.idl

As you can see, I am using the −d option to generate packages relative to the directory I am in (./ refers to the current directory). If all goes well, the cgen command above will generate a directory called Arith (which is the module name of the interface) with the following file hierarchy in it:

```
Arith:
    Add.java
    InOutAdd.java
    OutAdd.java
    AddPackage:
        InOutarray.java
    Outarray.java
```

The most important files here are Add.java (which is the interface name) and Outarray.java.

Based on the files that have been generated, we can now start developing our Voyager arithmetic client. We'll start by looking at the interface Add.java to get a clue for the type of objects (and their signatures) that are served by the CORBA server. The `Add.java` interface has lots of CORBA code, including the following important line:

```
void sum_arrays(int[] a, int[] b, Arith.AddPackage.Outarray c);
```

This line shows us the signature of the object served by the CORBA server. The method `sum_arrays()` takes three arguments, two of type array of int, and one of type `Arith.AddPackage.Outarray`. This information will help us in writing our Voyager arithmetic client. In the client, we first need to start Voyager as a client, then we need to read the IOR from the file arith.ior, which can then be passed to `Namespace.lookup()`. Then we can remotely invoke the method sum_arrays. The source code for the Voyager arithmetic client is shown in example 24.7.

Example 24.7 VoyClient.java

```
import java.io.RandomAccessFile;
import com.objectspace.voyager.*;
import com.objectspace.voyager.corba.*;
/**
 * @(#)VoyClient.java
 */
public class VoyClient {
    public static void main(String argv[]) {
        int a[] = {4, 4, 4, 4, 4, 4, 4, 4, 4, 4};
        int b[] = {4, 4, 4, 4, 4, 4, 4, 4, 4, 4};
        Arith.AddPackage.Outarray result = new Arith.AddPackage.Outarray();
        try {
            Voyager.startup();
            RandomAccessFile file = new RandomAccessFile("arith.ior", "r");
            String ior = file.readUTF();
            file.close();
            System.out.println("Arith IOR = "+ior);
            Arith.Add arith = (Arith.Add) Namespace.lookup(ior);
            Arith.sum_arrays(a, b, result);
            System.out.print("Sum = ");
            for(int i=0; i<10; i++) {
                System.out.println(result.value[i]+"     ");
            }
            System.out.println();
        } catch(Exception e) {
            e.printStackTrace();
        }
        Voyager.shutdown();
    }
}
```

To try this out, run the CORBA-based arithmetic server (shown in example 24.6) in a window, and run the VoyClient in another window, but make sure that the file arith.ior, which has the IOR, is in the directory from which you're running the VisiClient. If all goes well, you should see the client displaying the sum of the arrays (an array of 8s).

24.3.2 Voyager server and CORBA client

I will now show you how to build a CORBA client that communicates with a Voyager server. Again, in this example we will build an arithmetic CORBA client to communicate with the Voyager arithmetic server implemented in example 24.3. We already have the Voyager interface, IArith, which is shown in example 24.1. Its implementation, the Arith class, is shown in example 24.2. Our job here is to write a CORBA client using VisiBroker to communicate with the Voyager server.

In order to develop our CORBA client, we will need an IDL interface that shows what kind of services (and their signatures) are offered by the Voyager server. We need to generate this IDL interface from the IArith.java interface that is shown in example 24.1. This task is made easy in Voyager by using the cgen utility. Create a new directory and copy into it the IArith.java file, then use the cgen utility to generate the required IDL interface:

prompt> cgen IArith

cgen 3.0, copyright objectspace 1997-1999

This command generates a file named IArith.idl, and saves it in the same directory where IArith.java exists. The contents of the generated file are shown in example 24.8. Notice that the generated file contains a valid (syntactically correct) IDL interface.

Example 24.8: IArith.idl

```
/**
 *  IArith.idl
 *  <p>
 *  @version 1.0
 *  @author generated by cgen 2.0 at Sat Nov 21 16:16:06 GMT+00:00 1998
 */
interface IArith
  {
  typedef sequence< long > tmp1;
  typedef sequence< long > tmp2;
  typedef sequence<long > tmp3;
  tmp1 addArrays( in tmp2 arg1, int tmp3 arg2 );
  };
```

As you can see from the IDL file, the addArrays method takes two in (for input) arguments of type sequence<long> and returns tmp1, which is of the same type. The IArith IDL interface shown in example 24.8 gives us a clue of the objects offered by the Voyager server and their signatures.

Now, run the VisiBroker's idl2java compiler on the new generated file (IArith.idl) to generate the necessary stubs and helper files.

prompt> idl2java IArith.idl

We are finally ready to write our CORBA client. The client is similar to the one developed in example 12.5. However, here we will need to retrieve the IOR of the objects in order to invoke methods on them. Our CORBA client is shown in example 24.9.

Example 24.9: VisiClient.java

```java
import org.omg.CORBA.*;
import java.io.*;
/**
 * @(#)VisiClient.java
 */
public class VisiClient {
    public static void main(String argv[]) {
        int a[] = {4, 4, 4, 4, 4, 4, 4, 4, 4, 4};
        int b[] = {4, 4, 4, 4, 4, 4, 4, 4, 4, 4};
        int result[] = new int[10];
        try {
            ORB orb = ORB.init();
            BOA boa = orb.BOA_init();
            RandomAccessFile file = new RandomAccessFile("Arith.IOR", "r");
            String ior = file.readUTF();
            file.close();
            System.out.println("IOR = "+ior);
            IArith add = IArithHelper.narrow(orb.string_to_object(ior));
            System.out.println("Got Add reference");
            result = add.addArrays(a, b);
            System.out.print("Sum = ");
            for (int i=0; i<10; i++) {
                System.out.print(result[i]+"    ");
            }
            System.out.println();
        } catch (SystemException se) {
            se.printStackTrace();
        } catch (Exception e) {
            e.printStackTrace();
        }
    }
}
```

To run the application, compile everything, then start a Voyager server in one window and the VisiClient in another window. Make sure you have the file Arith.IOR (which will be generated by the Voyager server, which is shown in example 24.3) in the directory where you start the VisiClient from. If all goes well, you will see the sum of the two arrays (an array of 8s) in the client window.

24.4   SUMMARY

- Voyager has integrated native support for CORBA, and it can communicate with other ORBs regardless of their implementation language. This integration allows Voyager to be used as a CORBA client and server. This system generates proxy classes at run time so no stub generators, IDL repository, or helper files are required.
- Programming a `Voyager` CORBA application is made easy as the call to `Voyager.startup()` automatically CORBA-enables the program.
- As shown by the examples in section 24.3, in order for a CORBA client to communicate with a Voyager server, IDL interfaces must be generated from the classes in the application. For a Voyager client to communicate with a CORBA server, some Java interfaces must be generated from the IDL interfaces of the CORBA server. In both cases, you run the cgen utility to translate IDL to Java and vice versa.

bibliography

Books, articles, and papers

Berners-Lee, Tim. "World-Wide Computer" *Communications of the ACM*, Feb 1997.

Comer, Douglas E., and David L. Stevens. Internetworking with TCP/IP, Vol. II: Design, *Implementation, and Internals*. 2nd ed., Prentice Hall, 1994.

Coulouris, George, Jean Dollimore, and Tim Kindberg. *Distributed Systems: Concepts and Design*. Addison-Wesley, 1994.

Gong, Li.. Java Security Architecture. (Draft document from Sun Microsystems.)

Green, Shawn, Leon Hurst, Brenda Nangle, Padraig Cunningham, Fergal Somers, and

Richard Evans. *Software Agents: A Review*. Dublin: Department of Computer Science, Trinity College, 1997.

Hughes, Merlin, Michael Shoffner, and Derek Hamner. *Java Network Programming*. 2nd ed. Manning Publications Co., 1999.

Lewis, Ted. *The Next 10,000$_2$ Years: Part I & II*. Communications of the ACM, April 1996.

Lynch, Daniel C., and Marshall T. Rose. *Internet System Handbook*. Addison-Wesley, 1993.

Mahmoud, Qusay H. *The Web as a Global Computing Platform*. In the 7th International Conference on High Performance Computing and Networking Europe (HPCN99). April 12 – 14, 1999. Amsterdam, The Netherlands.

Nebel, Ernesto, and Larry Masinter. RFC1867: Form-based File Upload in HTML. Network working draft document, November 1995.

Orfali, Robert, and Dan Harkey. *Client/Server Programming with Java and CORBA*. 2nd ed. John Wiley & Sons, 1998.

Stevens, W. Richard. *UNIX Network Programming*. Prentice Hall, 1990.

Tanenbaum, Andrew S. *Computer Networks*. 3rd ed. Prentice Hall, 1996.

Vogel, Andreas, and Keith Duddy. *Java Programming with CORBA*. 2nd ed. John Wiley & Sons, 1998.

Online references

Aglets Workbench.
    http://www.trl.ibm.co.jp/aglets
ComponentBroker, IBM.
    http://www.software.ibm.com/ad/cb
DAIS, International Computer Limited (ICL).
    http://www.icl.co.uk
General Magic Inc. Mobile Agents White Paper.
    http://www.generalmagic.com/technology/
    techwhitepaper.html
Imaginary JDBC Driver for mSQL.
    http://www.imaginary.com/Java
Inprise Corporation. VisiBroker Programming
    and Reference Manuals.
    http://www.inprise.com
Java IDL.
    http://java.sun.com/products/jdk/idl
Java PC.
    http://java.sun.com/products/javapc
JavaSpaces.
    http://java.sun.com/products/javaspaces
Jini.
    http://java.sun.com/products/jini
Linda.
    http://www.cs.yale.edu/HTML/YALE/CS/
    Linda/linda.html
mSQL, Hughes Technologies.
    http://www.hughes.com.au
MsqlJava.
    http://www.hughes.com.au/software/con-
    trib/archive/mSQLJava

Object Management Group. IDL/Java
    Language Mapping.
    http://www.omg.org/techprocess/
    meetings/schedule
Object Management Group. The Common
    Object Request Broker: Architecture and
    Specification, Revision 2.0.
    http://www.omg.org/corba/corbaiiop.html
ObjectBroker, BEA Systems.
    http://www..beasys.com
ObjectSpace Inc. Voyager ORB 3.0
    Developer Guide.
    http://www.objectspace.com
OrbixWeb, IONA Technologies.
    http://www.iona.ie
PowerBroker, Expersoft.
    http://www.expersoft.com
RSA Laboratories.
    http://www.rsa.com.
Service Location Protocol.
    http://www.srvloc.org
Sun Microsystems Inc. object serialization.
    http://java.sun.com/products/jdk/rmi/
    serial
Sun Microsystems Inc. remote method
    invocation.
    http://java.sun.com/products/jdk/rmi
W3 Consortium. The World Wide
    Web Project.
    http://www.w3.org

index

ICustomer 257
identifier 174
IDL 165, 226, 285
  array 192
  boolean 187
  char 187
  definition 173
  interface 175, 193
  mapping 154, 156
  module 184
  names 183
  octet 187
  repository 279
  string 187
  struct 230, 231
  union 190
  wchar 187
IDL/IIOP 230
IDL/Java translation 279
idl2ir 224
idl2java 165, 183, 198, 199, 221, 287
IHello 261
IIOP 226, 230, 240, 279, 280
IllegalArgumentException 44
Imaginary 61
IMobile 263
IMobility 260
impl_is_ready()
impl_rep 211
implementation
  activation 157
Implementation
  Repository 210
implementing callbacks 130
implementing factories 126
incompatibility 88
InetAddress class 23, 28
information
  management 157
inheritance 256
initialize() 81

initSign() 81
initVerify() 84
inout 165, 170, 180, 184, 194, 221
Inprise Corporation 155, 163
InputObjectStream 75
InputStream 20
integer type 177
interactive software
  development 222
interface 8, 42, 130, 154, 175
Interface Definition Language
  (IDL) 11, 154, 156
Interface repository (IR) 154, 157, 223
  creating an IR 224
  irep 224
International Standard
  Organization (ISO) 4
Internet addresses 6
Internet Inter-ORB Protocol,
  (IIOP) 155
Internet packets 4
Internet Protocol (IP) 4, 5
Interoperable Object
  References (IORs) 280
interpretation 157, 239
interpreters 10, 222
Inter-process Communication
  (IPC) 8, 15, 16
InterruptedException 41
IntHolder 184
IOException 23
IONA Technologies 155, 164
IPayment 258
IPtoName 30
isAutonomous 265
isCompatibleWith 147

J

J/SSL 143
Java 2 13

Java Archive (JAR) 13, 148-149
Java
  bytecode interpreter 93
  compiler 12, 93
  interpreter's security
    manager 94
  package 147
  Secure Socket Layer
    Protocol 143
  security 12
  virtual machine 10, 70, 5, 106, 107
  WebServer 143
java2idl 226
java2iiop 225, 226, 230
JavaIDL 155, 164
JavaPC 11
JavaServer Toolkit 143
JavaSoft 143, 155, 164
JavaSpaces 11
javax.net.ssl 143
JCP Computer Services 143
JDBC 53, 60, 61, 65
  API 61
  DriverManager 61
  Security Model 61
JDK1.0 12
JDK1.1 13
Jeevan 65
Jini 11
JoinGroup() 24

K

key management 78, 134
keyboard 41, 237
KeyGenerator 78
KeyPairGenerator 78, 81
Keywords 181

L

LAN 4, 5
language mapping 157

lap() 276
learning 236
leaveGroup() 24
Linda 11
Lisp 156
live reference 108
loadNet 92
local vs. remote object
    location 204
localHost() 36
long 177, 188, 273
LongHolder 185
lookup 117, 120, 158

M

Manager 200, 202, 214
ManagerHelper 203
ManagerImpl 199, 202, 216
marshaling 108, 230, 249
MarshaledObject 145
MathObj 75
MAX_PRIORITY 44
measurement statistics 276
megacomputer 86
message digests 78, 134
method invocation 157
MIN_PRIORITY 44
Mobile Agents 236, 260, 264
    Applications 23
    mobility 236, 244, 260
    working with 265
Mobility.of 260
Mouse 237
moveTo() 260, 265
mSQL 60, 62, 65
    database server 60
    JDBC driver 61
MsqlException 60
MsqlJava 60
MsqlResult 60
multicast 107
    backbone (MBONE) 24
    group 24
    sockets 19, 23

MulticastSocket 23
Multiple failure modes 10
multiple transports 107
multithreaded server 97
Multiuser applications 10
MyAgent 268
MySSLSocketFactory 142

N

Namespace 282
Namespace.bind() 250, 280
Namespace.lookup 286
naming objects 202
naming service 157, 250, 251
narrow 205
native objects 272
NetClassLoader 90, 91
Netscape 54
network 4
    layer 5
    management 238
    mobility 12
    traffic 237, 260
    protocols 4
Network Information Center
    (NIC) 6
nice thread 45
NO_IMPLEMENT 210
Non-blocking
    operations 180
non-printable 174
NORM_PRIORITY 44
NoSuchGroupException
    146
NovaBank 202
NsLookup 29
null 184, 208, 245

O

oadutil 210
obj_is_ready 209
Object 241, 273
Object Activation Daemon
    (OAD) 208, 210

Object Adapters (OA) 154,
    157
    authority 272
    concurrency 158
    events 158
    externalization 158
    ID 159, 160
    implementation 155
    key 159
    naming 158
    persistence 70
    reference 157, 159, 160,
        208
    relationships 158
    security 158
    serialization 65, 69, 108,
        122, 134, 261, 268
    services 157
    transactions 158
Object Lifecycle 158
Object Management
    Architecture (OMA) 147,
        153, 154
Object Management Group
    (OMG) 11, 153, 160
Object Request Broker
    (ORB) 154
object_to_string 209
object-based model 7
ObjectInputStream 70
ObjectNotFoundException
    275
ObjectOutput 73
ObjectOutputStream 70
objects by value 159, 160,
    226
objects over sockets 74, 122
ObjectSpace 243
ObjectStore PSE 65
octet 177
Odyssey 240
oneway 160, 180
    messages 273
Open Systems
    Interconnection (OSI) 4

operating systems 40
operations declaration 180
ORBIX 155
OrbixWeb 164
osagent 169, 201, 202, 209, 229
OSAGENT_ADDR 170
OSI reference model 110
OurHttpSecurityManager 58
OutputStream 20
overhead 74, 122

P

Package versioning 147
parallel computing 7
Parameter declaration 180
passive 143
password 72
patent 240
peer-to-peer model 8
performance 86, 244
Perl 239
persistent 208
    object 158
    object references 209
    references 108, 143
    resource 29
    storage 64, 65
Phaos Technologies 143
ping 33, 38, 39
pipe 16
policy file 13
Polling 160
polymorphic 244, 256
port number 17, 21
    port 1099 11
    port 25 3
    port 7 3
    port 79 3
    port 80 54
portability 239

Portable Object Adapter (POA) 159, 161
postArrival 263
postDeparture 263
preArrival 263
preDeparture 263
preprocessing 181
    directives 174, 181
presentation layer 4
primary object 255, 256, 259
Principal 230
printStackTrace 49
priority 44
PrivateKey 81
private-key cryptosystems 78
proactivity 236
process migration 237
productivity 244
protection 78, 239
    domains 14
protocol 4, 8, 105, 122, 241
    connectionless 18
    connection-oriented 18
proxy 59, 119, 247, 250, 259, 279, 280
    servers 58
public key 79, 134
public-key cryptosystems 78
publish/subscribe 273
Python 156, 239

Q

Query 60
QUIT 34

R

raises expressions 180
random number generator 81
RDBMS 62
reactivity 236
readArray() 51
readLine() 26

readObject() 70, 75
readonly 176
rebind() 117, 120, 121
reference-counting 109
Reflection 241
    API 90
registry 119, 130
reliability 12, 238
Remote Method Invocation (RMI) 11, 106, 113, 124, 142, 143, 156, 165, 170, 226, 227, 240, 241, 248
    garbage collector 109
    registry 110, 113, 115, 117, 120
    specification 107
Remote Procedure Call (RPC) 8, 9, 106, 236
remote programming 236
remote reference 107, 109
RemoteException 114, 124, 145, 146
RemoteStub 146
replication 108, 273
repository identifier 223
Request For Proposals (RFPs) 158
resolveIt 90
resource manager 7
resource sharing 10
responsiveness 41
ResultSet 63
resume() 44
RFC 1288 36
RFC 822/823 34
rlogin 19
rmi compiler 106, 108, 109, 118, 126
RMI vs. sockets 122
rmiregistry 120, 126
RMISecurityManager 115, 116, 125
RMISocketFactory 139-141

root 17, 38
routing 6, 29
RSA 86, 143
run() 42, 49, 54, 91
Runnable interfgace 42, 43, 82
RunnerSecurityManager 95

S

sandbox 12, 13, 89, 241
scalability 71
scheduling 87
search engines 100
SecureRandom 81
SecurityManager class 12, 14, 57, 87
  checkAccept() 95
  checkAccess() 58
  checkConnect() 58, 95
  checkCreateClassLoader() 95
  checkDelete() 95
  checkExec() 95
  checkExit() 95
  checkListen() 95
  checkPropertyAccess() 95
  checkread() 58
  checkWrite() 58
  custom security manager 93
security 10, 38, 57, 87, 110, 134, 239, 244
  and mobile agents 239
  and object serialization 72
  of interactions 157
  policy 93
  risks 89
  vulnerability 93
seed 81
selfish thread 45
Sendmail 34
sequence 178, 191, 287

Serializable interface 69, 70, 72, 75, 79, 116, 135, 249, 262, 268
serialization 231, 241
  control 72
  versioning 73
serialVersionUID 73
servant 159, 160
server-per-method mode 208
ServerSocket 21, 57, 97, 140
Service Location Protocol 87
session layer 5
setAutonomous() 265, 268
setPriority() 44
setSocketFactory 141
setuid 38
shared server mode 208
shipDocument 56
short 177, 188, 273
ShortHolder 184
signature 78, 81, 134
signed 177
  applet 13
  code 13
  object 134
signedBy 14
SignedInterface 135
SignedObject 79, 135
Signing objects over sockets 134
Simple Mail Transfer Protocol (SMTP) 4, 33-35
skeletons/stubs 108, 109, 111, 118, 126, 226
Smalltalk 156
Smart Agent 165, 169
  See also osagent
Snapshot.from 276
Snapshot.getObject 276
Snapshot.of 276
SOCK_DGRAM 17, 38

SOCK_RAW 17, 38
SOCK_STREAM 17, 38
Socket 8, 11, 15, 16, 19, 20, 35, 57, 97, 105, 140, 165, 170, 227, 248
  closing 22
  opening 21
SocketType 140, 141
software agent 235
Space 273
spying 84
SQL 61, 63
SSL 139, 244
SSLava Toolkit 143
SSLTPool 208
SSLTSession 208
stack 40
Statement 63
static 90, 156
stop() 44
Stopwatch 269, 276
Streams
  creating an input stream 21
  creating an output stream 22
string 135, 176, 178
struct 177, 179, 189, 190
stub code 221
stub/skeleton layer 107, 108
subname 62
subprotocol 62
superuser 17
suspend() 44
synchronize 45, 46, 134
synchronous 160, 244, 273
  messages 273
System.getProperties() 149
System.setSecurityManager() 96
Systems management, 157